GLOCK

REFERENCE GUIDE

2ND EDITION

ROBB MANNING

Published by

Gun Digest® Books, an imprint of Caribou Media Group, LLC

Gun Digest Media
5600 W. Grande Market Drive, Suite 100
Appleton, WI 54913
www.gundigest.com

To order books or other products call 920.471.4522
or visit us online at www.gundigeststore.com

ISBN-13: 978-1-946267-79-5

Edited by Chuck Smock
Cover Design by Jordan Matuszak
Interior Design by Jon Stein

Printed in the United States of America

10 9 8 7 6 5 4 3 2 1

More Great Handgun Books from Gun Digest

1911: The First 100 Years

Gunsmithing Pistols & Revolvers

Gun Digest Book of Automatic Pistols Assembly/Disassembly

Gun Digest Book of Concealed Carry

Choosing Handgun Ammo

Tactical Pistol Shooting

Find these and many more firearms and knives titles at
GunDigestStore.com

DEDICATION

I would, first and foremost, like to thank my Savior Jesus Christ, through You all things are possible. I also want to thank my wife, Ty, for putting up with me and my gun problem, and supporting me in my writing endeavors. I'd also like to thank those in the industry who have helped my writing career: Mark Olis, J.J. Reich, Doug Howlett, Jason Mulroney and David Fortier. Your advice and help have been instrumental. Also, thanks to James Tarr and Patrick Sweeney for sharing your wealth of knowledge, and for letting me bounce my wacky ideas and theories off you.

I'd also be remiss if I didn't acknowledge the man who got me started in gun writing, the late Mike Strandlund. Back in 2010, I wrote him a long letter about an article written in one of the publications he was editor of, and he wrote me back, "Your letter was great, do you want a job writing for us?" The rest is history.

Glock is notoriously hard to work with and get answers out of, and while this hasn't changed much, and there are some questions Glock wouldn't answer, there are people at Glock who helped me immensely. They went above and beyond to help me get most of the answers I needed and/or product in my hand to test. Thank you, Brandie, for helping me out with this 2nd Edition. I also want to mention the Glock folks who helped me out with the first edition: Kie, Connie and Eric. The information from the first edition is the foundation of my Glock story, and still makes up a large portion of this book

One final thanks to Matt Bogues at MJ Gunsmithing (mjgunshop.com) for transfers and getting all the guns I need into my hands. Gun writers can't do what they do without guns in their hands, and it takes a great gun shop to do that.

TABLE OF CONTENTS

INTRODUCTION

When Glock pistols burst onto the scene, very few pistols on the market could do what the Glock did: excel out of the box.

The debate about polymer is over, or at least it should be. Polymer is the material of the era, and test after test has shown it to be as strong and as durable as metal in many applications. About the only thing metal is better at is being subjected to the high pressures associated with a cartridge being fired. Yes, most metals have a higher melting point, but polymer has a far higher melting point than what your skin can stand, even when wearing a glove, and the firearm has to be held in order to be fired.

I still hear people say, "steel or nothing" in regard to their choice in firearms. Hey, I love all firearms whether they are made of polymer, alloy, steel or whatever. To each their own. I have steel handguns in my collection, and I love to shoot them. Some I might even carry on occasion. But to say steel guns are better than polymer guns is like saying the all-metal cars of yesteryear are better than the mostly plastic cars of today. We can all get nostalgic for old cars, and I think they're great, but as for reliability, safety and function, they can't compete with today's cars. They're not even in the same league. I've seen crash tests comparing old metal cars to new ones and it throws conventional thinking out the window.

It's the same way with guns, all-metal handguns are great, but when it comes to out-of-the-box reliability, safety and function, polymer handguns have them beat. I'm sure this will torque some people off, and I'm going to preface it by reporting I'm a John Moses Browning devotee and love the 1911 handgun. If you want a great shooting range pistol and maybe even a competition gun, the 1911 is fine. If you want a fighting gun, buy a Glock.

I'm quite sure Browning would agree if he were still alive. He was a genius firearm designer whose innovations were ahead of their time. Which is why if he were still alive, he would be designing polymer pistols.

I've heard some people argue that the only reason companies make polymer guns is to save money. While polymer certainly is cheaper to produce than metal, the polymer used to make handguns has many qualities that are superior to metal. I know this is sacrilege, and those same people wouldn't admit it, but it is true. For one, a polymer frame absorbs recoil better. It just does. This makes for better handling, especially in follow-up shots. Second, it allows for more rounds to be crammed into the magazines that are fed into the grips. The walls of a polymer grip are much thinner compared to the metal frame with plastic grips attached to it. Third, it's lighter, which makes for more comfortable carry, especially if you carry all day, every day.

One top of that, if polymer is cheaper to produce and some of those savings get passed on to me, that's even better. If a Glock was an all-metal handgun with the same features it has now, it would easily be an $800 to $1,000 gun. One only need look at the SIG line of metal pistols versus its polymer pistols to back this claim. If one compares out-of-the-box reliability and function of a Glock to that of the various 1911s on the market, who knows what the price would be? I've owned 1911s, and I've been around them, and up until recently, you couldn't get one for a reasonable price with the reliability of a Glock. Eats through anything? Hardly. Maybe most hardball/FMJ, but getting one to feed reliably with hollowpoints wasn't something you would come by cheaply.

I bought my first handgun in 1993, a Government Model 1911, for $320 at the Base Exchange on Marine Corps Base (MCB) 29 Palms. Aside from crappy magazines, it ate hardball ammunition like it was going out of style, but I don't think I ever could get one full magazine of hollowpoints to feed through it. With that handgun, my method of carry was a hollowpoint in the chamber with the rest of the magazine filled with hardball. I knew the first round would do some damage, and the follow-up rounds would at least feed reliably. In the last few years, I've spent a lot of time with Ruger's SR1911, and have been very impressed at how reliably it feeds all sorts of ammunition. Still, at around $800, and Ruger has a reputation for being very reasonably priced, it's far more expensive than a Glock, and it's still not quite as reliable. Most quality 1911s are priced at well above $1,000 and they're nowhere near as reliable as a Glock.

Over the course of doing research for this book, I have fired every model Glock makes, except the G18 and G17L. Most models I have fired in both Gen4 and Gen3, and in the Short Frame models where offered; and I've fired all of the Gen5 and slimline models available. I have fired a lot of Glocks. And I've fired a lot of ammo through them, several thousand rounds. I've fired ammo from Federal, SIG, Black Hills, DoubleTap, Winchester and just about every major ammo maker available on our shores, plus some really good small manufacturers. My point in mentioning all of this is that after putting a lot of ammo through a whole bunch of Glock pistols, I have concluded that you can pull any Glock out of its box, put any brand or type of the appropriate caliber into it, and it will fire every time you pull the trigger. And it will last a long time, regardless of how you treat it.

NOTE TO THE READER:

In this book there will be instances where color is important, and this is a black-and-white photo book. In these instances, I'm going to post the photo on my Instagram feed, and in the book caption I'll make note: (instagram.com/robb_manning). Or you can go to Instagram and search: #robb_manning.glock.book

CHAPTER 1:
GLOCK TIMELINE

TIMELINE:

1963: Glock KG is founded by Gaston Glock. In Austria (as well as other German-speaking countries), KG is the abbreviation for Kommanditgesellschaft, or limited partnership. Gaston is a chemical engineer specializing in plastics and thermal molding. The company makes a variety of odds and ends, such as shower curtain rods, hinges and doorknobs.

1970s: Glock KG starts designing and producing miscellaneous products for the Austrian military, such as practice grenade shells, field knives and machine gun belt links. The field knives are still being made to this day in two models; one with saw (Model 81) and one without (Model 78).

1980: Glock receives a formal invitation from the Austrian Army to develop a new pistol for the Austrian Army and compete in the field trials for selection.

1980: Glock KG is reformed into Glock G.m.b.H, which is the abbreviation for Gesellschaft mit beschränkter Haftung, which means Company with Limited Liability, or what in the United States is called an LLC, or Limited Liability Company. This is the most common type of business in Austria and other German-speaking countries.

1981: Gaston Glock assembles a group of engineers to develop the new pistol. Weeks later a prototype is complete. The Model 81 Field Knife with saw goes into production.

1982: The Glock pistol competes in a rigorous battery of tests, and it distances itself from the other entrants. Glock comes in first and is awarded the contract.

1983: Glock delivers the first order of G17 pistols to the Austrian Army. The Glock E-Tool also goes into development and is still being made to this day.

1984: The Norwegian Army adopts the G17, and that same year deliveries begin.

1985: Export marketing is greatly expanded. Several companies vie for importation rights into the U.S. Glock instead chooses to form its own import entity, Glock USA, the following year.

1986: The G17 is accepted for import into the U.S. It's a hit in both the U.S. law-enforcement and civilian markets.

1987: Glock develops the G18 select-fire pistol for use in Austrian Special Forces and anti-terrorism units. Glock opens a second Austrian factory in Ferlach.

1988: Production begins on the G19 and G17L.

1989: Second Generation frames are released. Glock hits the 350,000 pistols sold mark, with nearly half (150,000 units) being sold to U.S. law-enforcement agencies. Glock pistols are now being used by entities within 45 different countries.

1990: Production on the G20 and G21 gets bumped out of the way, so production of the G22 and G23 can commence. Later in the year, the G20 goes into production, and by the end of the year the G21 also goes into production. Both pistols are large-frame Glocks and offer two calibers that pack a lot of punch: one new, the 10mm, and one old, the .45 ACP.

1991: The Captured Recoil Spring is released.

1994: Production begins on the G24 and G24C.

1995: Production begins on the G25 .380. Not available to civilians in the United States, it would leave American consumers clamoring for a Glock in .380 for nearly 20 years. This is also the year of the subcompact, as the G26 and G27 go into production. They would become affectionately known as "Baby Glocks."

1996: Production begins on the G28, another .380 that won't make it to the U.S., at least not for consumers. The G17T is also released, a training pistol which shoots marking and target cartridges. Six years after the full-size 10mm and .45 ACP pistols go into production, production starts on the subcompact G29 and G30.

1997: Gen3 frames go into production, also known as FGR frames (Finger Groove and Rail).

1998: Production begins on the .357 SIG pistols, the G31, G32 and G33. Two pistols, made for competition, also are released: the G34 and G35. (The G31 and G32 also are offered in compensated models.)

1999: Glock hits the 2 million pistols sold mark. The G36 goes into production, as does another training pistol, the G17T AC.

2000: Glock unveils its new headquarters in Deutsch-Wagram.

2001: Glock starts production on some pistols that incorporate an integral lock, for states that require such a device.

2002: Glock jumps into the tactical light/laser market, with various models available. The three-pin G17 goes into production.

2003: Glock introduces a new cartridge, the .45 G.A.P. (Glock Automatic Pistol), and starts production on the G37. The G19 three-pin is released.

2005: Production begins on the two other .45 GAP pistols, the G38 and G39.

2006: Glock USA celebrates its 20th anniversary.

2007: Glock begins production of the Short Frame (SF) variants of its large frame pistols: the G20, G29, G21 and G30. Glock also hits the mark of 5,000,000 pistols sold worldwide.

2009: Glock begins production of the Gen4 pistols, called the Rough Texture Frames (RTF).

2010: Glock introduces and begins shipping Gen4 pistols, starting with the most popular law enforcement models: G17, G19, G26, G22, G23, G27, G31, G35 and G37.

2011: Glock USA marks 25 years in the U.S. market.

2014: Glock introduces and starts shipping on the G41 and G42.

2015: Glock introduces the G40 Gen4 in the MOS (Modular Optic System) configuration, as well as expanding the MOS line to include the G34, G35, and G41. Glock also introduces the G43, a single-stack 9mm, something consumers have been requesting for years.

2016: Glock celebrates 30 years in the U.S. market. Glock wins FBI contract with G17M and G19M, which begin shipping in August.

2017: Glock announces 5th Generation, with the G17 Gen5 and G19 Gen5.

2018: Gen5 lineup expands to include G26 and G34 MOS. The G19X is introduced, a hybrid of the G17 frame with G19 slide assembly. Glock adds MOS and Front Serrations (FS) to G17 Gen5 and G19 Gen5. The G45 is introduced, a black, commercial version of the G19X. America mourns the loss of U.S. Marine, actor and Glock spokesman R. Lee Ermey.

2019: Glock releases two new Slimline 9mm pistols: the G48 and G43X. The G47 is introduced for the U.S. Customs and Border Protection agency. The MOS configuration is added to the G45. Glock names Chuck Norris as spokesman.

CHAPTER 2:
GLOCK SAFETY MECHANISMS

In order to fully understand the Glock, you must know how it functions and how the safety system operates. The Glock's introduction was revolutionary: For the first time there was a handgun that was completely safe, in the sense that it absolutely could not fire a chambered round unless the trigger was intentionally pulled. It cannot fire from being bumped. It cannot fire from being dropped. It has been dropped from six feet, and it has been dropped from six stories. It has even been dropped from hundreds of feet out of a helicopter. It has been tied to the back of a truck and dragged down a gravel road. All of these were done with a round in the chamber (generally a cartridge with no bullet, just the primer), and never has it fired.

In fact, the striker (firing pin) is almost completely encapsulated and simply cannot touch the primer of the cartridge unless the trigger is pulled. Even if there was no striker block preventing it from striking the primer, it would still be physically impossible for the striker to bump the firing pin because the striker spring is at rest, not under tension, and can never be cocked unless the trigger is pulled. As soon as the trigger is released and allowed to move forward, it is uncocked.

The first and most obvious thing about the Glock, is that it has no manual external thumb safety, as did nearly all semi-automatic pistols prior to its introduction. This intimi-

Most notable about a Glock; the absence of a manual thumb safety. This is both a selling point to some, and a detractor for others.

With proper training, Glock pistols are just as safe, if not safer than, other pistols. If you follow the commandments of safe shooting — chiefly, keep your finger off the trigger until ready to fire — there is no excuse for negligent discharge.

Train to properly clear your shirt from the mouth of the holster when re-holstering your pistol. This will prevent the shirt from entering the trigger guard and snagging the trigger. Also, take your time; there's no need to rush the re-holster.

dates many people who are new to shooting, and even those who have been shooting for a long time, but are unfamiliar with Glocks. I was leery when I first became interested in carrying a Glock. I've been around guns my entire adult life, and spent a considerable amount of time carrying one. When I carried in a military capacity, the service sidearm I carried was a Beretta M9, and that's the type of operating system I was used to: a safety/decocker SA/DA (single action/double action) pistol.

The first striker-fired pistol I purchased was a Ruger SR9, which has a thumb safety. When I finally decided to purchase a Glock, it was still not something I felt comfortable carrying. So, I put it to my own test. I handled it as much as possible and I carried it as much as possible, with no round in the chamber. As advertised, it never fired on that empty chamber. I started carrying it with a round in the chamber, and to my surprise, I found that I was more comfortable carrying it than I had been other handguns.

With handguns such as my 1911 being carried with the hammer cocked and the safety on, the thought of that safety being accidentally bumped in the holster, leaving it cocked and ready to fire was unnerving. I found myself constantly checking to see if the safety was on. I don't worry about that with a Glock. I know what condition it's in, and I know it's safe and cannot fire unless I pull it out of the holster, stick my finger in the trigger guard, and pull the trigger to the rear.

If you fall into this boat, interested in a Glock, but unsure about the lack of manual safety, don't be. Get some instruction, some range time, specifically "Glock-time," and you'll soon find your fears are all for naught.

I own a lot of Glocks, a Gen1, Gen2, Gen3, some Gen4s and some Gen5s, and have fired every model of Glock offered on the U.S. market, except for the G17L. Most models I've even fired every variant that is offered; Gen3, Gen4, SF (Short Frame), MOS, Gen5 and FS (Front Sight). Yet with all of those Glock pistols, not once has one negligently discharged. And they won't. They are designed to be safe, hence the name: Safe Action Pistol.

The key to safety with firearms, all firearms, not just Glocks, is training. I would never hand a firearm to a person without knowing their level of training. If you're handling a Glock, you must have finger/trigger awareness. You should know where your finger is at all times, and it should absolutely not be inside the trigger guard unless you are intentionally going to pull the trigger to the rear. The best place for your trigger finger is pointed straight ahead, alongside the frame, almost parallel with the bore. This is stressed in nearly every type of firearms training there is. If you keep your finger off the trigger until you are absolutely sure you are ready to fire a shot, (one of the 10 commandments of firearms safety) the lack of manual thumb safety is a moot point.

Probably the two most dangerous parts of firearms handling are unholstering and holstering. Negligent discharges while unholstering typically occur as the handgun leaves the holster and the trigger finger is not in proper position and the trigger is pulled. Some blame the holster in this, as it has occurred almost exclusively with holsters that require pressing a button or lever to release the handgun. The individual would press the button or lever with the tip of their finger, thus leaving their finger in a hook-shape, and as the pistol clears the holster the hooked finger enters the trigger guard. The answer is to leave the finger straight and press the button or lever with the underside of the finger, not the tip.

The other time of risk is holstering your Glock. If the shirt is not properly cleared from the mouth of the holster, as the handgun enters the holster, part of the shirt could enter the trigger guard, and become trapped between the trigger and holster, and as the Glock is pressed into the holster the shirt would press the trigger. The answer to this is to properly clear your shirt from the mouth of the holster by pulling it far enough away. This is an issue of training. Also, in a non-stress situation, there's nothing wrong with feeling the mouth of the holster, as you re-holster, to ensure there's nothing to snag. Just take your time re-holstering. This is real life, not a Hollywood Western, there's no need to rush the re-holster.

So, if it doesn't have a manual safety, what does it have? It has an automatic safety system consisting of three separate, passive mechanical safeties that come together to form the Glock "Safe Action" system. It is the purest safety available: In order to fire, one must deliberately stick a finger in the trigger guard and pull the trigger to the rear.

The trigger safety prevents the trigger from being pulled all the way to the rear. Notice I'm pushing on the trigger, but not the trigger safety.

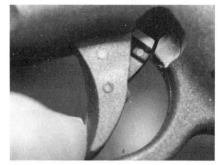

Here I'm pressing the trigger safety, and it has cleared the trigger.

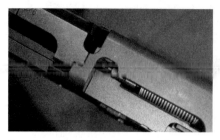

Top view of the firing pin safety at rest. It completely blocks the firing pin from moving forward and striking the primer.

The firing pin safety at rest. The trigger bar is also at rest and is not touching the firing pin safety.

The trigger has been pulled all the way to the rear, moving the trigger bar back, which pressed the firing pin safety up and out of the way, so that the firing pin may move forward to fire the gun.

The firing pin safety is up and out of the way, and the firing pin has moved forward to strike the primer.

SAFETY DEVICES

TRIGGER SAFETY

This is one of the first things people notice, after the lack of manual safety. It's one of the things that made the Glock famous when it first hit the scene. It consists of a lever incorporated into the trigger, and is, essentially, a trigger for the trigger. In its state of rest, it physically blocks the trigger from being pulled rearward. The trigger safety must be pulled to the rear at the same time as the trigger to disengage the safety and allow the gun to fire. If the trigger safety is not depressed, the trigger cannot be pulled to the rear, thus the weapon cannot be fired. It prevents unintentional firing as a result of being dropped or sideways pressure.

FIRING PIN SAFETY

The firing pin safety is a spring-loaded cylinder that in its untouched state presses into the firing pin channel, blocking the firing pin and preventing it from being able to touch a cartridge primer. The firing pin safety is disengaged by the trigger bar as the trigger and trigger safety are pulled to the rear. It prevents unintentional firing due to firing pin inertia.

DROP SAFETY

In order for the Glock to fire, the rear of the trigger bar must drop down, engaging the connector, thus releasing the striker. It looks like a step molded into the trigger mechanism housing (think of it as a drop safety) and prevents the trigger bar from dropping until the trigger is pulled rearward to a specific point. As the trigger bar moves rearward, the cruciform-shaped arm comes off the step and drops down. This is where you get the trigger break. The striker cannot be released until the trigger gets to that point.

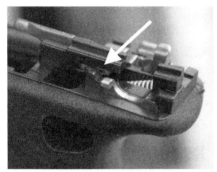

This is the trigger mechanism housing engaged (at rest) in the safe position. The trigger is forward. The trigger bar cruciform rests on the step, which prevents it from releasing down. The arrow points to the cruciform, in the safe position.

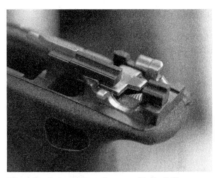

Here the trigger has been pulled all the way to the rear, and the trigger bar cruciform has moved all the way to the rear, passed the step, and drops down so the striker is released.

Here is another view of the cruciform all the way to the rear, where it dropped down. The arrow shows the "step" where the cruciform rests when the trigger is forward, in the safe position.

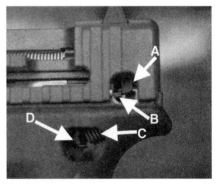

The firing pin lug (A) is resting on the rear of the trigger bar cruciform (B). The drop safety is engaged, in the safe position. Once the trigger is pulled, the cruciform will drop down out of the way of the firing pin lug, and the firing pin will snap forward, firing the Glock. You can also see the trigger spring (C) connected to the trigger bar cruciform leg (D).

CHAPTER 3:
PARTS IS PARTS

If you were alive from 1983 to 1984 you might remember a Wendy's marketing campaign called "Parts is Parts." In these popular commercials, a customer ordering food at a competitor's nondescript fast-food chain is told their chicken sandwich is made from parts of chickens. The customer asks, "Which parts?" to which the man behind the counter responds, "Parts is Parts."

The point is, it doesn't matter which parts of the chicken you use, because parts is parts. Though in the commercial Wendy's pokes fun at this, for non-food goods such as Glock pistols, this is a smart business practice. I doubt Gaston would have seen that commercial air in Austria, but you would think he had, because that's one of the brilliant manufacturing methods used by his company: make as many parts interchangeable between models as possible.

This interchangeability of parts is one of the hallmarks of Glock. For ease of manufacturing, the parts are standardized across the largest possible array of models. There are, of course, going to be some differences, but you can bet that whenever a new model is being developed, if it can use the same part as other models, Glock will use it. It's important, because anytime you minimize the number of parts in your company's inventory it streamlines the manufacturing process. Probably the most radical changes came with the G42 and G43 models, which Glock then incorporated those changes as the basis for the Gen5 models (more on that in later chapters). Glock is also very consistent about uniformity of parts. If you have 10 different G22s, you can completely disassemble all 34 parts (there are actually more than 34 parts, more on that later), put each part in its own bin, mix the parts up, reassemble the 10 G22s with the mixed up parts, and all parts will fit perfectly, and all handguns will perform perfectly. There is zero percent hand fitting needed.

That simplicity is part of the beauty of Glock. Everything about it is as simple as it possible. This is a boon for everyone. It's great for Glock, because it makes manufacture as simple and cost-effective as possible. It's good for the end-user, because the fewer parts there are, the fewer parts there are to break, and the more reliable the firearm. Plus, it's good for everyone in the entire supply chain, from Glock to armorers to the end-user, because as parts do wear or break, fewer parts makes it easier to get the part and fix it.

Furthermore, if a part is added to one model as an improvement, such as the locking block pin as a third pin to the .40 caliber models (G22, G23 and G27), it is often added to all models for standardization. And, just the same, when Glock decided (for the unforeseeable future) the Gen5 would not include any of the .40 caliber models, the locking block pin was removed from all Gen5 models.

Aside from the few parts that are not interchangeable, an armorer can have a tackle-box tray full of parts and when it comes time to fix a Glock, just grab the required part, swap it out and send the customer on his or her way.

It's important to note there are some parts that are listed as not interchangeable, and it's not because they wouldn't fit, it's because you just shouldn't swap them out. The perfect example are the compensated models, such as the 17C. It's not that you couldn't swap out the barrel of a 17C with a 17, but it would be completely unsafe to do so. You never want a compensated barrel on a non-compensated slide.

Glock officially lists 34 parts in its Gen5 pistol (Glock numbers it up to #35, but part #30, the locking block pin, doesn't exist in Gen5 models), but this isn't really an accurate number. First off, it lists the rear sight, front sight and screw as one part (#16, #16a, #16b, respectively). It's not really one part, and in inventory it used to be that they were sold together and couldn't be purchased separately, but now the front sight and rear sight can be purchased separately. This makes even more of an argument that they are separate parts. Second, the magazine floor plate and magazine insert used to be listed as one part (#32 and #32a, respectively), but are now two separate parts (#34 and #35). Plus, with the Gen5, the trigger spring (#25) is now in reality an assembly comprised of three parts. (Just because something is called an *assembly* doesn't mean it's only one part. Otherwise we could just call the slide and all the internal parts an assembly and list it as only one part.) Some people argue that the spring cup (#8) is two parts, but I disagree. It's one part with two halves.

Also, take into account the trigger with trigger bar is listed as one part (#26), but in reality it's an assembly that's comprised of four parts: trigger, trigger safety, trigger safety pin and trigger bar. This trigger assembly will never come as separate parts, and is considered

The original G17 Gen1 field-stripped into five major parts groups: the slide, frame, barrel, recoil spring assembly and magazine.

a permanent assembly, so Glock labels it as one part. But if you did consider it as four separate parts, this would put the total number of parts at 41. Forty-one doesn't sound as good as 34, but it's still an incredibly low number of parts.

To put this into context, you have to compare it to the number of parts other popular sidearms were comprised of in the era that the Glock was designed. The beloved 1911 Government Model has 52 parts. The Beretta 92F has 62 parts. In law enforcement, the firearms the Glock 17 replaced had even more parts. The Smith & Wesson J Frame revolvers have between 86 and 90 parts. Smith & Wesson semi-autos, the Series 39, 59 and 69, had 99 parts.

When the schematics of these firearms are held next to the one for the Glock, the simplicity of the Glock makes one question why these other designs require so many parts? Perhaps as manufacturers raced to outdo each other, their answer to "Can we make it better?" was to add more parts. Parts led to more parts, and soon there were handguns that had 99 parts.

I look at older models, such as the Colt Single Action Army with 47 parts, a respectable number, and see how, over time, as one safety mechanism is added here, another added there, those parts add up, and five decades later you have a revolver with 70 parts.

When I was just a little guy, I remember riding in my stepdad's 1974 Chevy Suburban. I would stand on the floor of the second row (this was before seat belts were mandatory) with my head peeking up over the front row bench seats. I don't know why this sticks in my head, but I remember at the bottom of his odometer was a label he had made that read, "KISS" (If you were alive back then you probably remember the gun-type label makers; you had to rotate a disk of letters until the one you wanted was centered on the tape and you would squeeze the handle and the letter would be imprinted onto the tape). I looked at this sticker for a long time before finally asking what it meant. "Keep It Simple Stupid," he told me. It was a reminder that no matter how complicated a situation can get, it's best to try to keep it simple.

Since Gaston Glock spoke little English at the time he developed the Glock 17, I doubt if he had heard of KISS, but maybe the Austrians have something similar in German, perhaps this: Halten Sie es einfach blöd. Either way, the Glock design exemplifies the KISS principle, not just in the pistol itself, but the entire manufacturing philosophy. It just makes sense to use the same part in as many models as you can.

Despite the standardization that Glock has, there are some optional parts that deviate from this, such as the New York trigger. The New York Police Department for the most part went directly from revolver to Glock; from an 8-pound revolver trigger pull to a 5.5 pound Glock trigger. New officers adapted quickly, but officers who had been using revolvers for years had a steep learning curve, and that led to some problems with negligent discharge. So, the NYPD wanted a heavier trigger, and since the NYPD is such a large department, Glock complied. Hence, the NY trigger was born. It makes the Glock trigger feel more like a revolver trigger.

At the armorer's course, I got to install and manipulate a New York trigger spring. The instructor told us parts will sometimes "get up and walk away" by the end of class, but they've never had a NY trigger come up missing. In fact, they once had an extra one turned in at the end of the class. I guess someone had an extra and didn't want it. I can honestly say I wouldn't wish the NY trigger upon my greatest enemy. For those who complain about the standard Glock trigger, try running a NY trigger in your Glock. It makes the factory 5.5-pound trigger feel like a custom aftermarket trigger.

It comes in two different models. The NY1 trigger spring is olive green with a silver spring, and adds 3 pounds to the overall trigger pull weight. The NY2 trigger is orange colored with a black spring and adds 5 pounds to the overall trigger pull weight.

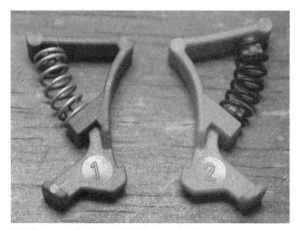

NY Trigger 1 (left), and NY Trigger 2. The greatest travesty perpetrated on Glock shooters.

A couple of notes on the NY trigger. First, never install either NY trigger with the 8-pound connector (marked with a "+"). Second, when installing the NY trigger spring, make sure the connector fits snugly in the trigger mechanism housing. If it doesn't fit tightly, the housing and/or the connector must be replaced to make sure it does fit snugly. Fortunately, the NY trigger isn't something Glock inflicts upon the general population, it's something for law enforcement only. However, if you really wanted one, they can be found online, but why would you want to?

The 3.5-pound connector has a minus sign on it, like this one. The 8-pound connector has a plus sign, and the standard 5.5-pound connector has nothing.

Another option is the connector. Standard Glock handguns ship with 5.5-pound connectors, but 4.5-pound (marked with a "-") and 8-pound (marked with a "+") connectors are also available, though you'll have to be an armorer to get one directly from Glock. During the printing of the 2002 armorer's manual, there is a reference to a 3.5-pound connector. That connector was closer to a 4.5-pound pull than a 3.5-pound

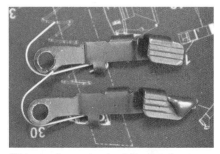

Slide stop lever, standard (top) and extended.

pull, so it was renamed 4.5-pound connector, but it is the same connector.

Glock also lists three different firing pin springs, the standard spring, a 28 Newton spring colored red, and a 31 Newton spring colored blue. Only the standard spring is available for the U.S. market. Glock also offers four different magazine catches: A standard,

Maritime spring cups on the right, standard on the left. Despite what your friends on the Internet say, do not fire your handgun under water.

an extended, an ambidextrous and an oval spring. You've most likely never seen an oval spring, those are also not available for the U.S. market.

One optional part more familiar to most people is the slide stop lever, which comes in two models, the standard and the extended. The extended has a little nubby on it, which makes quite a bit of difference in being able to release the slide, especially while gloved. Since I live in a climate in which I wear gloves about half the year, I'm a big fan of the extended lever.

Another option that you will never see unless you're a member of an elite water-born tactical unit, is the Maritime Spring Cup. You'll need a special letter from your unit commander for a set of these, because they can be potentially dangerous in the hands of the uniformed.

Standard polymer sights.

Standard steel sights. If your Glock gets knocked about quite a bit, switch to these.

Polymer adjustable sights. Great for competition, but not very rugged.

MH3 luminous night sights are made of steel and very rugged. They work great night or day.

Another Glock luminous night sight option. Great for day...

...or night.

Dangerous as in "lose your hearing for life, go to the hospital or even death for the user" danger. Internet commandos will tell you a set of these cups will allow you to shoot under water. That's a big no-no, and if one would be so inclined to do so, please re-read the preceding sentence. What it is for, however, is to allow the firing pin to function at full speed, with the firing pin channel filled with water, after the previously submerged gun has been brought out of the water, not *while* submerged. That's it.

Firing a pistol underwater while the user is submerged can lead to damage to internal organs, and potentially death, so don't do it. For those of us who don't train or conduct amphibious landings on a day-to-day basis, the conventional spring cups work just fine.

Sights are the area that Glock offers the most options. Sights can be had in polymer (rear sights can be adjustable or non-adjustable), steel, luminescent (steel), or self-luminescent dot (steel). Polymer sights are fine, and they function. They're OK for light housework. If it's a duty gun, or if your life could potentially depend upon placing accurate shots on target, get the steel sights. Steel is a lot tougher and won't be damaged nearly as easily. This is important not only for accurate shooting, but also if you're ever in danger and have an injured hand or arm, and need to use the sight to charge the slide.

For low-light conditions, I'm a big fan of the self-luminescent dot sights. They're brighter and don't require you to "charge" the sight with a light source beforehand. Since a lot of violent encounters happen at night, whether outside or inside the home, I recommend the night sights.

BARRELS

Glock barrels are hammer forged, a process in which a mandrel consisting of the reverse image of the rifling is inserted into an oversized, bored-out barrel, and both are inserted into a hammer-forging machine. Rotary hammers forge the barrel around the mandrel until it reaches the proper diameter, and the rifling is formed.

In Generations 1-4, the rifling is rounded polygonal, and is either hexagonal or octagonal, depending on the model. There is debate as to which is better, polygonal rifling or conventional rifling, and advocates on either side will tell you their way is better. Sound arguments have been made by both sides.

Glock barrels are cold hammer forged in a machine like this one being used for rifle barrels. (Photo Courtesy of Gunblast.com)

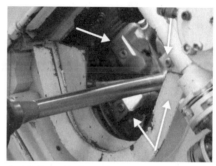

A rifle barrel being cold hammer forged, just like a Glock barrel. The arrows point to the four hammers that surround the barrel (The hammer at the four o'clock position is out of view from this angle). (Photo Courtesy of Gunblast.com)

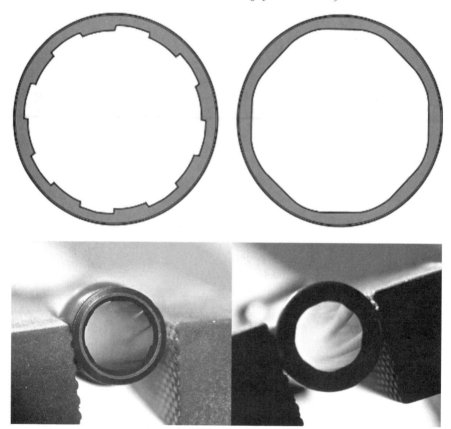

Conventional rifling (left) versus polygonal rifling (right). Note the more aggressive, squared-off rifling that is conventional, whereas the polygonal rifling is smoother and rounded off. Which is better? It's an age-old debate.

The barrel locking lug has been revamped in the Gen5 (bottom) and is now located farther to the rear. There's more wear in the finish of the Gen5, but it was used in testing for an article and has had far more rounds through it.

The advocates for polygonal rifling will argue there is a better bullet-to-barrel fit, making for a better gas seal. This leads to higher and more uniform velocities, as well as less bullet deformity. Better accuracy is also a consideration, though I've fired some really accurate handguns that have conventional rifling.

For me, the best argument is polygonal rifling is less aggressive, so when a bullet travels over the rifling there is less wear on the rifling, leading to longer barrel life. There's also less area for powder and jacket residue to build up, making it easier to clean. The one downside is that you cannot shoot un-jacketed lead bullets, which is the cheapest way to shoot, especially for reloaders.

I don't shoot cast bullets out of my semi-autos so I don't have personal experience in this issue. From what I've read, though, the issue is the polygonal rifling creates a better seal than conventional rifling, which means less gas escapes, so with an un-coated bullet the lead gets hotter and leaves behind more residue. Plus, polygonal rifling creates greater surface area on the bullet, also leaving behind more residue. This leads to potential pressure hazards.

When Glock released the 17M and 19M (and subsequently the Gen5), they equipped it with a Glock Marksman Barrel (GMB), which has conventional rifling which uses lands and grooves. This surprised the gun community, because Glock has espoused the virtues of polygonal rifling since inception, and many viewed it as acknowledgment that perhaps conventional rifling is more accurate. The addition of a muzzle crown is a good thing in my opinion, and the conventional rifling will be a good thing for those who reload. Accuracy is good, though I didn't see a huge difference between the GMB and the previous type.

The GMB looks different from other barrels. Why? The barrel locking lug is different from previous generation Glocks. This is why Gen5 barrels can't work with previous Gen Glocks, and why previous Gen Glock barrels don't work with Gen5 Glocks. This was done for sake of uniformity of parts, the G17 Gen5 now uses the same locking block as does the G19. The G19 has always used part number 7894 for the locking block (Gen1-Gen5), and the G17 has used part number 1447. But now the Gen5 G17 also uses part number 7894. Because of the locking block position change, the recoil spring is now longer on the Gen5.

PARTS UPGRADE

If you own or purchase an older Glock made prior to 1992, it could be subject to a parts upgrade, which, if returned to Glock, will be done free of charge. It only affects models up to and including the G23. Everything after that was made after 1992 and comes with the upgraded parts. The upgrade includes new firing pin, extractor, firing pin safety, spring-loaded bearing and trigger bar. To tell if your Glock can use an upgrade, look at the serial numbers' alphabetical prefix. The applicable prefix will be up to and including the following serial number ranges:

The 15-degree angle, started with Gen3 (bottom). Gen2 is on top.

- Glock 17: up to and including XG
- Glock 19: up to and including XK
- Glock 20: up to and including WX
- Glock 21: up to and including XM
- Glock 22: up to and including YB
- Glock 23: up to and including SL

If your Glock has a three-letter prefix, it already has the upgraded parts system. Additionally, for G21 pistols, all pistols prior to serial number ALD can be sent in for slide modifications, where the right rear edge of the ejection port is cut to a 15-degree angle, and the pickup rail is reduced.

Also, in 1995, Glock started to change the angle of the ejection port back face, and the extractors. The angle of earlier Glocks was 90 degrees (to the bore axis), but the change would cut the ejection port rear face back by 15 degrees. Due to the new angle, the extractor face would also have to be cut by 15 degrees. The change started with the G19, due to a malfunction that was caused by an empty case getting caught up between the barrel hood and the slide as it was coming into battery. The fix was the 15-degree angle, as well as a change to the barrel hood. Eventually the change trickled down to all models.

This affects models with the following serial numbers:
- Glock 17: up to and including BKK
- Glock 17L: up to and including BMD
- Glock 19: up to and including XK
- Glock 20: up to and including WX
- Glock 21: up to and including XM
- Glock 22: up to and including YB
- Glock 23: up to and including SL
- Glock 24/24C: up to and including BMT
- Glock 26: up to and including BMX
- Glock 27: up to and including BMY

If your serial number is after these, you have the 15-degree cut. Or, you could just look at your ejector port to see if the rear face runs parallel to the breech or if it's cut at an angle.

CHAPTER 4:
IT'S A GENERATIONAL THING

If you've ever been in a conversation about Glocks, you've no doubt heard discussion about the five different generations of Glock, starting with the Gen1 and ending with the current Gen5 models. Only the Gen4 and Gen5 are designated as such on the slide; previous generations weren't officially marked on the slide, even though they're often referenced by generation. This has led to a lot of confusion among those who aren't Glockophiles. Especially if you factor in that some models straddle the fence between Gen4 and Gen5 and aren't marked on the slide as either. Examples of this are the G45 and G19X and the Slimline Glocks (G42, G43, G43X and G48). Time to clear up some of that confusion.

Glock has had a shift in regard to its distinction between the various Glock generations. It's a little peculiar, but the company is no longer recognizing Gen1, 2 or 3 pistols. Before the first edition of this book, if you talked to a Glock salesperson about the current production lineup at that time, there was Gen3 or Gen4. Then the changed it so there was only a Gen4 pistol, and "previous generations." So, to call a pistol Gen1, Gen2, or Gen3 isn't in keeping with the "official" Glock policy. Honestly, I think this is kind of silly. Having a Gen4 and labeling it as such is acknowledging that there are three previous generations of pistols, and if there are three previous generations of pistols, it's natural to define what those generations are. I will do so in this book, even if Glock won't, because I need to differentiate between the generations.

Something else to bear in mind is that the changes made to mark each new generation of Glock are not the only changes made to the various models. Generally, each change to a new generation is marked by a change in the external, physical appearance, most specifically to the frame, while along the way changes have been made internally that do not mark a change in generation. Sometimes these internal changes are more important than the external changes that do mark a new generation. For example, the addition of a third takedown pin to improve strength is more important structurally than is the change in Gen1 to Gen2 grip texture. But the change in grip texture is more easily noticed and is what marked the new generation. It makes sense, since it's the external changes to the frame we notice most, as the frame is the interface through which we handle the handgun. Even though an internal change might be more important to the operation of the pistol, we don't notice the addition of a pin or a change to one of the parts. But what we notice immediately is how the grip feels in our hand, or whether we can put a flashlight on it.

FIRST GENERATION: 1982-1989

When I was first given the assignment for this book, one of the first things I realized was I had never fired a Gen1 Glock, and had only fired a Gen2 once, in 1994. I knew that was something I wanted to do for the book, so I set out to acquire one of each. I quickly learned the market is filled with Gen3 and Gen4 pistols for sale, but the first two generations were a little harder to find.

This earlier Glock took a lot of work to track down. I found very few, and the ones

Proof markings on the slide.

I did were asking what I thought was too much: $750 to $850. I didn't really know much about Gen1 Glocks, so I headed to some forums to find out about pricing. Everyone agreed: The Gen1 Glocks are becoming hard to find, and even rare. But this was followed with advice on where different people would draw the line on cost. Some wouldn't pay more than $550, some drew the line at $600, and others said they wouldn't pay more than $700. The free market was disagreeing with them though, as the $750 Glocks were selling on the auction websites.

I finally found one, just as I wanted it, stock sights, with box and manual, listed for $550. I made a bid that would take me up to $650 if need be. About an hour later I found another listing, this one for $600, so I bid on that one as well. I figured, as hot as these things are becoming, with bids on two, I'd still be lucky to get just one. And even if I did win both, they would be a good investment. I lost the second auction, but won the first, for $590. I was

Proof markings on barrel (serial number is just to the left, but has been blurred per owner request).

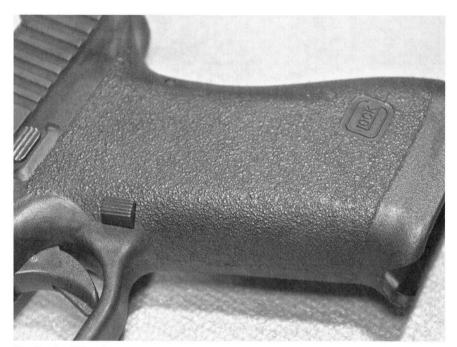

The Gen1 pebble grip texture.

Exploded view of a G17 Gen1.

happy with that, and happy with the condition. It has a born-on date of 1988, and with some cleaning it's in very good condition. Of course, that was all in 2014, but as I write this in 2019, searches of that same auction website show fewer listings of Gen1 pistols, and prices are above $1,000. I've seen some for around $1,250, even listings for up to $2,800 (though I haven't seen any sell at this price).

Theories abound on why there is a Gen1 shortage, but here's the skinny, right from Glock: There were just never that many of them sold in the U.S. Only about 25,000 Glock G17 Gen1s were ever sold here. If there is one Glock that is collectible and appreciating quickly, it's this one. If you find one for a good price, buy it now while you can.

As popular as the Glock was from the very start, there was one thing that shooters saw as a drawback: With wet hands, be it water, sweat, blood, etc., the grips became very slippery and hard to hold on to. As a result, an improved grip was one of the primary upgrades that led to the Gen2.

I really like the feel of the Gen1 while shooting; it feels very nice in the hand. It's comfortable, controllable and in general it is a pleasure to shoot. I had a buddy with me when I first fired it, a novice shooter with limited experience. I first had him shoot a 9mm in one of Glock's main competitors, and then the Gen1 G17. He loved the Gen1 and didn't care for the other one as much. He said the grips on the Glock were better, and it was more enjoyable to shoot. So after nearly three decades, even Gen1 Glocks are still a match for current competitor's guns.

SECOND GENERATION: 1989-1997

The benefits of the Glock are apparent and can be summarized by the statement "every time you pull the trigger it fires." Still, many point out the Glock's "ugly brick" appearance. However, as polymer pistols have become the norm, most have gotten accustomed to the look, and in fact have learned to appreciate its simple beauty. However, there are others, mostly the "I'll only carry wood and steel guns" type, who can't get past the looks. Most people couldn't imagine this "hunk of plastic" ever becoming a collector's item. But in fact, it has.

It took me just a couple weeks to lock onto a Gen2, and the one I found was in excellent condition with manual and box. I paid $450 for it. It's not uncommon to find them online for $500 to $600, depending on the condition and how early they were made. That's more than they cost new, and as much as a Gen3, which you can still buy new on the shelves (even as of this writing, in 2019). These prices certainly won't go down, and as more people see the Glock as something to collect, the prices will most likely go up.

The beauty of the Glock is that people have always bought them to use and shoot. Given their reputation as being nearly impossible to break, some even buy them to neglect. As in, "Hey, I'm going to throw this Glock in the back of my truck and drive around for 10 years, only taking it out when I need it." So even though you can buy an old Glock to collect, you can still shoot it, it's not a safe queen.

I well remember the time I saw and shot my first Glock. In 1994, I was plinking with a Marine buddy of mine. He had his Taurus PT92, and I had my Auto-Ordnance Government Model 1911. He said, "Hey check this out. This is one of those new Glocks." He then reached under his Jeep steering wheel, and with the unmistakable sound of Velcro ripping

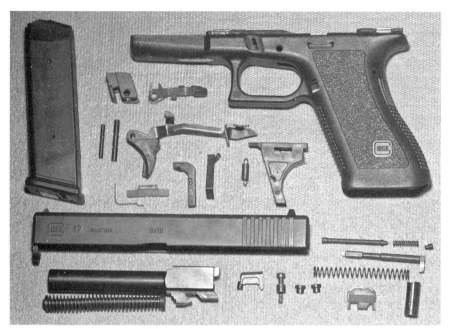

Exploded view of a G17 Gen2.

apart, he pulled out a pistol. I had no idea what he was talking about, but the pistol he showed me was one ugly gun. "This is one of those new plastic pistols," he said.

It dawned on me that I had heard about the airport metal detector controversy, and he explained to me how that was all a load of bunk. He handed me the pistol, pointing out that he had a strip of Velcro attached to the length of the slide. He said, "Yeah, I was talking with an MP (Military Police) the other day, and he asked me why I had Velcro on the slide of my gun. I told him because it sticks to stuff." My buddy then demonstrated how he kept it under the dashboard.

I found it peculiar, because I would never think of sticking Velcro to the slide of my prized 1911. We had a good chuckle about it, then we loaded it and started to plink at cans. His demonstration is a great example of the prevailing attitude toward the Glock, even back then. It's not a safe queen to be babied; it's a rugged workhorse that makes an excellent go-to gun. It's a gun to have by your side, even if it means sticking Velcro to it. At the time I was enamored with the 1911 and anything .45, so I didn't pay much attention to the 9mm G17, but looking back I wish I had.

My Gen2, which has a born-on date of February 1992, is a pleasure to shoot. It feels and handles nicely, a lot like a Gen3, it just doesn't have a front accessory rail. For a lot of people, myself included, that's not a big deal. I don't need an accessory rail on every handgun I own, and to be honest, with the exception of two handguns that I use for specific purposes, I rarely ever use it. I know in today's throwaway society where technology can be new and then obsolete within the same calendar year, we have a tendency to think that if something isn't the latest and greatest, we need to upgrade. However, with Glock pistols, there

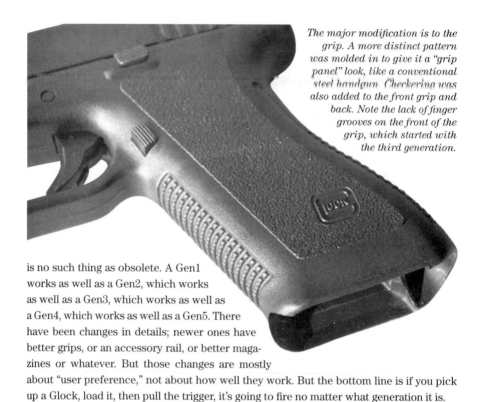

The major modification is to the grip. A more distinct pattern was molded in to give it a "grip panel" look, like a conventional steel handgun. Checkering was also added to the front grip and back. Note the lack of finger grooves on the front of the grip, which started with the third generation.

is no such thing as obsolete. A Gen1 works as well as a Gen2, which works as well as a Gen3, which works as well as a Gen4, which works as well as a Gen5. There have been changes in details; newer ones have better grips, or an accessory rail, or better magazines or whatever. But those changes are mostly about "user preference," not about how well they work. But the bottom line is if you pick up a Glock, load it, then pull the trigger, it's going to fire no matter what generation it is.

There were several changes made from the Gen1 to the Gen2, some more apparent than others. Not all changes were done at the same time. The major changes that occurred with each generation were first made to the G17, but some models made the change before the G17 (for instance, the G22 added the third pin before the change was made to all models). Most look at the release of the new grip style as the demarcation date between Gen1 and Gen2, but in reality, changes were ongoing, and Glock changed things as the need arose.

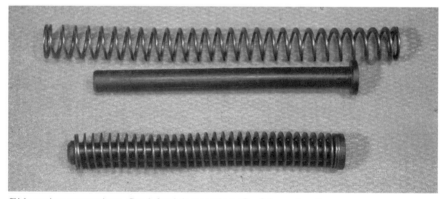

Slide spring comparison. Gen1 (top) is two piece, Gen2 is captured.

Firing pin safety, Gen2 (left) compared to Gen1. Very similar, but look at the base where the spring is seated. (This Gen1 part falls under the 1992 parts upgrade, but has not been upgraded on this pistol).

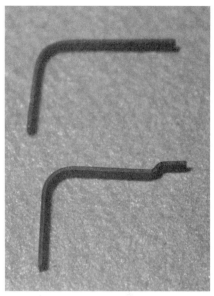

Change in the slide block spring. Gen1 (top) compared to Gen2.

Gen2 (left) ejector compared to Gen1. Shown are the front (top) and back of the ejector. (This Gen1 part falls under the 1992 parts upgrade, but has not been upgraded on this pistol.)

The most apparent change is the grip texture and the pattern in which it's applied. It doesn't just encircle the whole grip like the Gen1, it's been molded to represent side panels, like those found in a traditional metal pistol with screw-on grip panels. Then checkering was added to the front of the grip and the backstrap. The texture on the front of the trigger guard was also changed. All of this was done to improve grip, especially with wet hands. This texture and checkering pattern is continued in Gen3.

Barrel markings, Gen2 (top) versus Gen1. Note the Austrian proof marks on Gen1, which are gone in Gen2. Serial numbers are located just to the left on both barrels, but have been blurred per owner request.

Different firing pins; Gen2 (left) has changed a bit from the Gen1. (This Gen1 part falls under the 1992 parts upgrade, but has not been upgraded on this pistol).

Gen2 (left), Gen1 (right). Note the change to the frame — the length of ledge just to the right of the line annotation.

The barrel on the Gen1 (right) has a thicker hood and wider feed ramp.

The other major change is the slide spring, which was made captive. This is one of my favorite changes, as it's one less part to launch and lose. In fact, I view the captive slide spring as one of the important changes to semi-auto handgun design. This is such a vast improvement it always surprises me when I see a handgun maker release a new model that still has a non-captive spring.

There are a several minor changes to various parts, which can be seen in the accompanying photos. Those changes include firing pin, extractor, slide lock spring and the trigger bar.

After the first edition of this book came out, naturally I've talked to a lot of people about Glocks. For the people who've been around Glocks for a long time, I get more people telling me the Gen2 is their favorite, than I do any other generation. To them, they'd take a Gen2 over a Gen3 or Gen4 any day of the week, with the exception that some of them would add an accessory rail to the Gen2. But otherwise they wouldn't change a thing. Which, kind of interesting having these conversations a few years ago, when you fast forward to 2018 and the Gen5 frame is very similar to that: a Gen2 type "straight" grip (i.e., no finger grooves), but with an accessory rail added. (I use the term, "similar," loosely; there are many differences between the Gen2 and Gen5 frame other than the accessory rail.)

THIRD GENERATION: 1997-PRESENT

The Gen3 Glock was introduced in 1997 and is still in current production, as of 2019. This generation had more changes made from the previous generations than any other model.

Third generation Glock, exploded view.

The Gen3 frame is also known as the FGR Frame, a.k.a. Finger Groove Rail frame. This one is in Flat Dark Earth.

For many, the Gen3, often referred to as the FGR frame (Finger Groove and Rail), was the first Glock they owned or fired, and they still prefer it to the Gen4 or Gen5. It offers similar features to the Gen4, except without the aggressive grip texture, which many people don't care for. Good news for those people: Glock has no current plans to stop production of the Gen3, it will continue to be made and offered alongside the Gen4 and Gen5. No other generation of Glock has such a devoted following. With the Gen4 and Gen5 it seems you either love them or don't care for them, but everyone loves the Gen3. A lot of changes were made to arrive at the Gen3, solid changes that cemented Glock's position as the foremost innovator in handguns.

As the FGR frame name describes, one of the biggest new features of the Gen3 is the accessory rail. Glock knew the rail was becoming the next big thing, so it was wisely incorporated it into the new frame. At the time of its introduction in 1997, I was still in the Marine Corps, and the center of my handgun universe was the Beretta M9, which didn't have a rail. I did very little civilian shooting and had very little exposure to what civilians were carrying. The result is that I knew very little about what was happening in handgun design at this time, and knew nothing about rails. I got out of the Corps in late 2000, and it was around 2002 that I started to get into civilian shooting. Those next few years would see us enter two wars, and see the evolution of special police units into high-speed, low-drag terrorist combating teams. As a result, accessory rails, on rifles as well as handguns, became huge.

Since about 70 percent of U.S. police departments issue Glock pistols, it is common to see Glock pistols equipped with tactical lights or lasers. The next five years would see the growth of accessory rails to the point where hardly any pistols are offered without

The Gen3 ejection port rear face got a 15-degree angle cut into it.

them. Even some revolvers and 1911s now offer rails. (The biggest exception to this trend is the micro handguns designed for concealed carry; most do not have rails, because the very purpose of these guns is to be as small as possible, so people usually don't add accessories to these.)

The other change is the finger grooves, the other component of the FGR frame name. The Gen2 front grip was straight, but the Gen3 incorporated finger grooves to enhance the grip (Gen5 would see the finger grooves go away). Checkering is found between the grooves. Additionally, the finger notch at the bottom front of the magazine well went away with the Gen3 (and then came back with the Gen5, only to go away again with the Gen5 MOS FS (Front Serrations), and then later be removed completely from all Gen5 models). This notch was to assist in grasping the magazine to pull it out, and dates back to when the magazine wasn't drop-free.

A third change to the frame came in the form of a thumb rest. It was primarily done for import reasons, and has little impact on gripping the handgun or control.

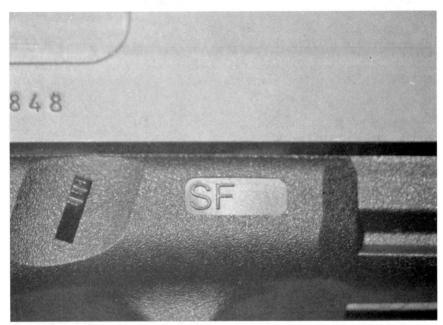

The "SF" means Short Frame, and designates a smaller grip length (measuring fore to aft).

The third generation grip texture is mostly the same as the second generation, but with the addition of a thumb rest.

Other important changes were also made, such as the shape of the extractor. The Gen3 extractor is cut to give it a loaded chamber indicator, which, when in position and with a round in the chamber, protrudes from the slide enough to give tactile confirmation of a loaded chamber. A third takedown pin was also added, this one the locking block pin. This was initially added to the G22, but was later introduced to almost all models. Another change came in the form of a modification to the ejection port. Previous guns had an ejection port rear face that was cut at a 90-degree angle to the bore. The Gen3 had the ejection port rear face cut back at a 15-degree angle (15 degrees from where it was, not 15 degrees from the bore).

Other minor changes include the firing pin, firing pin safety, the trigger bar, slide-stop lever, slide-lock spring, magazine catch (it was skeletonized), front sight, spring-loaded bearing and the locking block. Another minor change was to the trigger mechanism housing: A punch hole was added so the connector could be pushed out without damage.

Something else that you might notice if comparing generations of Glock; starting with the Gen3 there is a change in the color of some of the internal components. Most of the parts I'm referring to are the springs, but it also includes the extractor plunger and firing pin. These parts went from a darker, blued metal, to more of a metallic color. The new parts each weighs slightly more on the scale, and under closer inspection they look more porous. The only answer I got from Glock is that they don't make the springs, but I got nothing from them on the firing pin or plunger.

Also introduced in the Gen3 was a version of large frame pistols that are labeled with an "SF" on the right side of the frame. These are short-frame Glocks. More on that in subsequent chapters.

Most models are still made in Gen3, unless it came out after the introduction of Gen4 in 2009, which includes the G40 and everything after. Some models, the G30S, G36 and all of the .45 GAP models, are only available in Gen3, their sales never justified making them in Gen4. For large-frame models chambered in 10mm and .45 ACP, the Gen3 models only come in "SF" configurations and are designated as such. Glock doesn't designate Gen3 models as Gen3, they just don't include a "Gen4" or "Gen5" in the name. So, for example, the Gen3 G20 model is designated as "G20 SF." Compared to the Gen4 version, which is designated as "G20 Gen4."

FOURTH GENERATION: 2010-PRESENT

Introduced in 2010, while not the newest generation of Glock, Gen4 offers the most models at this time, making it the most commonly found. Externally, one of the first differences most people notice is the grip texture. Gone is the pebble grip texture, replaced by the new Glock RTF (Rough Textured Frame) textured grip. The RTF texture is on both side grip panels, the backstrap (and the additional modular straps) and on the front grip between the finger grooves. It is more aggressive than any previous grip, giving better purchase with slippery hands or in wet conditions. Some like it, others don't. Those who don't, argue that it's a little too aggressive. I like it a lot, especially when shooting large calibers like the 10mm out of little guns like the G29.

A Gen4 Glock, exploded view.

However, I will concede that if you're carrying it and it's rubbing against your skin, it does burn after awhile. I've found that with the holster I use, it's not an issue in most of my daily activities. It bothers me most when I'm sitting in my car with the seat belt connector pushing the grip into my side. However, tucking a piece of my shirt between the grip and my skin easily alleviates this. Another issue is one made by law enforcement officers who carry a firearm throughout long shifts: The aggressive grip can wear a hole through uniform shirts.

Also, the grip texture on the front panel of the trigger guard has changed. Gen3 texture was a raised step-type pattern, but with the Gen4 it's now just a series of raised lines that go left to right.

The next external change is the enlarged magazine catch. It is bigger, making it easier to thumb, and internally has also been made reversible for right- and left-hand shooters. That's a great move by Glock. It was an easy fix, but it can make many shooters much more efficient. To go along with this change, Glock has configured the magazine to work with the reversible mag catch. You'll notice a notch on both sides now. Along with this change is a change to the mag catch spring recess in the frame mold. It now resembles a "V" instead of half a V, so the mag catch spring has a full range of motion when used in right- or left-hand configuration. To accommodate the reversible mag catch, the magazine was also changed. The addition of a notch to the left side is for when the magazine catch is in the left-hand position.

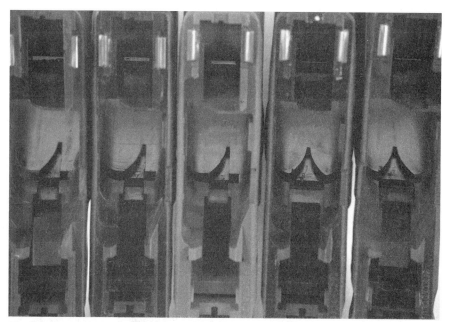

The evolution of the mag catch spring cutout (in generational order, Gen1 left, Gen5 right): Gen1 through Gen3 do not have an ambidextrous mag catch, whereas the Gen4 and Gen5 do.

The Gen4 magazine (right) now has a notch on the right side to accommodate the reversible magazine catch. It will still work with previous generations of Glock pistols.

Despite initial reports, older non-ambidextrous magazines will still work in Gen4 pistols, as long as the mag catch is in the right-hand (factory) position (which is on the left side). If you're a lefty and have the mag catch in the left-hand position, you're out of luck with old magazines. Another thing that has been misreported at times, the new Gen4 mags will also work with previous Glock generations. I've heard more than one gun-counter "expert" say if you have an older generation Glock and lose the magazines you're out of luck, because Glock won't be making them anymore. While he was correct in that Glock isn't making those magazines anymore, no one is out of luck because Gen4 mags will work in those older Glocks. Plus, those magazines (especially the 9mm and .40-calibers) were made in such vast numbers, you can find used ones all over the Internet.

The Gen4 magazine release button has been enlarged (bottom).

The Gen4 magazine release button (right) is larger than the Gen3 — plus it's reversible.

The Gen4 magazine release button (left) compared to the Gen3.

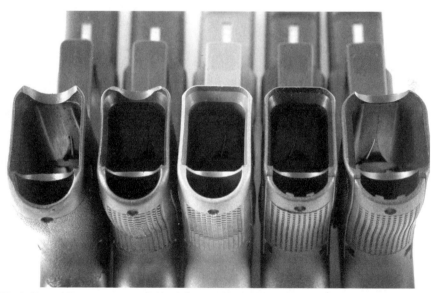

The bottom of the magazine well, Gen1 through Gen5 (left to right). The original Glocks didn't have a drop-free magazine, and you can see the finger notch in the front of the mag well for gripping the magazine to pull it out. This stayed with the frame until Gen3. Oddly enough, the Gen5 saw the return of the finger notch, despite having drop-free magazines.

The inside of the mag well, showing the difference in the reversible mag catch notch between Gen3 (left) and the reversible Gen4 (right).

One of the major external changes made, which might or might not be as readily apparent just by looking at the pistol, are the Gen4 modular backstraps. In my opinion this is the most important change, because it allows the user to customize the grip to fit his or her hand size. Glock was a little late to the game when it comes to customizable backstraps; all of the major competitors already offered it. Better late than never.

The backstraps that come in a Gen4 box vary depending on the model. Some models come with two backstraps (offering three different grip options), while some come with four backstraps (two standard and two beavertail, offering five different grip options). The grips also come with an additional trigger mechanism housing pin which is longer than the one that comes inserted from the factory to accommodate the wider backstraps.

Another external difference of note is the guide ring at the muzzle end of the slide. It's much larger, almost twice the size, of the Gen3 guide ring. The larger hole makes for a thinner guide ring hole wall, which will make the guide ring more prone to damage if the slide is dropped on it while disassembled from the frame. This is about the only time the slide can be damaged, when disassembled from the frame, so just don't drop it while it's disassembled, and it won't be a problem. Still, it's a small price to pay for the trade-off; the reason for the bigger guide ring is the more robust, captured recoil spring/rod.

The Gen4 recoil spring/rod is more robust. It is dual spring. It's also captive, so no more separate parts to get lost or launch into orbit. There are 12 different springs used for the various Glock models (up through Gen4), including two different ones for the G42 and G43.

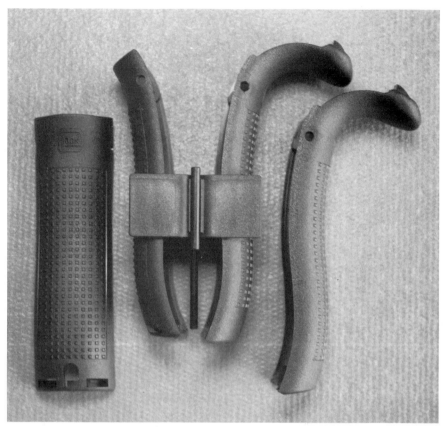

Gen4 pistols come with backstraps; this one comes with two sizes of standard, and two sizes of beavertail. A longer trigger housing pin can be seen attached (center).

The ejector, located on the trigger mechanism housing, is another change from the Gen3. Previously there were three different ejectors, one for the 9mm and .380, one for the .40 and .357 and one for the 10mm, .45 Auto and .45 GAP. The Gen4 ejectors have been expanded to four ejectors, splitting the .40 and .357 into two different parts. The shape of the ejector has also changed; previous models came to a point, but Gen4 models have more of a squared-off tip, with the exception of the 10mm/.45/.45 GAP model, it still has a point. The squared-off tip makes it look more rugged, though I don't think that was ever an issue with the ejector.

Until recently there was, on the right side of the frame just behind the accessory rail, a three-letter code, "MBS" (Modular Backstrap System). However, in the spring of 2014, Glock decided the marking was unnecessary and discontinued it.

I heard grumblings from some people about the Gen4 when it came out, that they don't like it, or that they've heard of someone having problems with one. I think this is to be expected with any gun on the market. Gun owners are a particular lot, and we can be critical

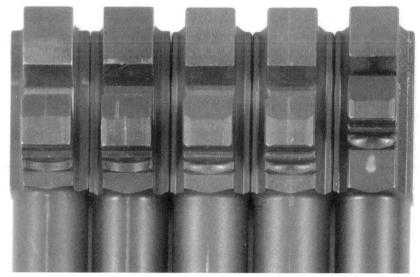

Barrel lug comparison Gen1 through Gen5 (left to right).

when it comes to what we're looking for in a handgun. I think many people who don't care for the Gen4 were expecting more changes when it was released. They were left feeling like, "This is it?"

I'm not really sure what they were expecting, but I've also heard and read more than one quip like, "If the previous generations were "perfection" then why does Glock keep having to upgrade their "perfection" with new iterations of "perfection?"

There's a simple explanation for that: Times change, as do the tastes of shooters. What's desirable now might not be as desirable in 10 years, or perhaps some previously unknown innovation comes along.

A good case in point is the accessory rail, which wasn't around when the Gen1 and Gen2 came out. But somewhere between the release of the Gen2 and the Gen3, they hit the market and became popular, which is why the Gen3 version of "perfection" has them. Interchangeable backstraps are another example. They weren't common when the Gen3 came out. Now, everyone has them. What was "perfection" in a Gen1, Gen2 or Gen3 suddenly isn't perfection unless it has an interchangeable backstrap. You can look at almost every change made in the Gen4 and see that it wasn't popular or even a known quantity when the Gen3 was introduced.

In addition, there are always going to be small improvements made and incorporated into newer model. That's a good thing.

For all the people who chuckle about Glock's next iteration of "perfection," the alternative is a company that doesn't improve upon its products and has a reputation for stubbornly putting out the same product without listening to what consumers are demanding. That's not a good thing.

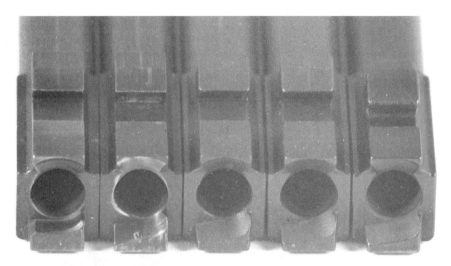

Barrel hood changes, Gen1 through Gen5 (left to right). The barrels are upside down. In this photo, the barrel hood is below the chamber.

The grip backstraps through the generations, Gen1 through Gen5 (left to right). Note the similarity between Gen2 and Gen3. Also, Gen4 and Gen5 look similar from the rear.

The inside of the frame has gone through some changes, especially the Gen5. Gen1 through Gen5 (left to right).

During the Gen4 reign as the most up-to-date generation of Glock pistols, Glock introduced a couple of pistols that are kind of hard to categorize as Gen4, because they aren't really Gen4, even though they were introduced during that timeframe. These are pistols that lead to the development of the Gen5. I'll cover these in greater details in their applicable chapters, but these guns include the G42, G43 and M-series (G17M and G19M). The G42 had a number of changes from the original Glock design (see Chapter 12), many of which were implemented so all of the Glock design features would fit into such a small handgun. The G42 design changes were incorporated into the G43 for the same reason, so Glock design features would fit into a small 9mm package. When Glock was looking to meet the FBI's requirements for the new handgun it was looking for, the company took those same G42/G43 design changes and incorporated them into the G17M and G19M duty pistols. Glock soon released the G17M and G19M to the commercial market as the Gen5 pistols we know today.

MOS

Though not a separate generation, during the Gen4 timeframe, Glock released the M.O.S. variant. No, it's not Military Occupational Specialty, it's Modular Optic System. Competition shooters have been having their slides machined for optics for some time now, and it's definitely an added expense and hassle. So, Glock offered these optic-ready slides from the factory, in the form of the MOS line, and they've been good sellers.

It ships with one plate for when no optic is mounted and only the open sights are used, and four additional plates that work with seven of the most popular red-dot models, including EOTech, Leupold, Trijicon, Meopta, Insight, Doctor and C-More.

With the MOS configuration, there is the option of adding tall iron sights, which can be co-witnessed with the optical sight. If your optical sight fails, you always have a backup ready to go. This is also important when using optical sights that don't always function effectively in every circumstance. For example, Trijicon sights are outstanding sights, however they have a reputation for not working well when the shooter is inside a dark environment, and your target is outside in glaring sunlight. No worries with a co-witnessed open sight. With the co-witness, both sight and optic are always on target, so there's no switch over.

With the MOS line, the most important thing is that the Glock will maintain reliability. When engineers design a slide, they work their engineer magic and come up with an optimal weight at which the slide will cycle reliably. But with an MOS slide, they cut out a section of that slide. For stock, open sights they include a plate (Glock calls it a plug) that will get that slide back to the optimal weight, it's the same weight as the part they machined out.

The reliability issue comes into play, though, when you start factoring in the different weights of the other potential optics that could be mounted on the slide. Glock is factoring this in and has designed the four optics plates to be approximately half the weight of the plug that fills the space for open sights. The optic plate, plus the optic itself will weigh just slightly more than what was removed for it. Glock says this will fit within the parameters and the slide will still cycle reliably.

The MOS line initially included only the long slide/competition guns, but the popularity of optics by the shooting public, including those that carry for duty and self-defense, has made Glock expand the lineup. Current MOS offerings include G17 Gen4 MOS, G19 Gen4 MOS, G34 Gen4 MOS, G17 Gen5 MOS FS, G19 Gen5 MOS FS, G34 Gen5 MOS FS, G45 MOS, G35 Gen4 MOS, G40 Gen4 MOS, G41 Gen4 MOS.

FIFTH GENERATION

We're generally under the notion that subcompact models are just scaled-down versions of their full-size kin, sometimes with some tweaks. In many cases, that's not true, it's more complicated than just "scaling down a handgun," and making it reliable. It's mostly true with the G42, in general it's a scaled-down version of the G17. To make it small, there were some considerable changes, such as the trigger spring, trigger bar (the "dog leg" is gone), firing pin safety, slide stop lever and slide lock spring.

The Gen5 (right/front) frame grip has several differences from the Gen4. Most noticeably, the finger grooves are gone. It also has a half-moon cutout that helps with removing a stuck magazine. Notice also the different magazine baseplate. It's longer in the front and more rounded, also to aid in stuck-mag removal. Later models would do away with the half-moon cutout.

The Gen5 (front) grip has a beveled/flared mag well for faster reloads. The half-moon cutout is uncomfortable in the G19; the corners cut into the little finger. It goes away in the FS version and would later be completely eliminated from all Gen5 models.

The Gen4 guide rod nose ring (center) had to be enlarged from the Gen3 (left) to make space for the larger dual-spring recoil spring assembly. It could be damaged if dropped when disassembled, so the Gen5 (right) got an overhaul and is more robust.

What's interesting though, is that Glock liked those changes so much, it incorporated them into the Gen5. So, in many ways the Gen5 is a "scaled-up" version of the G42, (with some tweaks, of course). As I wrote in an earlier paragraph, the G42 led to the G43, which lead to the G17M and G19M, which became the Gen5.

The very first thing that jumps out at everyone, is the grip. The finger grooves that were introduced with the Gen3 are gone, and instead the Gen5 grip has a straight front that terminates in a flared mag-well for faster reloads. Some people are happy to see the finger grooves go, others aren't (for those who prefer the finger grip, Gen3 and Gen4 models are still available). The straight grip is a throwback to the Gen2, as is the half-moon mag-well cutout that the Gen5 reintroduced. It's supposed to make it easier to rip a stuck mag out of the mag well, but I've never had a problem with a stuck mag in a Glock. This same half-moon cutout is done away with when Glock introduced the Gen5 MOS FS (Front Serrations) version, which I cover later in the book. Then, in August 2019, Glock announced all Gen5 models would now be FS, and the half-moon notch would be done away with completely. All Gen5 non-FS versions with the finger notch cutout will be phased out.

Another thing that's noticeable to long-time Glock users is the color. Gen5 slides are a noticeably darker shade of black, thanks to the nDLC finish. The nDLC finish is a Glock proprietary ion-bonding finish that has properties that near those found in a natural diamond, high hardness, low friction and corrosion resistance. Glock doesn't like to define what nDLC stands for, and I've seen all kinds of names for it online. Two of the most common are "near-Diamond Like Coating" and "near-Diamond Like Carbon." Both are based off of non-

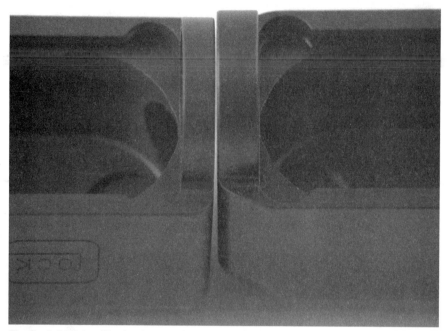

The Gen5 (right) guide ring is more robust than is found on the Gen4.

proprietary "DLC," which is Diamond Like Carbon. But that's not what Glock's nDLC means, and I have it straight from a source at Glock. It means: nitride Diamond Like Coating.

Glock decided on a more streamlined approach and gave the Gen5 a tapered muzzle. It's for easy holstering. It kind of ruins the whole "block Glock" aesthetic that Glock is famous for.

The Guide rod nose ring on the Gen5 is more robust than the Gen4. One of the things I cover in the Maintenance/Disassembly chapter is that when the slide is not on the frame, and it were to drop, the nose ring can get bent/damaged. It's one of the few times a Glock can be hurt by dropping it. It was a potential problem with the Gen4, because the nose ring was enlarged significantly from the previous generations, to make room for the larger captive dual-spring recoil spring assembly. So, the Gen5 nose ring got an overhaul and is a thicker ring.

Another difference is there are only two pins now, the locking block pin was removed. In the armorer's course we referred to this as the "first pin" because during disassembly it's the first pin to be taken out, and during assembly it's the first pin to be inserted. The locking block pin was added when Glock introduced the .40 S&W lineup, because the extra support was needed. But with the consumer demand for .40 S&W drying up, Glock chose not to include the locking block pin in the Gen5, which would lead one to believe there won't be a .40 caliber Gen5. Not to say there never could be. We never know how consumer tastes will change, and the .40 could hit a resurgence. Then Glock would have to add the pin back.

Notice the locking block pin found in the Gen4 (top), and lack thereof in the Gen5.

One of the most important changes is one that improves overall service life, but will probably be the least talked about: the disengagement ramp. In fact, in all the reviews I've read, I don't recall anyone noticing the change. The change stems from a potential problem with big-caliber Glocks (such as .357, .40, .45, 10mm, etc., but possibly ones that shoot a steady diet of +P) that have been fired a lot. Ones that have seen hard duty over the course of many years, not just the typical gun owner or police officer. People whose job it is to train *a lot*; multiple times per week, if not daily. What happens is when the large-caliber Glock recoils, the firing pin bounces off the firing pin safety plunger, and after years of the firing pin getting beat up, it starts to get "dings" in it. Eventually the dings add up and enough of the firing pin has been chiseled away that it causes "push by." The firing pin is able to push by the firing pin safety plunger. To fix this, Glock molded a disengagement ramp into the trigger mechanism housing. It keeps the firing pin safety plunger up and out of the way, so the firing pin doesn't get beat up during the slide cycling. One result of this new design that has alarmed a few people is that when the slide is locked to the rear, gravity will pull the firing pin forward so that it is protruding from the firing pin hole. Their fear is that when the slide captures a round and pushes it into battery, there can be a slam fire. The fears are unwarranted, because as the slide moves forward, the firing pin safety drops

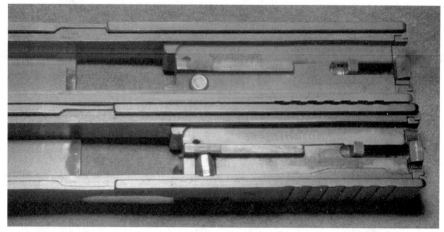

The firing pin safety has changed in the Gen5 (bottom).

The Gen5 slide cover plate (left) has a larger right notch to provide clearance for the disengagement ramp.

down once it clears the disengagement ramp, and the firing pin moves into its proper place and is safely to the rear. It's the addition of the disengagement ramp that lead to the change in the slide cover plate. The right notch is now larger and squared off to provide clearance of the disengagement ramp.

Also new is the firing pin and firing pin safety. The firing pin safety went from being round and fitting into a round hole, to being shaped more like the head of a shovel when looked at from the top. It's flat on one side and rounded on the other side. Which means you can't just fit it in any way, it only fits one way. Glock did this because the safety now has a shelf cut into one side, and it needs to mate up with the firing pin. The new firing pin has a notch cut in the front that mates up with the shelf in the firing pin safety, and this makes an even better barrier to keep the firing pin contained. The tip of the firing pin has also been changed to a more robust tear-drop shape, and the firing pin hole in the slide has changed to accommodate it. This is why the firing pin of a Gen4 and earlier won't work in a Gen5, and a Gen5 firing pin won't work with previous Gens.

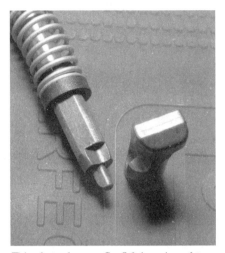

This photo shows a Gen5 firing pin safety and Gen5 firing pin. The cutout notch on each one mates up to prevent the firing pin from moving past the firing pin safety.

This photo shows how a Gen4 firing pin safety mates up with the Gen4 firing pin to block it from moving past.

The Gen5 (right) firing pin is tear-drop shaped and more robust than the Gen4. The firing pin hole in the breech face has also changed to accommodate the new firing pin.

The Gen5 firing pin safety (right) is redesigned and more secure than the previous generation. It also fits in only one way, since it's not round like previous generations of firing pin safeties.

The Gen5 slide stop lever w/spring (right) is now ambidextrous. The spring is now a coil type spring and is integrated better into the spring. It pushes up on the front of the lever, while the previous spring pulled down on the rear of the lever. It's much easier to install.

The slide stop lever is one of the major changes, as far as parts. Which makes sense, since it's now an ambidextrous lever. The slide stop lever now has a coil type spring that's incorporated into the front of the lever, whereas previous generations had a rod-type spring. The old slide stop lever used the spring to push *down* on the back of the spring (the portion that interacts with the shooter's thumb). The new one pushes *up* on the front of the lever (located next to the slide lock and slide lock spring). Because of the change in spring type, Glock had to change the frame. There's now a cavity for the new slide stop lever spring to nestle, just in front of the slide lock spring.

Speaking of the slide lock spring, for the Gen5 Glock changed it from a leaf type spring, to a coil spring. There could be pros and cons, I suppose, but to me a con is that it's far more likely to get lost during disassembly/assembly. Whereas the original spring had to be pried out, the new one is easily launched. The old spring, you could remove the slide stop, and the spring stayed put. The new one, it will not stay put, and you're lucky if it doesn't launch. The old spring had a potential to break in half, and then the half would get stuck in the frame, unable to be pulled out, which meant the frame was ruined. This usually isn't a problem unless the spring is pulled out frequently (and incorrectly). But there isn't really a need to pull the spring out, even for an armorer. So, to counter this hypothetical problem that could potentially happen, Glock incorporated a coil spring that holds a high likelihood of being launched and lost. In the armorer's course I took, with about 40 people, the spring was either launched or rolled off the table no less than a dozen times.

Another big change is the Glock Marksman Barrel (GMB), which I covered in Chapter 3 in greater detail. In sum, it uses conventional (lands and grooves) rifling instead of polygo-

The Gen5 (top) frame has changed to accommodate the new ambidextrous slide stop lever, which is now easier to install.

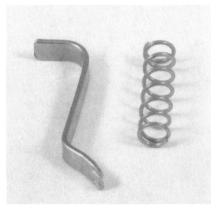

The Gen5 slide lock spring (right) is a coil type that replaces the leaf-type spring of previous generations. It has pros and cons, including that it is easily launched during disassembly.

nal rifling and has a muzzle crown. It also has a revamped barrel locking lug, which is back farther on the barrel. Because of this, Gen5 barrels do not work with previous Gen pistols, and vice versa.

Pull the trigger on a Gen5 Glock and one thing you'll notice is the improved trigger. It's not a match trigger, but it is a noticeable difference from previous generations. The pull weight is slightly lighter so that it's closer to the advertised weight, plus it's smoother. I've fired all the new Gen5 models except the G34 Gen5 and G47 Gen5, and the triggers have less overtravel, and a shorter reset. If you've spent a lot of time on a Glock trigger, the Gen5 improvements are immediately noticeable.

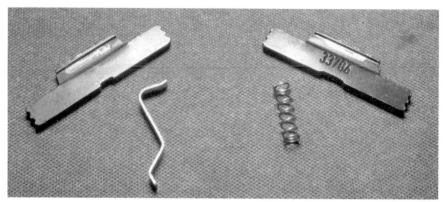

The slide lock spring went from a leaf-type of spring (left, Gen4), to a coil spring in the Gen5. If you're going to be taking apart Glocks, you might want to have a couple extras of these.

After four generations of Glock pistols, the Gen5 GMB has changed the barrel locking lugs.

Glock replaced the S-shaped coil trigger spring with a three-part assembly – technically it's listed as one part, because that's how it's sold, but in reality, it's three parts – the trigger spring bearing, rod and spring. In general, I'm not a fan of replacing one part with multiple parts, I like the KISS principle. At first, I felt that way about this change, however I'm starting to come around. On older Glocks, I've seen the wear that removal of the old S-shaped trigger spring can cause on the trigger housing, and this would alleviate that. Plus, it takes out of the equation the error that the old spring could be installed backward. The change in the trigger spring necessitated a change to the trigger mechanism housing, which now has the same barbell-shaped notch cutout that I write about in the later G42 chapter.

If you look at the specs of the Gen5, you might notice it's listed as being 0.8 inch wider than previous generations. It is, but not really. The slide and grip are both the same width, it's just that the Gen5 has an ambidextrous slide stop lever, which makes the overall width a little wider. It's not going to feel wider, and it's not going to carry any differently.

The Gen5 saw some magazine changes, as well, which I go over extensively in Chapter 15, so I'm just going to quickly touch on the changes here. Glock incorporated an orange follower to improve visibility of the follower, and a base pad with an extended front to aid in removing stuck magazines. The sleeve cutout of exposed metal, above the mag catch notch, is now gone.

If you have a lot of earlier Glock mags, fear not. If you're a right-handed shooter, all previous generations of magazines will work with your Gen5 Glock. If you have the mag catch set up for left-handed shooters, only ambidextrous magazines (Gen4) will work, all previous Gens will not.

The Gen5 trigger spring (right) is a three-part assembly that replaces the S-shaped trigger spring of previous generations.

To accommodate the Gen5 trigger spring, the Gen5 trigger mechanism housing (right) now has a barbell shaped notch cut out that was first introduced with the G42. Note also the new disengagement ramp at the top right of Gen5 housing in photo.

G17 ALL GENERATIONS
SIDE-BY-SIDE COMPARISON
(NOTE: ALL PHOTOS ARE GEN1 THROUGH GEN 5, LEFT TO RIGHT.)

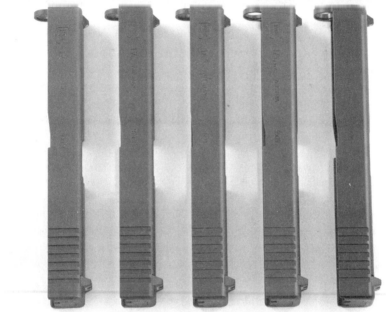

1. Slide (left side)

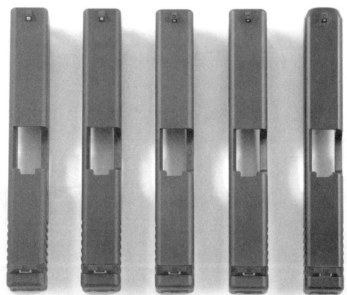

1. Slide (top)

1. Slide (right side)

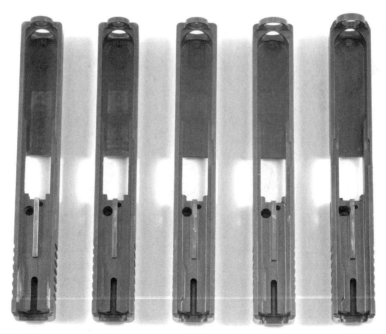

1. Slide (bottom)

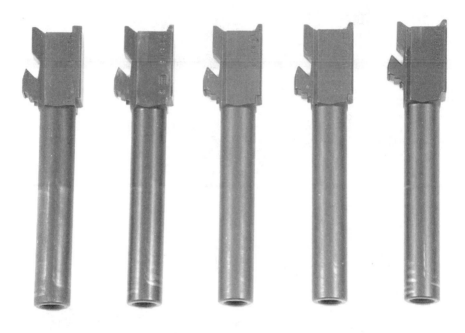

2. Barrel (side)

2. Barrel (bottom)

3. Recoil Spring Assembly

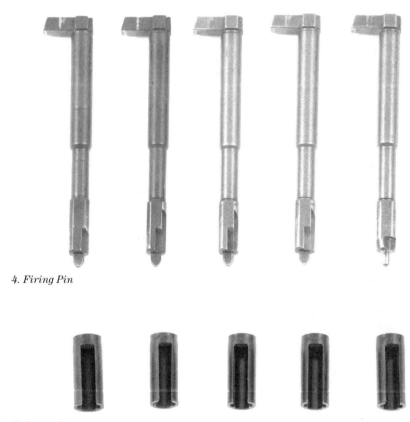

4. Firing Pin

5. Spacer Sleeve

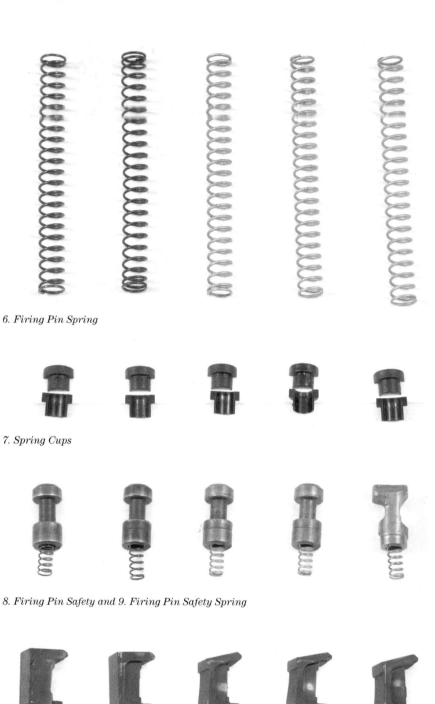

6. Firing Pin Spring

7. Spring Cups

8. Firing Pin Safety and 9. Firing Pin Safety Spring

10. Extractor (bottom)

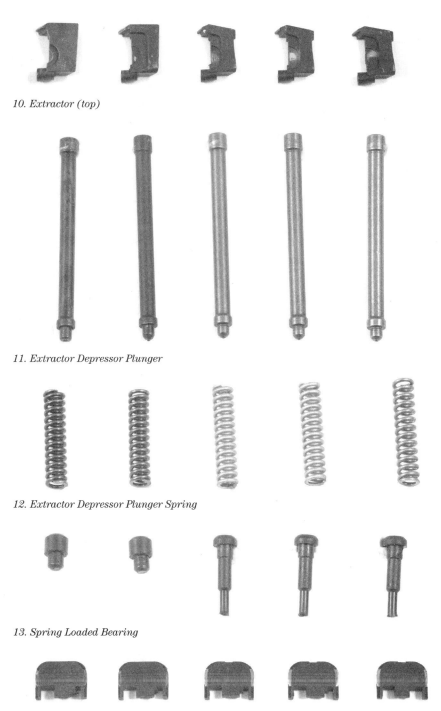

10. Extractor (top)

11. Extractor Depressor Plunger

12. Extractor Depressor Plunger Spring

13. Spring Loaded Bearing

14. Slide Cover Plate

15. Rear Sight

16a. Front Sight

16b. Front Sight Screw

17. Frame (right side)

17. Frame (left side)

17. Frame (inside)

18. Magazine Catch Spring

19. Magazine Catch

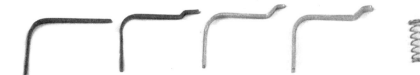

20. Slide Lock Spring

21. Slide Lock

22. Locking Block

23. Trigger Mechanism Housing with Ejector (right side)

23. Trigger Mechanism Housing with Ejector (front)

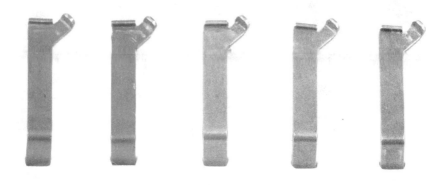

24. *Connector*

25. *Trigger Spring*

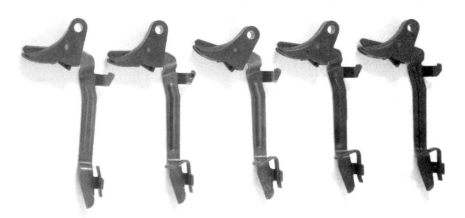

26. *Trigger with Trigger Bar*

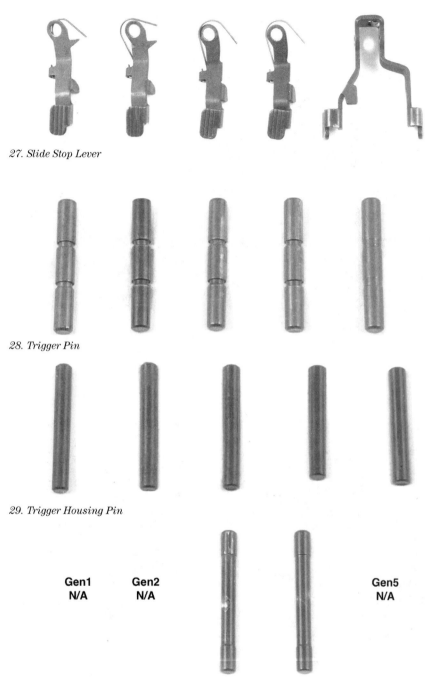

27. Slide Stop Lever

28. Trigger Pin

29. Trigger Housing Pin

Gen1
N/A

Gen2
N/A

Gen5
N/A

30. Locking Block Pin (a.k.a. "First Pin"). Note: Gen1, Gen2 and Gen5 Glock pistols do not have the Locking Block Pin.

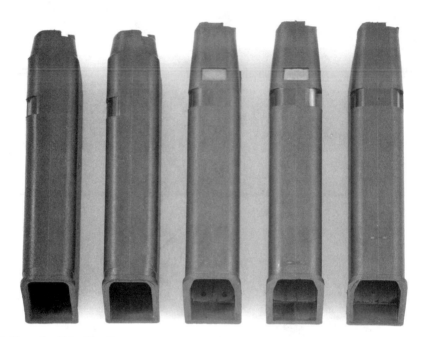

31. Magazine Tube (front)

31. Magazine Tube (left side)

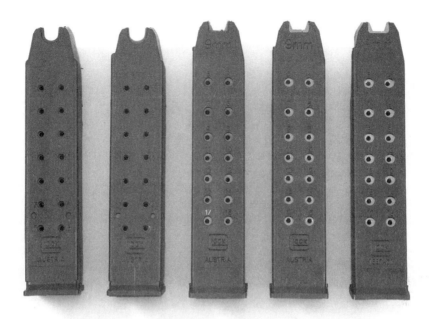

31. Magazine Tube (back)

31. Magazine Tube (right side)

32. Follower

33. Magazine Spring

**Gen1
N/A**

34. Magazine Insert

35. Magazine Floor Plate

CHAPTER 5:
THE G17

This is the first model Glock brought to market. The original. The one that started it all. The Glock 17 is the most innovative handgun design since John M. Browning's 1911, and when you add to that the way that Glock revolutionized handgun manufacturing, the G17 is probably the most innovative handgun ever.

The G17 was developed by Glock for the Austrian Army to replace the P-38, a gun that had been in use since World War II. Glock beat out eight different handguns from world-class firearms makers including: Heckler & Koch, FN, SIG Sauer, Steyr and Beretta. The Austrian Army adopted the G17 in 1982 as the P80 (or Pistole 80). Word quickly got around about this new upstart that beat out established gunmakers. By 1985, Glock had a contract with the Norwegian Army (for the G17 as the P80) and suitors by the dozen vying to import the G17 into the U.S.

(As an aside, for collectors, if you can get your hands on a P80 marked Glock, buy it. Or if you don't want it, drop me a line. I want one. They're rare in the U.S., but can be

A G17 Gen4.

A G17 first generation. Incidentally, the two clips on the web belt are made by Glock, too.

found. The magazine alone can fetch premium dollars. For example, I've seen Norwegian P80 magazines listed for $600 online.)

Glock decided to go its own route, however, and Glock USA opened its doors in 1986. From there, Glock would capture around 70 percent of the U.S. law enforcement market and become one of the (if not the) most popular handguns in the U.S. civilian market. No other handgun brand is as recognizable by shooters and non-shooters alike. Today Glock is used in an official military or government capacity in more than 42 countries. This does not include non-national police forces.

Gaston Glock designed his masterpiece for the Austrian Army contract, which he won. Designated the P80 (or Pistole 80), it pre-dates the G17 Gen1 that would later be imported into the U.S. (Photo by Shane Hicks)

In the early days there was confusion and incorrect information as to why the first model was called the 17. To this day some of the confusion still exists among new Glock owners. Some sources said the reason was that the Austrian Army laid out 17 requirements that must be met by the potential service pistol to be considered for adoption. Other

Some would argue this is the best Glock ever made: the third generation G17.

A G17 is a great handgun for beginners. It's soft on recoil, and the lack of a manual safety makes the shooter especially mindful of finger awareness.

sources stated it was due to the 17-round capacity of the Glock magazine. Both make sense, but neither is correct. Popular fiction perpetuated these myths.

In the novel *Killing Floor*, by Lee Child, the protagonist, one Jack Reacher, is confronted with a Glock 17. In his mind he goes over everything he knows about the weapon, which he says he knows well, with one of those things being, "Seventeen rounds to a magazine, hence the name."

Reacher got a lot right about the Glock, but this wasn't one of them. The true reason the first Glock is named the 17 is because it was the 17th patent filed by Gaston Glock.

Still, it's interesting to watch movies and read articles from that era and read the various theories as to the origin of the name. The other thing Lee Child got wrong was that Reacher recommended rejection of the Glock for the U.S. Army, and instead recommended the Beretta 92F. In reality, the G17 was never entered into the official army trials. The U.S. Department of Defense did receive from Glock four samples for unofficial testing and evaluation, but when they invited Glock for an official submission, Glock declined. It would

A field-stripped third generation G17. The Flat Dark Earth frame is a special run that is made periodically.

have required extensive retooling of manufacturing equipment, which was something Glock wasn't going to do at that time.

In another famous and hilarious Hollywood moment that was indicative of the perception of Glock pistols at the time, in *Die Hard 2*, John McClane (played by Bruce Willis) said of the Glock, "That punk pulled a Glock 7 on me. You know what that is? It's a porcelain gun made in Germany. Doesn't show up on your airport X-ray machines here, and it costs more than you make in a month." Sure, this was before the age of the Internet and Wikipedia, but that is just lazy script writing. Almost every aspect of that was incorrect: It's not the model 7, it's not porcelain and it isn't made in Germany. It *does* show up on airport X-ray machines because the majority of it is metal. I do not know the price of a G17 in 1990, but it wasn't more than the current (approximate) street price of $550; and the average starting monthly salary for police officers in large cities in 1990 was about $2,917 (BJS.gov).

Amazingly, after all these years, the G17 is still Glock's most popular model for law enforcement and military/government sales (which are generally large contracts), and second in overall sales to the G19 for civilian sales. I've gone back and read books and magazine articles written at the time of the introduction of the .40 S&W G22 and the .45 ACP G21, and at the time some writers discussed the demise of the 9mm G17 and G19 because of the introduction of these other calibers, especially the .45 ACP. We are a .45 ACP nation, after all.

How often have you heard someone say, "If it doesn't have a '4' in front of it, it's not big enough for self-defense." But the G17 and the G19 didn't become obsolete, and they weren't replaced by the .40 S&W or .45 ACP. In fact, their popularity has only increased right along with the Glock itself.

There have been spikes in popularity of other models, especially when they are first introduced, but, after the hoopla is over, the G17 9mm charges on. This is particularly amazing, given the popularity the G22 had among law-enforcement agencies, and the numbers of those sold. It's really quite remarkable how well the G17 still sells and is a testament to the handgun.

In the first edition of this book, I wrote I personally thought the 9mm cartridge was just starting to come into its own in America, and it's doing so even harder than anyone could have predicted. It's kind of a curiosity that it took so long, but over a century after it was

The culmination of nearly 30 years of Glock design: The G17 Gen4.

introduced, we're just starting to appreciate it. I believe we're in the Golden Age of the 9mm in America. There's a lot of irony in the fact that those writers wrote about the .40 S&W and .45 ACP leading to the demise of the 9mm, when in fact the 9mm has led to the demise of the .40, and even taken huge chunks out of the all-American .45 ACP's popularity.

A Gen4 G17 is 7.95 inches in length, 5.43 inches in height and 1.18 inches in width, with a slide width of 1.00 inch. It weighs 25.06 ounces unloaded and 32.13 ounces loaded (in this book, "unloaded" weights include an empty magazine). The barrel height is 1.26 inches, which is low, and has a lot to do with the minimal muzzle flip compared to other handguns. The lower a barrel sits above the shooter's hand (bore axis), the less it will rise as a bullet is fired. The Gen3 is identical in dimension, with the exception that it is 8.03 inches in length, which is .08 inches longer.

In 2017, Glock introduced the G17 Gen5 using a pretty unique marketing method. It secretly shipped G17 Gen5 and G19 Gen5 models to select ranges around the country, and when Glock announced the Gen5, it mentioned to head to your local range to shoot the new models. I don't know if it worked better than what the company normally would do for a new product launch, but I thought it was clever. I covered the Gen5 in detail earlier in the book, so I won't go over all the changes here. A Gen5 G17 is 7.95 inches in length, 5.47 inches in height and 1.34 inches in overall width. The extra width is due to the addition of the ambidextrous slide stop lever, which is now the widest part of the gun. The slide width

A third generation G17 with FDE frame, being fired at THE RANGE, a new shooting facility in Richfield, Wisconsin. Notice the state-of-the-art computerized target controls.

The G17 Gen5 did away with the finger grooves, bringing back the straight grip, something not seen since the Gen2.

is still 1.00 inch. It weighs 25.25 ounces unloaded. It's about 0.19 ounces heavier than the Gen4, which isn't significant, and is probably due to the change in parts and addition to the ambi slide stop lever.

All of the standard-frame, full-size Glocks (G17, G22, G31 and G37) are nearly identical in dimensions, with one minor exception: the G37 has a slightly wider slide, and the height is 5.51 inches, which is .08 inches higher. There is also a difference in weight, though not significant. Unloaded, the G22 weighs 25.59 ounces, the G31 weighs 26.12 ounces, and the G37 weighs 28.95 ounces.

Most shooters love the extended mag well on the Gen5 (left) compared to the Gen4, but I haven't found anyone who prefers the finger notch cutout. The cutout goes away in later Gen5 models.

For this book, I've shot a lot of Glocks in a lot of calibers and a lot of sizes. Almost all of them, in fact. The very first two I fired for the book were the G17 Gen1 and Gen2. Then I shot everything else, with the very last pistol I fired being the G48.

After shooting everything else, I forgot how nicely the G17 shoots. The recoil is handled very well – still even more so than 9mm guns from competitors, despite everyone else trying to catch up to Glock. It's just a great gun, one of the all-time classics. I've put a lot of rounds through the various generations of G17; some loads from Federal, including: American Eagle 115-grain FMJ, AE 124-grain non-toxic primer TMJ (Total Metal Jacket), Federal Premium 124-grain Hydra-Shok JHP (one of my all-time favorite carry loads), Syntech 124 grain, Speer Gold Dot +P 124 grain (another favorite carry round); as well as loads from DoubleTap, SIG Sauer, Black Hills, G2 Research, SuperVel to name just a few.

For carry ammo, I used to be all about just the Federal HST or Hydra-Shok JHP; but now, I've found so many excellent choices on the market. I still carry those offerings from Federal, but you can also find my carry (and/or "go-to" guns') mags filled with Speer, Black Hills, DoubleTap, SIG ammo, G2 Research and SuperVel. All are outstanding, and I say this with pretty good authority; I get to test a lot of ammo. For articles and books, I work di-

The Gen4 and Gen5 offer two different grip styles.

rectly with almost all of the ammo makers on the market, which means I have access more vast array of ammo, compared to a law-enforcement agency/department which might have just one type, or a competition shooter who can use only what his or her sponsor offers. Not that I'm an expert on ammo, by any stretch of the imagination.

As I explained in the chapter discussing the different Glock generations, when I was first assigned this book, it became important for me to get my hands on all generations of G17, and preferably to shoot them. At the time, Gen3 and Gen4 models were simple to get, they both were on the shelf of almost every gun store you'd walk into. (You can still find those on shelves, with the Gen4 being most common of the two, but now everyone wants the Gen5). The first two generations were not so easy. None of my friends or acquaintances had them, and it's not like you can check them out on loan from Glock. I knew my only course of action would be to track them down and buy them. With a lot of research and a little work, I did just that.

Those two Glocks, which are both becoming very collectable, are still just as good as they were when they were released. They could be placed against any competitor's guns on the market and still fare well. They are timeless designs and built to be workhorses. I have since decided to collect the G17 generations, since this is the only model that spans all five generations.

In September 2018, Glock released an update to the Gen5 G17 (and the G19), with MOS, and designated it as the "FS" model, for Front Serrations (not to be confused with "SF" models, which stands for Short Frame). The primary feature that sets the G17 Gen5 MOS FS apart is, as the name implies, the front serrations found on the slide, like the G45. (The G45 was released before the MOS FS version of the G17 Gen5, and I cover the G45 in Chapter 6.)

The slide front serrations are identical to the ones at the rear of the slide. Some people love them, some people hate them, I find I'm impartial. I've never not bought a gun because it has them, nor have I ever bought a gun just because it does have them. I honestly don't care either way. I understand both sides of the argument, but I think the debate is overblown.

Front slide serrations are to rack the slide, but some use it to aid in press checks (when the slide is pulled back just enough to check if there's a round in the chamber). Proponents argue it makes it easier to conduct the press check or rack the slide with serrations at the front of the slide. Those against it argue three points.

First, it could lead to someone positioning a portion of their hand in front of the muzzle while manipulating the slide. I don't fully buy into this. I agree, you never want to put a part of your hand in front of the muzzle, because you never want the gun pointed at something you don't want to destroy. I sure hope no one wants to destroy his own hand. But placing serrations on the front of the slide is not going to lead to people blowing off their own hands. People should learn/train how to manipulate the slide safely, it's not difficult. Just as people had to learn/train how to safely use a Glock handgun with no manual thumb safety, I'm sure most people will figure out how to safely use front slide serration. Also, the act of doing a press check is not going to cause the shooter's trigger finger to wildly flail about, entering the trigger guard, and pressing the trigger.

Second, using the front serrations could lead to your hand covering the ejection port of the pistol, and when racking the slide to clear a malfunction or unload the gun, a round that's ejected won't fly free but could bounce of the hand, back into the chamber as the slide closes, causing a malfunction, or worse, the slide closing and the ejector striking the primer causing the round and gun to go boom, and not in a good way. It might sound like a reach, but this does happen, there's plenty of video evidence online, and it's frequently at shooting matches, so it's people who handle guns a lot, not just a mistake made by novices. This is a point that goes beyond front serrations, and is an education issue. A lot of people aren't aware that this can happen and need to be educated and should seek training. But, to the point of this paragraph, for a right-handed shooter, using the front serrations with the hand positioned properly (thumb and index finger on the serrations, pointed forward toward front of gun, small finger toward rear of the gun) does not block the ejection port, while those who use the rear serrations with the hand positioned improperly (thumb and index finger on serration, pointed rearward on slide, small finger pointed forward) will block the ejection port.

The third point made by detractors of front slide serrations is that it tears up holsters when holstering, or it can cause friction and/or snag when drawing the handgun.

Generally, the best course of action, if you don't want front slide serrations on your Glock, don't buy one of the variants that have it. Glock is smart in that for the most popular models (G17, G19 and G34) that have front serrations, it offers the same model without. It is one of the few companies that does that, most companies either have them or don't have them, the consumer doesn't get a choice. For now, and this could change, the only models that come only with front serrations are the G45, G43X, and G48. These three models do not come in a configuration without front serrations.

The lastest version of "perfection" – a G17 Gen5 MOS FS. FS is for Front Serrations.

When you pick it up, aside from it being MOS and having front slide serrations, you'll also immediately notice something else about it. Glock got rid of the half-moon cutout found on the grip of the Gen5 models. The half-moon cutout is probably the most complained about part of the Gen5 models. You don't notice it as much on the G17, but you'll definitely notice it on the G19, and it's not comfortable. The edge of the notch is kind of sharp, and it digs into your little finger. It was easy enough to take a fingernail file and round out the sharp edge, so to me it wasn't a huge deal, but Glock should have discovered it and fixed the problem before it ever hit shelves, so the end-user doesn't have to. Either way, Glock must have received enough complaints that it omitted the notch from the MOS FS version.

In August 2019, Glock announced all Gen5 models would have front serrations on the slide and the half-moon finger cutout would be removed from all models. All non-FS versions with the finger notch cutout would be phased out. So, on the Glock website, you won't see just a G17 Gen5, it's going to be G17 Gen5 FS. At least for the time being. I'm going to miss the ol' slab sides, (non-FS version) Glock.

G17L

The G17L was designed for one thing: competition. It was the third Glock model released to the civilian market, after the G17 and G19, and began rolling off the line in April of 1988. It would be produced in small quantities, on and off until the last ones were made in April 1999.

The final dagger that killed it off was the very thing it was designed for: competition. More specifically, the International Practical Shooting Confederation (IPSC) decided to limit the size of the pistols used in competition, so it designed a box with internal dimensions of 225x150x45 millimeters. The competitor must place his or her handgun into the box, and it must fit wholly in the box. The G17L does not fit in the box, so Glock changed the size of the G17L so that it would fit in the box and called it the G34.

After the introduction of the G34 in January 1998, the G17L just wasn't selling, and really wasn't needed. As of this writing, the G17L is out of production, but in the past Glock has had an occasional production run of them.

There are only seven models of Glock that I have not shot, this being one. The others are the G24, G25, G28, G18, G46 and G47. There are still G17L handguns on the market, and I even found one source that has them new in box. As with a lot of firearms that were once popular and are now not as common, I'm sure someday this will be a collectable.

The G17L shipped with a standard trigger pull of 3.5 pounds, which is 2 pounds lighter than most other Glock triggers. The overall length is 8.85 inches (0.7 inches longer than the G34), which gives it a sight radius of 8.07 inches. The barrel is 6.02 inches long. The front quarter of the slide has been machined open on top to reveal the barrel beneath. Glock did this to keep the weight down, a lot of additional weight would affect the cycling of the slide, and thus make it less reliable. In all other aspects it's the same as the G17. It even uses the same frame.

The G17L was an early attempt by Glock to name a variant of one of its models, but shortly after that the company went a different route and started to name every variant with a different model number, like the .40 long-slide version of the G17L was named G24, not G22L.

Because everything else since then has been named something completely different, the G17L is an oddball in Glock naming convention. It throws off the entire Glockiverse. I wonder if Gaston had to do it all over again, would he have named this the G20? Then all subsequent models would have moved up a model number (the 10mm would now be the G21, the .45 the G22). Of course, now Glock has added a couple more oddballs to the Glock naming convention with the G19X and G43X. Glock has completely messed up the Glockiverse with recent names. The G19X is a crossover of the G17 frame (with shortened, G19 length dust cover) and G19 slide, but if it's black with a few other minor changes it's called the G45. Then to come full circle, Glock took the G45 frame (again, shortened G19 length dust cover), mated it with the G17 slide, and called it the G47.

CHAPTER 6:
THE G19 AND OTHER 9MM GLOCKS

I t's been more than 100 years since it was introduced, but in case you haven't noticed, the 9x19 (9mm Luger) has been taking the U.S. by storm in the last decade. No other handgun round is as popular right now as the 9mm. I love just about every cartridge, even the ridiculous ones, and I frequently carry other cartridges such as the 10mm and the .357 SIG.

But my go-to guns, the ones I keep in my safe, at the ready, are all 9mm. You can get dropped anywhere in America, or anywhere in the world, and the ammo you're most likely to find is 9mm.

While Glock handguns perform well with all cartridges in which they are chambered, they really shine in 9mm. It is, after all, what the design was intended for.

G19

The G19 was the second Glock pistol released to the civilian market, with production beginning in March 1988 (it beat the G17L by one month). The G19 is one of the two pistols that has been around for all five generations, though first generation G19 Glocks were only prototypes, so they are extremely rare. After all these years, the G19 is still the second most popular Glock model in overall sales (which includes military/agency/law enforcement), after the G17. If you don't include military/agency/law enforcement sales and just look at civilian sales, the G19 is number one.

This compact 9mm Glock is just a G17 that has been made 0.67 inches shorter in length and 0.56 inches shorter in the grip. It has a 4.02-inch barrel and is about 1.4 ounces lighter.

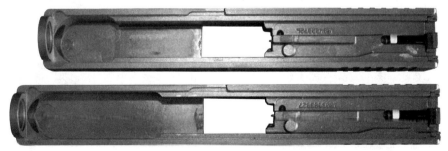

The difference in length between a G17 and G19 is nearly 0.7 of an inch. It doesn't sound like much, but when carrying it's a lot.

The popularity of the 9mm is at an all-time high in the U.S. So when advancements are made in handgun cartridge design, they are going to hit the 9mm first.

It is an excellent compromise between the full size and the subcompact. The definition of a "compact" pistol can sometimes get a little murky, because if you look at the G19 it looks like a full-size handgun. The designation is relative, and really differs from company to company. What one company calls a full-size, another calls a compact. This is especially true for companies like Glock, which manufactures combat/duty pistols that are often larger than other pistols.

The Glock pistol sizes can be summarized by how they are used within police departments. The full-size pistols (G17, G22, etc.) are generally issued to uniformed police officers who open-carry. The compact pistols (G19, G23, etc.) are generally issued to plainclothes officers, where concealment is not necessary, but being discreet is.

The subcompact pistols (G26, G27, etc.) are generally issued to undercover officers, where concealment is needed. Of course, this is a generalization and not always the case; some departments just issue the compact pistol to everyone.

If I could only own one handgun, which is thankfully not the case (God bless America) it would be this one. It's big enough that it handles and shoots much like a full-size handgun, yet compact enough that it can be concealed with a jacket, vest or even a properly designed shirt. It's roughly the size of a 1911 Commander, though a little bit smaller and lighter. It makes for an excellent "go-to" handgun.

The 9x19 cartridge is the most common handgun cartridge in the United States, and aside from the popularity among civilians, it is the U.S. military standard cartridge, the NATO standard cartridge and the choice of many police departments. Plus, since it also uses G17 magazines, with the sheer number of G19s and G17s in the U.S., magazines will always be plentiful.

Whether real or perceived, and I'm going to refrain from entering into politics here, the threat to "high capacity" magazines (or what we in the gun community call standard capacity) has led to a boom in sales of these magazines, with boom being an understatement.

The G19 is still one of Glock's top sellers.

A G19 barrel and spring (the top barrel and the top spring) compared to a G17 barrel and spring.

A field-stripped G19.

So, there are a lot of them out there.

Glock engineers have always been excellent at stuffing the maximum number of rounds into their magazines. To compare magazine capacity one must consider height, which is determined primarily by grip height, and this, along with grip width, is one of the biggest determinants of magazine capacity. In the first edition, I wrote that this becomes evident when you compare the same-class offerings of other manufacturers from that time, such as the Ruger SR9c, Smith & Wesson M&P9c and Springfield Armory XD(M) 3.8 Compact. Things have changed, and most of these manufactures have upped their capacity.

Of the compact models, the G19 has a 15-round capacity, with a 4.9-inch height and 1.26-inch overall width (the Gen5 G19 has an overall width of 1.30 due to the ambidextrous slide stop). The Springfield Armory offerings are kind of difficult to compare to the G19, because they don't offer something with quite the same dimensions, only subcompact and service size. Through most of the XD(M) and XD Mod.2 lineups, they've taken a category of slide/barrel length (subcompact, compact, etc.), and added the grip/frame of the next larger category (like the Glock G45, which mates a G19 compact slide with the G17 standard-size frame). So, the subcompact slide/barrel now comes with a compact grip/frame, and the compact slide/barrel comes with a full-size grip/frame. This method boosts the capacity, but you lose barrel length and it's harder to conceal without printing. The grip size that's the same height as the G19, which is the XD Mod.2 (4.75-inch height), comes only with a 3-inch barrel and is marketed as a subcompact. It has a standard mag capacity of 13 rounds, two fewer than the G19, and the barrel is an inch shorter.

The original Smith & Wesson M&P compact was 4.3 inches in height with a 12-round capacity. It's 0.6 inches shorter than the G19, and it lost three rounds. It's not a terrible trade-off, three rounds for just over half an inch. The M&P9 M2.0 Compact has bumped the capacity up to 15 rounds, the same as the G19, and has a height of 5.0 inches, so it's very comparable.

The Ruger SR9 series has been replaced with the Ruger American Pistol, which is its answer to the Army's MHS program. It's comparable in size to the G19, with a height of 4.5 inches and a barrel length of 3.55 inches. It boasts an impressive magazine capacity of 17 rounds, but that's for the extended magazine (which the G19 can accept a 17-round magazine as well). The standard magazine is 12 rounds, three fewer rounds than the G19.

The G19 is truly the workhorse of the Glock lineup, and probably the most popular handgun in the U.S., if not the world.

The G19 Gen5: Perfection…almost. The finger notch cutout near the mag well isn't very comfortable if you have large hands; the edges are a bit sharp. Glock would later remove this finger notch cutout from all Gen5 models.

Especially amongst civilians. I'd venture to say, if someone is being issued a gun and doesn't have a choice, it's going to be a Glock G17. If the person is buying the gun and/or has a choice in what they carry, it's usually going to be a G19. It's my number-one, go-to gun, and it's my primary carry gun. If I can fit it in the attire I'm wearing, it's what I carry, and I'll generally choose my attire to dress around my G19.

For a long time, my choice for carry guns was the G26 or G43. The G43 based just off size, but the G26 I rationalized that I had 10 rounds in the magazine, but could easily reload my spare with 17 rounds. Why carry a G17 when you could just carry the G17 magazine in a smaller G26 package, right? Then I attended a training event led by Dave Spaulding. He

The author's preferred carry gun, a G19 Gen5 MOS FS.

addressed this issue directly. With a subcompact, the mag well doesn't extend past your palm, which means during reloads your palm could get pinched between the mag well and mag baseplate, preventing sure reloads. You don't have this concern with a compact pistol that your hand fits on. Another thing, a grip you can get your whole hand on is a whole lot easier to grip when drawing from your holster. Finally, they're far easier to shoot. With a subcompact you're controlling muzzle flip and recoil with two or three fingers on the grip, but with your whole hand on a G19 grip, the whole hand can control it. The little finger goes a long way toward controlling the torque created from muzzle flip. After Spaulding's course, I started carrying the G19. For the exact same reason, I was pleased to see when Glock came out with the G43X and G48 (discussed in later chapter).

The G19 is now available in the Gen3, Gen4, Gen4 MOS, Gen5 FS (as of August 2019, Glock phased out standard Gen5 models, and replaced them with FS versions) and Gen5 MOS FS. The G19X is a slightly different beast, and I'm going to cover it separately. The Gen5 variants have the same changes as the G17 Gen5, which I wrote about in the Generations chapter. The one thing I don't care for with the G19 Gen5 is the half-moon cutout on the front of the mag well. The forward edges come to sharp points that dig into the hand, and I found completely uncomfortable during range sessions, because I don't typically wear shooting gloves. It's not as bad an issue with the G17 Gen5, because the bottom of my hand doesn't quite reach the cutout. The problem was fixed with the introduction of the G19 Gen5 MOS FS version that did away with the half-moon cutout. In August 2019, Glock announced all Gen5 models would not have the half-moon cutout, and all would have front serrations. There will no longer be a standard model called the G19 Gen5, it will be called G19 Gen5 FS.

My go-to carry gun, unless I have to carry something smaller, is now the G19 Gen5 MOS FS. I'm a big fan. The finger grooves on the Gen4 and Gen3 never bothered me, but I do prefer the straight grip of the Gen5. For now, I don't plan on putting an optic on it, but who knows, if I train more and become comfortable with an optic, that could change.

The G19X is Glock's commercial release of its entry into the Modular Handgun System (MHS) competition for the U.S. Army. (instagram.com/robb_manning #robb_manning.glock.book)

G19X

What do you get when you slap a G19 compact slide on a G17 full size frame? The G19X. (Given the title of this section, I'm sure you saw that one coming.) Glock proudly proclaims on the G19X page that it's "Glock's first ever 'Crossover' pistol," except that it's not. More on that later. First, to clarify, Glock didn't literally take a G17 frame/grip and put it on a G19; the dustcover would protrude past the muzzle. The dustcover/accessory rail on the G19X is the same size as the G19, so it's more like they lengthened the grip/mag well on a G19, so it was the same size as a G17. (Remember what I wrote in a previous chapter: Glock models, with the exception of single-stack Slimline models, are essentially the same from the ejection port back, but with different lengths of the grip, depending on if it's a subcompact, compact, standard or long slide.)

A lot of people didn't really *get* this pistol. It's advertised as having the compact concealability of a G19, but the magazine capacity and long grip of the G17. For me, if I wanted the magazine capacity of a G17 in my G19, I would just use the G17 magazine. It worked fine for me, and I never had any issues. But apparently there was a pretty big hankering for this configuration. It does make sense for law-enforcement officers, who spend a lot of time sitting in squad cars. The G17 slide can be long, and when you're sitting down it can cause the pistol to dig into your side and not be that comfortable, and it pushes up your belt, making it feel all jacked up.

However, everyone I've talked to would prefer the opposite configuration: a G17 slide on a G19 grip. Because for concealability, the biggest issue is printing, and it's the grip that prints. Which is why I don't quite understand Glock's reasoning behind it, from a concealed-carry perspective. But then again, it wasn't initially designed for civilians, it was designed to meet the U.S. Army's requirements for the MHS (Modular Handgun System)

The coyote-colored G19X is Glock's first factory-finished model. Glock says it's the company's first crossover model, but it's not. That would be the G30S. (instagram.com/robb_manning #robb_manning.glock.book)

The G19X was a Gen5 before there was a Gen5, with just a couple Gen5 features lacking.

program. Glock submitted this pistol as the G19 MHS, from which Glock later removed the thumb safety, changed the roll-mark and released to the commercial market as the G19X. And from a fighting perspective, the G19X *does* make sense. It's compact, accurate, but with a full grip. The G19 slide gives all the benefits of the compact slide, but the full-size grip really gives you a lot to hold, and it's very noticeable with gloves on. A G19 grip is good when wearing gloves, but the G17 is even better.

And about that MHS program: Glock did not win. But that's not a knock on Glock pistols. Glock is proven with around 70 percent of U.S. law enforcement, SOF units, government contractors, U.S. government agencies and foreign militaries. Yet, Glock was beat out by a new handgun, only a few years old, with very little track record. According to Military.com, DOD reports show in PVT (Product Verification Testing) the SIG Sauer M17 and M18 both failed reliability testing, primarily double ejecting (a spent case ejecting at same time as unspent round). In Mean Rounds Between Stoppages (MRBS), using the same standard 115 grain ball ammunition used by U.S. and NATO forces for more than 20 to 30 years, the M17 got a 75 percent and M18 got an appalling 61 percent. MHS requirement is 95 percent. Glock passed reliability testing. However, Glock was underbid by $102 million. To be fair, the M17 and M18 did very well when using special-purpose ammo (147-grain jacketed hollow point), but so did Glock. The Army's response was that if a handgun is designed to fire special-purpose ammo, it's not going to fire ball ammo as well. I've never heard of a Glock having issues with any type of ammo, it shoots everything. The tests support this as fact, because Glock passed both tests. But, that's water under the bridge, and at least it can be reported the M17 and M18 are more modern and more suited to today's mission than was the Beretta M9.

The most noticeable MHS feature is that it has a coyote-colored (aka desert tan or flat, dark earth, FDE) nPVD coating, Glock's first full-gun, factory in-house, color-coat job (previously Glock has made frames of different colors, but this is the first time for the slide), designed to meet the MHS requirement for non-reflective, neutral-colored coating. Additionally, it has a finger tab on the front of the mag well (like the one found on the G26), and a lanyard loop on the back of the mag well (filling the famous grip hole that Glock pistols have).

Glock doesn't label the G19X as a Gen5 model, it predates the Gen5, but in reality, it is pretty much the Gen5. The only difference I've seen is it doesn't have a flared mag well. All of the other Gen5 features and upgrades covered previously are present in the G19X.

The G19x ships with three magazines, two are extended capacity (17 plus two rounds), and one is a standard G17 magazine. The included magazines are not full Gen5 magazines, as noticed by the black follower (Gen5 magazine followers are orange) and the baseplate (Gen5 baseplates have a longer, rounded front, whereas previous generations have a flat front). The magazine tube is Gen5, it has ambidextrous mag release cutouts, however it doesn't have the visible metal notch above the mag release cutouts.

G19X magazines are dark-earth colored and use a Gen5 tube with a Gen4 follower and baseplate.

Gen5 magazines do not work with the G19x because the longer, rounded baseplate front can't get passed the mag well finger tab, so it won't properly seat. It's not an issue with pre-Gen5 magazines, and it's not an issue with aftermarket magazines I've used, including Magpul, Jagemann, Elite Tactical Systems (ETS) and ProMag, because they don't have that extended-front baseplate. It's not a huge issue, but something to be aware of. If you already own some Gen5 mags, and you're incorporating a G19X into your ready bag, or bugout bag; or if you're carrying it as part of your EDC, be careful not to use Gen5 mags as your spare mags. If the proverbial poop hits the fan, you don't want to empty your magazine, and then when you go to reload, find out none of the other 10 magazines you have in your bag will work with your G19x because they're all Gen5. That would royally suck. If you're in a situation where you really need that reload, you probably won't be around to make that mistake again. If you don't yet own Gen5 mags and you're looking to purchase extra mags for your G19X, try to find some pre-Gen5 magazines. Just look for the rounded baseplate front, and the orange follower, if you see either, don't buy it.

If you have some Gen5 mags, or that's all you can find in the stores, don't worry, there's an easy fix. There are companies that make aftermarket baseplates for your OEM Glock mags. I have a whole bunch of TangoDown baseplates, and those work great, and fit the G19X just fine. They are a littler wider than Glock OEM baseplates, so you have something to grasp if you have a stuck magazine and need to rip it out of the mag well. Another great option I've personally used is the Magpul Speedplate. If you're familiar with the Magpul

The finger tab found on the G19X prevents Gen5 mags from seating fully because of the extended-front baseplate. Pre-Gen5 magazines work fine, or you can replace the baseplates on your Gen5 mags.

The baseplate on the Gen5 mag (left) has an extended front. The G19X uses a Gen4 baseplate.

Ranger Plate, an AR15 magazine baseplate that made it easier to pull your magazine out of your mag pouch, the Speedplate is the same thing, but for Glock mags. It's very convenient and works great, plus it makes a Glock Gen5 mag compatible with the G19X. It only works with Glock OEM mags, though, not with Magpul Glock mags. Additionally, you cannot take the baseplate off of a Magpul Glock mag and use it on a Glock OEM mag, it won't fit.

Another option: I've seen photos of G19X pistols where people have cut/filed the finger tab off, so it's not a concern. The ones I've seen look pretty good, at least from the side. It's a good solution if you want the G19X, but don't want to concern yourself with the magazine compatibility problem. I wouldn't do it, because I hate making permanent modifications, but to each their own.

Now, about the "Glock's first ever 'crossover' pistol" thing. Everyone forgets the G30S that I cover in Chapter 8 of this book. The G30S is a Slimline G30. Glock took a G36 Slimline slide and put it on a G30 Frame. If Glock defines crossover as taking the slide/barrel from one model and mounting it on the frame of another model, then the G30S is truly the first crossover model from Glock.

G45

The folks at Glock were kind enough to include me in on receiving three new models prior to them even being released to the public, one being the G45. (Being the editor of a gun magazine can have its privileges, as does writing books). The necessary NDAs (non-disclosure agreement) were circulated and signed, to me and my FFL dealer who would receive them. A big deal was made about secrecy. I was pretty stoked about the possibilities, especially for this mysterious G45, thinking maybe it was a single-stack 10mm cousin to the G36, or maybe that .22 LR everyone has been waiting for, or maybe the Internet

The G45, essentially a black G19X, but with a couple Gen5 features the G19X doesn't have.

The G19X (left) has a finger tab on the front of the mag well (like the G26), the G45 does not. The G19X has a lanyard loop for military use. The G45 has the Gen5 flared mag well.

rumors were true and a Glock carbine had come to fruition.

I received the promotional materials, and nope, none of the above. The G45 is a black G19X, a G19 slide on a G17 frame. Yes, that's an oversimplification, because there is more to it than just that (like the G19X, it's not an exact G17 frame, but one with a shortened dust cover), but I was a little underwhelmed with the announcement. Not underwhelmed in the G45 itself, it's a great pistol, but given all of the secrecy, I thought for sure it was going to be something huge. The G45 isn't marked as a Gen5, but it is, with the addition of "FS" features, serrations on the front of the slide, and the loss of the much-maligned half-moon cut out on the mag well. Maybe the G45 was a harbinger of things to come, because later Glock announced all Gen5 models would get these updates: addition of FS, removal of the half-moon cutout.

The G45 is very similar to the G19X, so there's really not tons to cover in this section, but there are a few things. When it was first introduced, everyone thought it was just a "black G19X" but that's not the case at all. Not to understate the significance of it being black, that is important. "Why?" you might ask, but what you're really asking is what's the point of the G45 if the G19X already exists?

I got into a related conversation last year with a law-enforcement officer from a rural area out West. We were discussing lever-action rifles for law enforcement versus an AR15. I didn't understand why a cop wouldn't want an AR15 in his squad car as backup, and I

Like other Gen5 Glocks, the G45 has an ambidextrous slide catch lever.

Nope, it's not a .45 ACP; it's a G45, a crossover that blends a G19 slide with a (modified) G17 frame. (instagram.com/ robb_manning #robb_manning.glock.book)

was curious as to why he thought a lever action was better. Don't get me wrong, I lover lever-action rifles and carbines, but I'm thinking that if I'm a cop in a rural area, and I need something more than a handgun, an AR offers fast shots with fast follow-up shots, and super-fast reloads. I'm not a cop, and don't think of all the variables that cops have to look at, so for me his answer was unexpected. It had absolutely nothing to do with capabilities of the gun or firepower. He told me, "Well, if I showed up carrying an AR15, and townsfolk drive by and see me carrying a military-style rifle, it's going to freak them out and scare people. A lever action doesn't do that, it makes them feel comfortable."

That's why the G45 exists. The G19X has a lot of features that law-enforcement officers want, but the public image of cops running around with flat dark earth (FDE) guns, a color associated with military operations overseas, isn't an image LEOs want. Especially in these times with the police getting a bad rap for excessive use of force, and with some already talking about law enforcement becoming too paramilitary.

Though it's not marked as such, the G45 is full Gen5 (unlike the G19X), which means the G45 has a flared and beveled mag well. That's the only Gen5 feature that the G19X is lacking. Aside from that, the other difference from the G19X is the mag well finger tab is missing, as is the lanyard loop.

A G45 MOS variant is also available for those that want to mount an optic.

Why would someone choose to buy a G45 over the G19X? It comes down to the three main differences: 1. You want black, not FDE; 2. You want a flared mag well; 3. You don't want the mag well finger tab (magazine compatibility).

G26

The G26 and G27 were introduced at the same time in July 1995. They were the first of the subcompact Glocks, often affectionately called "Baby Glocks." The G26 is chambered in 9x19 and the G27 is chambered in .40 S&W. It was only natural to go with these two calibers for the first of the subcompacts, for two reasons. First, these were the two most popular calibers in total Glock sales at that time. Second, these were the two most popular issue calibers for police departments.

As with all standard-frame Glocks, the beauty is in the universal controls. It doesn't matter if you're handling the long slide G34, the G17 or G19, the G26 or G27, the .45 GAP pistols, .357 pistols or any other standard-frame pistols, the controls are in the same location. The only Glocks that are different are the large-frame Glocks (like the G20), and the Slimline Glocks (like the G42). Even those have the controls located in the same relative place on the frame, the only difference being that the differing thicknesses of the respective frame changes how your thumb interacts with those controls.

The G26 was my everyday carry (EDC) pistol for a long time, until I switched to the G19, as I discussed previously. Being a gun writer, I've had the luxury of testing out many different concealed-carry pistols. I started with wanting the smallest pistol I could find, which ended up being a little .380. Then I wanted something with more horsepower, which landed me a compact .45. Except that it wasn't that compact, and I tired of trying to prevent it from printing. That's about the time all the micro-nines hit the market, and I've tried most of them. My initial carry 9mm was a nice little pistol, and reliable. But some of the parts on it seemed to wear out fast. The second one I tried is one of the fanciest on the market, but is the least reliable pistol I've ever owned. One failure per magazine is terrible, and this wasn't just mine, but a widespread problem. I tried a couple of other micro-nines, and found one that is really great, except I don't care for the trigger.

About that time, rumors were swirling about the new Glock G42 coming out, which everyone thought would be a single-stack 9mm. If it was, it would be exactly what I was looking for. If you know one Glock, you pretty much know them all, and I like what I know about Glock pistols. But when it was released, it wasn't a 9mm, but a .380 ACP. So, I turned to the G26. It's not quite as thin as I would like, but in exchange, it holds 10 rounds in a standard mag, with the ability to use full-size G17 magazines (and will also work with G19 magazines). So, I carried the 10-round magazine loaded, with a 17-round magazine on my belt.

The G26 is 6.41 inches in length, and 4.17 inches in height. That puts it at 0.9 inches shorter than the G19, and about 1.5 inches shorter than the G17. In height it's about 0.8 inches shorter than the G19 and almost 1.3 inches shorter than the G17. At 21.17 ounces, it's approximately two ounces lighter than the G19, and almost 3.5 ounces lighter than the G17. Given the difference in size, that's not a lot of weight difference.

For the most part, though, there's not going to be a lot of weight difference, and there shouldn't be. There are three parts to the Glock that are reduced to make for the compact and subcompact models: the frame (the bottom of the mag well and the front of the dust cover), the slide and the barrel. The only part that can be shortened with impunity is the frame, but that's only half an inch of polymer shell in two different places. The weight difference between the three frames is three-eighths of an ounce each.

The thing is, the 9mm cartridge creates basically the same recoil when fired, whether it's from a G26, G19 or G17, which means you still need the same force to counter the force of recoil. The barrel and the frame comprise one of the two ways to counter the force of recoil, the other being the slide spring. You can't have a significant reduction of weight in the slide and barrel, because you still need that counterweight.

Each model has a specific slide weight it needs to cycle properly, and to achieve that a portion of the slide wall is reduced so it is thinner. The G17 reduces the slide wall

The G26 field-stripped.

The G26 with 10-round magazine. Two fingers fit on grip, but the third dangles. This is the case with all subcompact pistols unless there is an extended grip.

about three-fourths of an inch from the front of the ejection port. The G19 doesn't reduce it until after an inch and a half. The G26 doesn't reduce it until as far forward as possible, which actually ends up being at the same place as the G19. To make up for the extra mass the slide lacks, it uses the slide spring.

Unlike the compact and standard-frame Glock models, the G26 and other subcompact models do not have an accessory rail on the dustcover. This means you won't be able to mount a flashlight on it, and if you're looking to add a laser it will have to be mounted in a different manor, such as on the grip or the slide spring. The front of the slide is also beveled, which, I think, makes it look nice, and not so boxy. The lack of a rail (and thus accessories) and the beveled slide front make for a really smooth, easy slide into a carry holster.

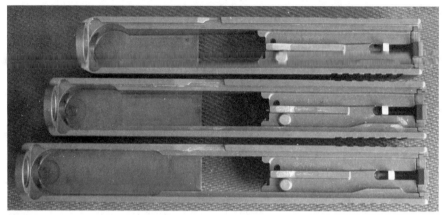

(Top to bottom): G26, G19 and G17 slides. Notice where the wall thickness reduction starts on each model.

(Top to bottom): G26, G19 and G17. The difference in frames is a reduction off the bottom of the mag well and a little off the front dustcover. Not a lot of weight removed.

(Top to bottom): G26, G19 and G17. The difference in barrel length is a reduction in the hollow barrel, which is, once again, not a lot of weight reduction.

Since the G26 comes with a mag well finger tab, the Gen5 will have the same magazine compatibility issue as the G19X: Gen5 mag baseplates will not work with it. So, the G26 Gen5 ships with Gen5 mags with a Gen4 baseplate. The finger tab on the G26 also precludes the half-moon cutout that other Gen5 models have.

Like all Gen5 models, in August, Glock announced the G26 Gen5 would come only with front serrations, non-FS models

(Top to bottom): G26, G19 and G17. The difference in weight of the three different slide springs isn't a lot, either.

would be phased out, so it's now available in Gen3, Gen4 and Gen5 FS. As of now, no MOS configuration is available for the G26.

For the Custom and Boarder Protection service contract Glock won (see chapter 14, Specialty Glocks and Glocks You Can't Have, about the G47) alongside the G47, Glock

You have to love the magazine flexibility of Glock pistols. Here is the G26 with a G19 15-round magazine (top left), with a G17 17-round magazine (bottom left) and, for maximum pleasure, with a 33-round magazine (right).

also (allegedly) designed a G26 model with front serrations, slightly longer grip, flared mag well, the absence of the finger tab found on the other G26s and an 11-round magazine. Glock hasn't confirmed this at the time of this writing, and like anything else, details about the pistol are subject to change before the order is actually filled.

G34

The G34 was introduced in 1998, as a long-slide variant to the G17, and a replacement for the G17L. It was designed specifically to fit in the IPSC box that made the G17L obsolete. Glock made sure to make the G34 as long as possible so as to maximize sight radius, yet still fit in the box. It was introduced as a third generation Glock, but is now offered in Gen4, Gen4 MOS and Gen5 MOS FS.

The barrel length is listed as 5.31 inches, which is .83 inches longer than the G17. The slide length comes out to just over 8 inches, which gives it a sight radius of 7.55 inches.

Not to point out the obvious, but the G17 was designed to fire a 9mm projectile, which it does quite well. If Glock were to change the weight of the G17 slide, it would change the dynamics of slide operation and wouldn't function as reliably. The G34 is a long slide sitting atop a G17 frame, and thus the question becomes: How does one make a long slide weigh the same as the standard-length slide? There are different answers to this, as I will discuss later in the chapter discussing the G41, but for the G34, Glock went with the simple solution of machining out an opening on top of the slide (it resembles the sun roof

The author's limited-run G34 Gen4 MOS with OD Green frame.
(instagram.com/robb_manning #robb_manning.glock.book)

The G34: It was designed for competition, but has practical/tactical use.

Glock machined out the slide to keep the weight the same as the G17. A change of more or less weight will affect the cycle speed, which decreases reliability.

of an automobile) to remove some of the weight. I like how it looks, some people don't, but either way it's a simple solution that works.

I purchased my G34 Gen4 MOS as part of the Glock Shooting Sports Foundation (GSSF) purchase program, so mine is a blue box model (if you don't know what that means, please refer to the GSSF Chapter 17). It's a limited run that came with an OD Green frame. Mine came with the extended slide catch lever and a 5.5-pound trigger (standard trigger comes with the 3.5-pound connector, designated with a minus symbol) that averaged about 4.9 pounds on my Lyman digital trigger scale.

The 3.5 connector-equipped Glock is actually

a very nice trigger, one preferred by a lot of competitive shooters. My G34 Gen4 did not come with the adjustable sights, like other G34s, but instead came with the fixed polymer sights.

The G34 is a competition animal, but as you would guess, it's not a very good concealed-carry gun. I've carried mine in open carry situations and it's fine, but for concealed carry it doesn't work as well.

The G34 Gen5 MOS FS incorporates front serrations into an already outstanding competition platform. (Photo provided by Glock.)

Carried inside the waistband, the long slide is going to pry against the upper part of your leg, dig into the bone and generally not be very comfortable, especially when sitting. I found it to be the opposite of comfortable. Carried outside the waistband, it's going to be too long and will stick out from under the bottom of the shirt. When you go to sit

The extended slide stop lever.

down, the muzzle will bury into the seat and force your belt up, which is again, not very comfortable.

There is a place for it in the tactical world, whether in military special-operating forces, or special police units. Some of these units have no issues with carrying a pistol the size of a 1911, and if you factor in the 1911 grip safety, the G34 is just a bit shorter than the 1911, except it has a longer sight radius. Of course, if a unit wants a .45, the best choice is the G41, but for something in a 9mm, the G34 would make an outstanding choice. This would be going in the opposite direction from the shorter slide of the G19X.

When it comes to 9mm, compared to hammer-fired duty 9mm handguns, the G34 is shorter than most, despite the long slide, especially when you start to factor in the added length of the beavertails most hammer-fired guns have. Factoring that, the Beretta M9 is about a half-inch longer, however, the sight radius of the G34 is over one inch longer. Another favorite 9mm, the CZ-75B, is also longer.

The G34 uses standard G17 magazines and extended 9mm magazines, but just like the G17 it cannot use G19 compact or G26 subcompact magazines.

CHAPTER 7:
THE 10MM GLOCKS

THE G20

My first Glock was a G20C, and it's still my favorite. There's a lot of power in the 10mm cartridge, making the G20 a very effective handgun. A weakened 10mm load, dubbed the "FBI load," handicaps it to .40 S&W power, but there are a few manufacturers that make the full-power load. If your intent is to shoot the "FBI load," you're better off saving the extra girth of the G20 and grabbing a G22 in .40

Four of Glock's 10mm lineup (bottom to top): G29 Gen4, G29SF, G20C (discontinued) and the G20SF.

S&W. Ammunition is cheaper and generally easier to find. I say generally, because during times of ammunition shortages, often the only ammunition I could find on store shelves were chamberings that not many other people shoot, and I could always find 10mm.

If you're not familiar with the 10mm, you should reconsider, it's essentially a .40 Magnum. The 10mm produces 775 foot-pounds of energy, which means that power-wise, it's not quite at the .41 magnum level, but it does edge out the .357 Magnum in all but the hottest loads. With 15 rounds in a Glock G20 magazine, that's the firepower equivalent to carrying three magnum-power revolvers with you. With the three magazines that come with it, it's 45 rounds of grizzly-be-good.

It's the 10mm cartridge that is responsible for turning me into a Glock guy. It started during a weekend hunt on the Ted Nugent ranch. Ted and I were discussing the 10mm, which he carries. I had read a lot about it and was intrigued. After talking with him, I searched around the Internet for guns chambered in 10mm. I saw a few, but the Glock's reputation of reliability, ability to handle the powerful round and the price, all had me leaning in that direction. So, I contacted Glock and had them send me one for testing and evaluation. I also contacted Buffalo Bore for some of its full-power loads. I shot some off-the-shelf loads first, and was impressed, but when I shot that Buffalo Bore 180-grain

Here is how I measured the girth of the grip, where your hand encircles it.

JHC (1,350 feet per second) and 200-grain FMJ-RN (1,200 feet per second), I fell in love. It's wicked, to say the least, and I love wicked.

My feelings for the Glock 20 ran parallel to the 10mm cartridge. It always worked, without any problems, it could handle abuse, plus it was easy to take care of. I thought "this will be the only Glock I ever need." Right. How naive we can be.

Interestingly enough, the G20 was not released before the G22. During the 1980s, the Federal Bureau of Investigation (FBI) was looking to replace its antiquated revolvers with something more powerful, and in semi-auto. FBI leaders designated the 10mm as the caliber they wanted, and gun makers scrambled to develop handguns in that chambering. Eyeing an opportunity to arm one of the leading law-enforcement agencies in the world with its handguns, Glock was one of those makers.

The problem, however, was the G17 didn't have a big enough frame to handle the magnum round, so Glock had to increase the size of the handgun proportionally to the round it would shoot. Glock engineers went to work, and soon the G20 was born. Just as the G20 was set for production, the FBI switched gears and decided to go with an even newer round, the .40 S&W. Glock then scrambled to get that to the FBI, fortunately, this one could use the G17 frame, so engineers focused all their efforts on developing and producing the G22, which delayed the G20. The G20 was released in late 1990 (along with the G21), two months after the G22 and G23 (the compact .40 version of the G19).

The G20 Gen3 is 8.22 inches long with a height of 5.47 inches. The barrel length is 4.6 inches long and it has a bore axis of 1.26 inches. It's 1.27 inches wide and weighs 30.89 ounces. The G20 Gen4 and SF are 8.03 inches long, all other measurements are the same as the Gen3. They both weigh 30.71 ounces.

The third generation G20 has been discontinued in the full-frame configuration, and now only comes in the Gen3 SF (Short Frame) version, which I cover in the next section. It makes sense, because the standard-size, large-frame grip is pretty big, and because Glock was able to cut down the girth to make the SF, and then the Gen4, it allows it to fit in the hands of a larger number of shooters.

The Gen4 is the most current generation of G20 as of this writing in 2019. It has all the Gen4 changes discussed in Chapter 4. I am a big fan of Gen4's RTF in the 10mm Glocks. The rougher texture gives a little more grip when firing the large 10mm, which allows for better control. In fact, since getting a Gen4 10mm, I don't shoot my Gen3 as often, though I still enjoy watching flames shoot out of the compensated barrel in low-light conditions. Only time will tell if the Gen5 will trickle down to the G20. I'm sure Glock will calculate the sales estimates and decide if those numbers will justify the change. I think people who don't own a G20 would choose a Gen5 over previous generations, however, I don't believe many G20 Gen4 owners would sell their gun to buy a Gen5.

The grip of a Glock G20 SF Gen3 (left), compared to the standard frame grip of the G20C Gen3 (discontinued).

G20 SF (SHORT FRAME)

The G20 SF is the short-frame version of the Gen3 and is now the only version of the Gen3. Glock started production in 2007 of SF variants of all four large-frame pistols: the G20, G21, G29 and G30. The difference in girth between a G20 SF and full-frame G20 is a little more than .25 inches. The length of the grip is shortened by about 0.13 inches, fore to aft. This is accomplished by slimming down the trigger mechanism housing and reducing the amount of

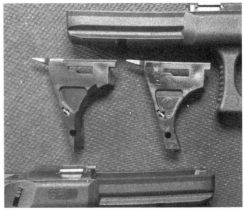

The trigger mechanism housing has been trimmed in the SF (left) so it can fit into the narrower grip. A standard trigger mechanism is on the right.

space in the empty backstrap channel. I took the measurements around the portion of the grip that's the biggest determinant of how you grip the pistol, starting with your thumb, wrapping around with the web of your hand and continuing around where the second finger comes around under the trigger guard. This seemed like the best place to measure, since this is where the most pressure is applied while gripping the handgun. The girth

Marking on a short frame compared to the lack of marking on a standard frame.

Where the road ends and the wilderness begins is where you'll truly appreciate the G20.

of the G20 is 6 inches, and the grip is 2.22 inches long, while the G20SF is 5.75 inches, and the grip is 2.09 inches long.

On paper, it doesn't look like there's much of a difference, and if you look at it, the difference is barely noticeable, but when you hold it, you can feel the difference. I'm right at the borderline of holding a standard G20 Gen3 pistol and not needing to twist the pistol to put my thumb on the magazine release. I can do it, but just barely, and I have to stretch my thumb. With the G20SF, I don't have to stretch my thumb at all, it's right there. I've always found it interesting how in the world of firearms, one-eighth of an inch can make such a big difference.

Internally, there really isn't much difference between a SF and a standard frame, because the only difference is the length of the grip fore to aft. The one part that this has a direct effect on is the trigger mechanism housing, which, as I mentioned earlier, had to be trimmed down so it would fit in the narrower grip.

One thing you'll notice for the G20, the SF version is offered only in Gen3; there is no Gen4 SF. That's because the Gen4 *is* an SF. In order to make the Gen4 fit a broader range of hand sizes, Glock first made the frame shorter (which, "short frame" as I just mentioned, in the Glock-o-sphere means, "smaller grip") for those with the smallest of hands, then offered various backstraps to make it as hand-filling as the shooter wants it. Since the Gen4 is a short frame, it made the SF version obsolete and only available in Gen3 Glocks.

There is an elite Danish naval unit called the Slædepatruljen Sirius (Sirius Sledge Patrol), whose mission is to protect Danish sovereignty in the arctic wilderness of northeast Greenland. The entire unit consists of 14 men (the unit is open to women, but none has ever applied), and they're stationed among four outposts scattered along the coastline of the Danish-controlled region. Throughout the year, they conduct long-range recon patrols in sled teams of two men and 11 to 15 dogs. Their patrols are approximately four to six weeks long in autumn and up to four months long in spring. During these patrols, and I stress, they are up to four months long, the only contact an individual has with another person is with his one teammate. They have limited supplies, with about 750 pounds carried and the sled, and additional supplies provided by air and boat located in 50 huts scattered throughout the patrol area, which is approximately 375,000 square miles (that's about one-tenth of the United States). Each member is a trained expert in survival, shooting, demolition, engine repair, reconnaissance, firefighting, communications, first aid, sewing and truck driving. The average high temperature for the year is 7.7 degrees Fahrenheit, (December through

Hold on tight to that G29; she produces a little bit of recoil.

March it never gets above -10) and the average low is -0.7 (January through March it averages -26, -26 and -27, respectively). Polar bear sightings are frequent.

These are rough men doing a rough job. These men are issued the G20. The G20 is the sidearm of choice with men who could potentially need to put down a polar bear. It's the sidearm of choice for men who are alone for four months, and must fix their own injuries, must repair their own gear and must be self-reliant.

There are but a handful of police departments across the United States that issue or authorize the use of the G20, but most of the users belong to units such as Special Weapons and Tactics teams and the FBI Hostage Rescue Team.

THE G29 (G29 SF, G29 GEN4)

The G29 is the subcompact version of the G20, meant for concealed carry. It's like what the G26 is to the G17 for the 9mm lineup. Glock does not have a compact model (like the G19) for the 10mm lineup (or the .45 ACP lineup, either), and only offers standard (G20) and subcompact (G29).

To quote fellow writer Patrick Sweeney, "And for those who simply must have the loudest of anything, we have the G29." (Gun Digest Book of the Glock, 2nd Edition). The G29 is not for the faint at heart, to say the least. To one-up the old adage, "Speak softly and carry a big stick," the G29 is like carrying a little stick with a Claymore strapped to the end of it. Mr. Roosevelt would be proud.

The G29 has some rather stiff recoil. Not that it's unmanageable, because it's not. In fact, with the way the Glock polymer frame flexes, it's nowhere near what some people have made it out to be. The Glock is a modern pistol, with modern properties, and it is efficient at minimizing recoil.

Picture a Shelby 427 Cobra. It packs a lot of engine into a small package. When you press the gas pedal to the floorboard, you best hold on tight. The G29 is a lot like that; it packs a lot of power into a small package. For some shooters, a full-power 10mm in the full-size G20 is too much gun to shoot comfortably. That same full-power 10mm loading in a subcompact Glock is something many aren't willing to try. Not only is the shooter slinging lead out of a package that's about seven ounces lighter when loaded, it has less weight in the 1.2-

The G29: Glock in "Beast Mode."

The trigger bar cruciform leg is where it attaches to the trigger mechanism housing, via the trigger spring. In the left picture, the G29 Gen4 is on top, the G29 SF is on the bottom. In the right picture, the G29 SF is on the left/bottom, the one with a notch in the tip of the leg.

Both the Gen3 Short Frame and the Gen4 use the same trimmed trigger mechanism housing.

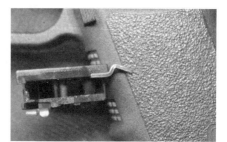

The Gen3 10mm ejector.

inch shorter slide, thus giving it more muzzle rise. The shooter has to hold on to the package because it's one inch shorter in height, meaning that your pinky is going to dangle.

In my estimation, most G29 owners are people like me, who own and love the G20, and want a 10mm in a concealed-carry gun. For as much as I love my G20, and it's an awesome open-carry woods gun, it's just too big for concealed carry, unless you have on a jacket. While the G29 is still thick, it measures 1.27 inches wide, it's the smallest 10mm handgun on the market.

Introduced in 1996, the G29 is 6.88 inches long, 2.15 inches shorter than the G20. In height, it measures 4.45 inches, which is about one inch shorter than the 5.17 inches the G20 is listed at. The width is the same, though it is about 3.9 ounces lighter, at 26.83 ounces. When shopping for a new G29, there are now two variants to choose from: G29 SF, and

G29 Gen4 (the Gen3 G29 full frame, like the G20 full frame, has been discontinued). The G29 SF is what most of us call a Gen3, but Glock is using it as a "standard" model. When comparing the grip measurements between the two models, it's going to be the same as the comparable G20 model measurements, the G20 SF and G20 Gen4. Internally, the differences in parts between the G29 SF and G29 Gen4 are minimal, aside from the Gen4 changes, of course. It looks like the parts in the G29 SF, at least in the late model I tested, carried over to the G29 Gen4.

It's easy to see the short-frame models had influence in the design of the Gen4. The G29 Gen4 is the culmination of everything that's great about the different Gen3 models. It's hard to justify buying one of the two Gen3 models when the Gen4 includes everything they do, plus more. Unless, of course, you just don't like the aggressive Gen4 grip texture. The Gen4 gives you the option of different backstraps, so you can go short frame, medium frame or you can use the backstrap that is the equivalent to a standard Gen3 grip. It also has a third magazine, which I like. Two magazines are the bare-bones minimum that should come with a handgun, but three or more is even better.

Everything I wrote about the G20 Gen4, and speculation about a Gen5, is applicable to the G29, as well.

G40

Glock introduced the G40 shortly before I finished the first edition of this book, (and after the G41 (.45 ACP), as part of the M.O.S. (Modular Optic System) line of handguns. The G41 shipped on time, and I was able to include it in the book, but the G40 did not. Glock released the specs for the G40, which I included in the "New Glocks" chapter of that book, Chapter 15; but I was never able to confirm specs or test the gun prior to going to print. Then the G40 was delayed. Then it was delayed again. Finally, around August 2015, the G40 shipped. I quickly discovered it was not the same dimension specs Glock had advertised pre-launch, and the specs listed on the website reflected this. In particular, the width of the slide.

The G20 slide width is 1.12 inches, as is the G21 (.45 ACP). The 9mm model's slides are 1.00 inch, which is also the same width as the Slimline G36 (.45 ACP). The G41 slide width is 1.00 inch, which makes it the same width as the Slimline G36 and the 9mm model slides. The G40 was supposed to be the same width, and that's what I based a lot of that 1st Edition chapter on, but when I actually received the G40, that's not the width of the slide, it measured 1.135, which is more in line with the G20. The overall width is 1.35 inches, measured at the widest part, the mag release.

I have no facts, I can only surmise, but I believe the wider-than-advertised slide gives a clue as to why the G40 was delayed. My theory is the G40 was originally intended to have a Slimline slide like the G41, but engineers possibly had problems with it in testing. This would explain the delay, they were trying to make it work, but couldn't.

With all of that reported, and set aside, the G40 is an outstanding Glock. It's designed to be used for hunting, duty, and self-defense, but not for competition. Yes, you could use it at GSSF competitions, but for IPSC it won't fit in the box. It's designed in the spirit of the G17L and G25, with the extra-long barrel, not like the G34, G35 and G41, which are designed to fit in the box.

This is a smart move. Since no one is going to use the G40 for serious competition. It's not conducive to a lot of practice time; the cheapest ammo you can find is $30 per box and there's not a lot of companies out there making cheap ammo. Why not make the slide and barrel as long as possible? The other three competition Glocks cover everything that needs to be covered in competition, and practice ammo is much cheaper.

The G40 has a 6-inch barrel, about a half-inch longer than the G34, G35 and G41, and approximately 1.5

The G40 is a beast, designed for hunting. Here it is equipped with a SIG Romeo1, a perfect combo.

inches longer than the G20, with an 8.19-inch sight radius when using the open sights. That's right: two-thirds of a foot. That's a long sight radius. Aside from that, MOS gives you the option of mounting a reflex sight for even more accurate shooting. With the optics added, the G40 will really reach out with that 10mm.

The overall length is 9.49 inches, about 0.6 inches longer than the G41 and .75 inches longer than the G34 and G35. To put the length in perspective, the difference between the different Glock categories (subcompact, compact, standard, competition) is generally between 0.6 to 0.8 inches. So, the difference in length between the G40 long slide and the competition-length G41 is about the same difference in length between the G17 and the G19, and between the G19 and G26. It's not just a little bit longer, it's in a new category of length. If the G17L and G25 were still in production, it would be in this category, as the G40 is the large-frame version of those two models.

The weight of an unloaded G40 with plate is just over 32 ounces, roughly 4.7 ounces heavier than the G20. Just like all the other long-slide Glocks, the G40 is just a longer slide fitted on top of a standard-category Glock frame, in this case the large-framed G20. If you compare the frames of a G20 to a G40, aside from the Gen3/Gen4 difference, they're virtually the same, dimensionally. Since it is the same frame, it also has the same 5.47-inch height as the G20 and G41.

I watched the product release from Glock, and one of the things stated by the PR gentlemen is that the longer slide is going to cut down on recoil from the G20. It does make sense, a longer barrel and slide do put more weight out in front, so in general there will be less muzzle rise. In my non-scientific, side-by-side comparison of my G20C and G40, I'd concur there is noticeably less felt recoil. I found the G40 to be a pretty sweet shooter. I have a SIG Romeo1 red dot mounted to it, and it makes for a potent package. The Romeo1 has a huge field of view, so there's no blind spots.

As a fan of the 10mm, I appreciate Glock's dedication to the cartridge. Judging from the 2015 SHOT Show, that loyalty will pay off, because it appears the 10mm is making a comeback. Several companies introduced new handguns in 10mm, including SIG Sauer.

AMMO: FEED THE BEAST

In the first edition of this book, I predicted the 10mm would hit a resurgence in popularity, and I was correct (not because I'm particularly brilliant, but because the 10mm is an outstanding round, and it was an anomaly that it fell out of favor in the first place). In 2017 and 2018, a flurry of new 10mm models were released, from companies including SIG, Ruger, Kimber, Wilson Combat, Dan Wesson, EAA, Rock Island Armory, Para USA, Remington, etc.; and with it a smorgasbord of ammunition to feed them.

As soon as ammo makers saw the renewed interest in not just 10mm, but *full-power* 10mm, they have been more than happy to jump on the 10mm train. When you consider the advancements in bullets and powders we've seen in the last 10 years or so, the 10mm ammo on the market today is lightyears ahead of what was on the market just four or five years ago. We hear so much about how the 9mm self-defense ammo of today is in a whole different league compared to 9mm ammo from a couple decades ago, which has led to the downfall of the .40 S&W in popularity. But now consider all of those advancements are now being poured into the 10mm. Wow.

Full-power loads available when I wrote the first edition were somewhat limited, and at the time I wrote: For me, the tried and true that I have used and tested the most is the Buffalo Bore 180-grain and 200-grain loads. Those were loads I had used since I got my G20, and I never had any issues, and since I had fired it the most and trusted it, it was what I used when I carry my G20. It was a great round then, and it's still a great round. In fact, I still carry it. However, now, it's not the only load I use when carrying the G20 or G40.

I received a batch of Underwood Ammo, and that's some great stuff. I'm a fan of the 180-grain XTP JHP that comes in at 1,300 feet per second. But what's even more impressive is Underwood's 140-grain Xtreme Penetrator, made with an all-copper bullet that travels at 1,500 feet per second. If you like speed, Underwood also has a 115 grain Xtreme Defender that screams along at 1,700 feet per second. It's based off the Xtreme Penetrator, with a CNC machined all-copper bullet, and is designed to consistently get 18 inches of penetration, and to maximize the permanent wound cavity (PWC). I haven't tested it in ballistic gel, yet, but Underwood engineers say they get two-times the PWC as any other expanding bullet on the market. I'll have to see that for myself.

I still haven't fired any, but I'm told Winchester also makes some pretty good stuff in a Super-X 175-grain Silvertip HP. The muzzle velocity is a very respectable 1,290 feet per second with 649 foot-pounds of energy.

Another company that's been making some excellent full-power loads is Double Tap, and I've shot a lot of it in the last couple of years. So much in fact, it's become one of my go-to choices for carry, and not just for 10mm. I've become pretty good friends with Double Tap owner Mike McNett, and he's sent me quite a bit of it for testing. Double Tap markets under three different lines: DT Hunter, DT Defense and DT Tactical; plus, it manufactures for Colt Defense Ammunition. The DT Hunter is a 200-grain controlled expansion JHP that leaves the barrel at 1,250 feet per second. You wouldn't be wrong in using this one for self-defense, too. The DT Defense is a 190-grain Equalizer moving at 1,210 feet per second. The Equalizer consists of two bullets in one, a 135-grain JHP in front of a 55-grain hard-cast solid that is designed to leave two wound channels, increasing your odds of neutralizing

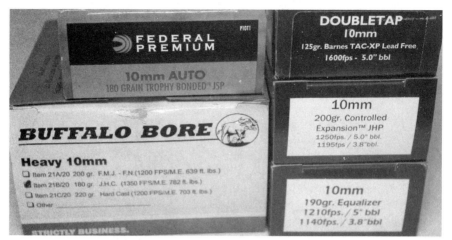

A sampling of some great full-power 10mm loads: Federal, Buffalo Bore and Double Tap. All are excellent. The author hasn't had malfunctions with any of them.

the threat. The DT Defense chambering is a 125-grain Barnes TAC-XP bullet fired at an impressive 1,600 feet per second. Ouch, that's got to hurt.

Since the first edition of this book, there's been an old gun company that's become a new ammo maker: SIG Sauer and its Elite Performance Ammunition. SIG brings a lot of manufacturing might into its new U.S.-based, ammo-production facility. I've fired a lot of SIG ammo since it's come to market, and it's some very good stuff. I've been trying to find fault with it, but can't. Sometimes when you see stuff like this it is kind of a novelty, but not the case with SIG ammo, the company is very serious. One of my writers got to tour the facility and wrote an article about it for me, and it's impressive. It's become one of my go-to carry ammo makers that I trust, and with the 10mm I really like the 180 grain V-Crown JHP.

Another new addition to the ammo scene is a small company called G2 Research. The company made some waves and ruffled some feathers with its R.I.P. round: Radically Invasive Projectile, designed to maximize the dissipation of energy into the target. I've fired quite a bit of it, and it's been very reliable with good accuracy, but I haven't been able to do ballistic-gel testing on it. I have used the 300 BLK R.I.P. cartridge to dispatch sizeable four-legged vermin that were causing damage to my cabin, and I'll just report the results were devastating. To the point where I wouldn't show the pictures in this book.

With all the fancy self-defense ammo on the market, people forget about the Speer Gold-Dot; it's still the standard for law enforcement and FBI. Its 200-grain GDHP has a velocity of 1,100 feet per second, which is pretty impressive for that size bullet. Since 2018, I've spent a good amount of time shooting it so far, and it's working its way up my list of go-to 10mm rounds. It's pretty high on my list of 9mm loads. I'm also a big fan of Federal Ammunition's HST loads.

For years, people were saying the 10mm was dying, and perhaps for a while it was struggling. I'm not sure why, because it's an outstanding cartridge (perhaps it would have had better reception had it been called the .40 Auto Magnum, instead of the European-sounding 10 millimeter). But now it's back, and in a big way.

CHAPTER 8:
THE G21 AND OTHER .45 ACP GLOCKS

Ahhhh…the mighty .45 ACP. It is as American as apple pie and baseball. When it comes to modern-day combat rifle cartridges from 1900 to the present, the United States rules with several different classics, from the .30-06 Springfield and 7.62x51 NATO (.308 Winchester) to the 5.56x45 NATO (.223 Remington). However, when it comes to pistol cartridges, there's only one: the .45 ACP. For decades, when it came to semi-automatic pistols, the .45 ACP received all the affections from American shooters. There were other calibers, but none as adored as the .45.

It's not as easy today for the .45, which now has competition from fans of the 9mm, .40 S&W, and the resurging 10mm Auto. Yet the .45 is still going strong and is still incredibly popular, as demonstrated by the sticker one of my neighbors has on the back window of his truck. It reads ".45 ACP: Because shooting twice is just silly!"

Glock has a very extensive line of .45 ACP models, more extensive than the 10mm models. There are standard size, competition, subcompact, slimline, hybrids, etc. What it does not have, like the 10mm lineup, is a compact model (comparable to what the G19 is for the 9mm line). It offers standard size and subcompact, but no compact.

G21

The G21 started life as the G20 10mm. As I wrote in the chapter about the G20, the FBI wanted a 10mm, so Glock put all its efforts into making what would become the G20. Just like a .357 Magnum revolver can handle any .38 Special load, if the G20 could handle a 10mm load, the .45 ACP would be child's play.

With this in mind, Glock was set to launch the G20 and G21 at the same time, just as the FBI changed its mind and decided to go with the popular new kid on the block, the .40 S&W. So, the G22 and G23 were introduced first, and the G20 and G21 had to wait. Within law-enforcement circles, the 10mm and .45 have been playing second fiddle to the .40 ever since. In truth, according to sales of the .40 and the 9mm, the .45 has been playing third fiddle.

The G21 has the same dimensions as its large-frame G20 brother, at 8.03 inches long and 5.47 inches in height. It has a width of 1.27 inches, 0.1 inches wider than the standard-frame Glock models. Despite having a larger frame, the G21 has the same bore axis as the smaller, standard frame models, at 1.26 inches. The sight radius is 6.77 inches and the barrel is

The G21 doesn't have to handle the force of the 10mm, so the slide can be machined thinner (top, at the pointer) to cut down on weight. Compare it to the G20 (bottom), which has not been machined thinner.

4.6 inches long. Unloaded, it weighs 1.5 ounces less than the G20, at 29.3 ounces. In regard to the trigger, it has the same pull weight and length of travel as all other Glock pistols with the standard connector, at 5.5 pounds and .49 inches, respectively. The magazine capacity is 13 glorious rounds of hate and discontent.

Giving new meaning to the term "heater."

The 10mm Auto has a SAAMI maximum pressure of 37,000 PSI. Full power loads, such as the Double Tap 200-grain jacketed hollowpoint speed out of a five-inch barrel at 1,250 feet per second. The .45 is on the opposite side of the pressure spectrum, with the SAAMI maximum pressure at 21,000 PSI. The bread and butter of the .45 ACP, the 230-grain bullet, is a subsonic round, with most maxing out around 830 to 900 feet per second. I've seen some 200-grain +P offerings hit 1,080 fps, but it doesn't get much faster than that for the .45. The point is: If it can handle a 10mm, the .45 is good to go.

However, when you chamber a less powerful cartridge in a semi automatic designed for a more powerful cartridge, it's not going to cycle properly. Glock solved the problem by taking some mass off the slide just forward of the ejection port. Not much, but apparently

The G21 vs. 1911. The Glock has almost twice the ammo capacity in one magazine. This particular 1911 is the first handgun the author ever purchased, back in 1993.

it doesn't take much. The G20C I have access to has a little more slide taken off than does the standard G20; there are two compensated slots taken out of the front, but it weighed 1 pound, 7/8 ounces. The G21 Gen4 weighed 1 pound, 3/4 ounce. The G21SF weighed 1 pound, 1/2 ounce. I'm unsure why Glock had the G21 Gen4 weigh .25 ounces more. I don't even know if that is significant, but there is a larger area milled out of the slide around the front sight area of the G21SF.

The thing that has always hindered the G21, and the same thing that has always hindered the G20, is the massive grip. It's big. It's entirely possible for a shooter in the market for a .45 to take a look at the G21 and like it, but upon feeling how big the grip is end up looking elsewhere.

Grip size, however, is a small price to pay for what you get in return. And what you get is a .45 that shoots flawlessly. If you're looking for a .45 for personal protection or home protection, skip the 1911 and take a look at the G21. I know this is going to make some 1911 fans mad, but don't be. I'm a big fan of the 1911. As I've written elsewhere in this book, it was the very first pistol I bought when I turned 21. It's what my childhood TV hero, Magnum P.I., carried. It is the finest pistol ever made, and it has influenced, in one way or another, almost every pistol that comes off the assembly line today.

However, while the 1911 was reliable in its day, it's not reliable by today's standards. Yes, you can make it reliable, but it will cost you. To make a 1911 reliable by Glock standards, it's going to cost at least $1,000 for pistol and customization, and that's at the low end. Most likely it will cost at least $1,200, but some people pay more than that.

Glock gives you that out of the box, for about two-thirds to half the price. My 1911, which I loved, but would never carry, was fraught with problems. It didn't like hollow points. Ball ammo worked decently (but even that wasn't 100 percent), but hollowpoints were about a 50/50 proposition whether they would feed correctly. That's why I loaded a hollowpoint in the chamber with the rest of the magazine filled with FMJ. This leads to the other problem with the 1911: the magazines. Magazines for the 1911 were terrible back then. At any given time, the welding on the baseplate could give out, sending the rounds shooting out the bottom. Yes, I know I could have done this, this and this, and could have bought that, that and that. But this is exactly my point: You don't have to do this and that to

The author's favorite ammo: American Eagle FMJ for practice and Federal Premium Hydra-Shok JHP for carry.

The number of .45 ACP offerings on the market is second only to the 9mm. This offering from Sellier & Bellot makes an excellent choice for plinking on a budget.

an out-of-the-box Glock. I paid $320 for my 1911 at the base exchange. This was what I had saved up as a Lance Corporal during my three-plus months in Somalia. I needed an out-of-the-box pistol, not one that I needed to spend more on to customize. As a lowly Lance Corporal, paying more wasn't in the equation, but at the time I was set on the 1911. In 1993, a Glock G21 would have fetched around $350 to $400. I could have paid a little more than I did for the 1911, and not have had all those headaches.

I will admit basic 1911s have improved since 1993. Magazines are worlds better, and even basic 1911s feed better. Still, they're not Glock reliable. You can put absolutely any brand or type of ammunition (excepting lead cast bullets) into a G21, and it will function flawlessly. You can't say that about a 1911.

One firearm accessory that's been huge the last few years is the suppressor, so much so that I've devoted an entire chapter to it. Sales are through the roof on suppressors, yet we're still at the beginning of the trend. It's this author's humble opinion that with the rise in popularity of the suppressor, there will be a corresponding resurgence in the popularity of the .45, which is a great cartridge for suppression. While other cartridges require special subsonic loads, the .45 ACP does not, as it's all subsonic.

Conduct your own research test. Go the store and see how many boxes of ammo you find marked "subsonic" or something to the effect of "suppressor ready." Now go to the .45 ACP section. Everything that doesn't have a +P on the box might as well read "suppressor ready." That's a lot of choices.

The G21 (Gen3) as it was, has been discontinued, like the G20 Gen3, and is now only available as the G21 SF version. Once Glock slimmed down the grip for the SF version and subsequently, the Gen4, I'm sure the large grip found on the Gen3 fell out of favor, given its massive size. The SF and Gen4 grips just fit a larger array of hands more comfortably.

G21 SF (SHORT FRAME)

Ever since the U.S. military adopted the Beretta 92FS as the M9, chambered in 9x19mm NATO, there have been critics of the caliber. It's a traditional organization, and there are those who don't like change, especially when it comes to weaponry. For example, dur-

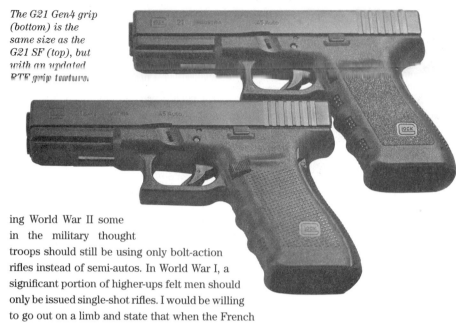

The G21 Gen4 grip (bottom) is the same size as the G21 SF (top), but with an updated RTF grip texture.

ing World War II some in the military thought troops should still be using only bolt-action rifles instead of semi-autos. In World War I, a significant portion of higher-ups felt men should only be issued single-shot rifles. I would be willing to go out on a limb and state that when the French invented the cased cartridge, some in the U.S. military probably fought tooth-and-nail to keep the cap-and-ball muzzleloader. I'm sure even smokeless powder had its detractors. I can hear the pro-black powder slogan, "If, after a volley of fire you can still see your enemy, you're just not shooting effective charges. Say no to smokeless powder."

The G21 trigger mechanism housing (left) compared to the G21 SF.

The slot in the frame that the trigger mechanism fits in. The G21 (left) trigger mechanism housing is squared off, and you can see the larger hole. The G21 SF (right) has had the bottom of the trigger mechanism housing "shaved down" so the bottom is tapered, and thus smaller. This allows for the back of the frame to be taken in so the grip is shorter.

Along with the critics of the 9mm, there are military units that argue for their specific missions, they need the stopping power of the .45 ACP. So, while the current official U.S. sidearm is the SIG M17 in 9mm, there are still plenty of .45 ACP pistols being used. Glock knows this, and if ever the military would go back to a .45 ACP as the official sidearm, it would love to fill that order with the G21. One of the major issues preventing the military from adopting the G21, aside from the lack of external thumb safety, is the grip size. The 1911 government model has a grip that is 5 and 3/8th inches around. This is relatively small for a full-size combat handgun, and it fits the hands of pretty much everyone. Then when the Beretta 92FS was adopted, small- to average-sized personnel said its 5- and 5/8-inch grip was too big. One major thing happened between the adoption of the 1911 and the M9: the acceptance of women into the military, and especially the issuance of weapons to female military personnel. So, the number of people with small hands went up exponentially in the military, and the M9 could be a little large in the grip for those people.

If the difference of one-fourth of an inch could make such a big difference to those with small- to average-sized hands, the G21 grip comes in at 6 inches around, a difference of three-eighths of an inch between it and the M9, and five-eighths between it and the 1911. So, Glock shortened the G21 frame, by shortening the grip one-fourth of an inch, and in 2007 the G21 SF was born. A quarter-inch doesn't sound like much, but as we can see from the difference between a 1911 and M9, it does make a difference that can be felt. To accomplish the grip reduction, Glock changed the shape of the trigger mechanism housing, making the bottom tapered, instead of squared off.

Even with the grip reduction, I suspect that if the M9 grip is a problem, the even larger G21 SF grip will be, too. It would be tough to envision the U.S. military adopting a Glock .45 handgun for general issue with the grip as large as it is.

The shooters I previously mentioned who might be put off by the grip size of the G21 could definitely be brought back to the G21 SF if they were to give it a second chance. It's still big, and it's still not for everyone, but it fits much better into medium-sized hands.

As I wrote in the previous section, if one prefers the Gen3 Glock, the G21 SF is still being produced, with no plans in the immediate future of stopping production. In fact, like the G20, Glock stopped production of the full frame G21, so if you want a G21

The Gen4 RTF (Rough Texture Frame) grip texture gives you a very secure grip on your Glock.

Gen3, the only way you can get it is in the SF frame. If, however, one wants the most current model of Glock, the G21 Gen4 really makes the SF Glock obsolete. Out of the box, it's the same size grip as the SF, with the option of two additional backstraps to make it a larger grip if one prefers. I think this would be something someone of Arnold Schwarzenegger stature would prefer. The G21 Gen4 uses the same tapered trigger mechanism housing as does the SF.

G21 GEN4

Just like the G20, there aren't many differences between the G21SF and the G21 Gen4, aside from the standard Gen4 changes. With other calibers and models, including the G21 standard frame, you notice a difference in the grip when you pick up a Gen4. A G21SF feels the same as the G21 Gen4, other than the grip texture. I really like the G21 in the Gen4 configura-

Two .45 ACPs: the G21 (front) compared to the G41. Whichever variant of G21 or the G41 you choose, when equipped with night sights and an extended threaded barrel and a suppressor, it is the ultimate .45 combat handgun.

tion; it handles great, and it feels great. If a shooter is looking at a .45 Glock for the first time, and the Gen4 is the first one he or she handles, it's going to leave a good impression. You can really sink your mitts into it and get a very positive grip. If I were on the market for a full-size .45, I would go the route of the G21 Gen4 over the Gen3 SF, though I would most likely go with the G41 Gen4.

I'm able to get a good, solid grip on the G21 and manipulate all the controls with my thumb, but just barely. I can reach the magazine release and the slide catch with my thumb, but I have to stretch my thumb for all it's worth. I'm at the borderline. I find that if I let myself get sloppy, I'll tilt the pistol in my hand to better reach the controls. With that admission, though, I operate a G21 (and G20) just fine, the G21SF and Gen4 are a better fit. I feel like I have a little better control of those manipulations.

The Gen4 is the most current generation of G21 as of this writing, and like the G20, it has all the Gen4 changes discussed in Chapter 4. It's hard to say if and/or when Glock will make a Gen5 G21. As far as priority, it's likely not high on Glock's list of Gen5 upgrades, but it does have the added bonus that it would get a two-fer, because the G20 would be updated at the same time.

G41

The G41 is a competition-length .45 ACP that follows in the footsteps of the G34 and G35, but in a large frame. Glock separates the "Competition" category of guns like G41, G34 and G35, from the "Long-Slide" category which includes the G17L, G24 (both are obsolete) and G40.

It is a long-slide version of the G21, but built in the slimline spirit of the G30S, which is a large-frame, subcompact frame with a G36 slimline slide on it. The G41 slide is 1.0 inch in width, which is the same width as the 9mm/.40 slides, as well as the aforementioned G30S and G36, as mentioned earlier in this chapter, the G21 slide is 1.12 inch in width. The narrower slide of the G41 makes it lighter than the G21. Despite the slimmer slide, the G41 is listed with the same overall width as the G21 at 1.28 inches (actually the G21 is listed as 1.27 inches) because the frame on both is wider than the actual slide. The G41 is .9 inches longer, at 8.9 inches, and the same height of 5.47 inches. The sight radius is 0.8 inches longer, and the whole package weighs 27 ounces, 2.3 ounces lighter than the G21.

Just like the other long-slide pistols, Glock has dubbed the G41 as "practical/tactical." What it means by that is, even though it has been designed for competitive shooting, it will also serve well in a practical role, as a carry or home defense gun, or a tactical role: S.W.A.T. (Special Weapons and Tactics) teams, S.O.F. (Special Operating Force), etc. In fact, for SWAT and SOF units looking for a .45 ACP, I don't think there is a better choice.

The benefit to the practical/tactical user is twofold: The longer sight radius allows the shooter to more accurately place rounds inside the intended target, and the longer slide makes the weapon more balanced so there isn't as much muzzle flip. This allows shooters to get their sights back on target faster after a shot. Equipping it with a flashlight on the rail makes it even better in this regard.

Though the G41 slide looks abnormally long compared to other Glocks and other polymer pistols, it's the same approximate size as a 1911 Government model pistol, which was the U.S. sidearm for more than 70 years. The overall length of the G41 is .65 inches longer, but if you hold them grip to grip, it's only about a quarter-inch longer.

As expected, I found the G41 to be an excellent shooter. It handled well, with much lighter recoil than my G20. I didn't notice much difference between how it handled recoil compared to the G21, despite the longer slide. This is most likely due to the slimline slide. The increase

The G41 is built on the same premise as the hybrid G30S, which took a slimline G36 slide and mounted it on a large-frame G30 bottom, except the G41 is much bigger than the G30S.

in barrel size will show an increase in velocity, though not much. With standard .45 ACP ammunition, the increase will most likely be around 75 feet per second, depending on ammo. The extra slide length does give you about an extra 0.8 inches of sight radius, which improves accuracy.

Let's go back to that slide: When I first picked up the G41, it didn't occur to me right away that the slide was a slimline slide like the G36, and it's not something that is mentioned on the G41 data page. So aside from the thinner slide, something I found interesting about the G41 is it is actually lighter than the G21, even though it's close to an inch longer. I didn't have a G21 on hand to weigh, but I did have the 10mm model, the G20C. The slide of the G20C weighs 1 pound, 7/8 ounce, the G21 slide is 16.75 ounces, and the G41 is 14.125 ounces. This is only one ounce heavier than the G34. So, I pulled out my calipers and scale and did some investigating.

I used as my baseline the G20; the frame that the .45 Glocks are built off of. The slide thickness on my G20C is .236, forward of breech, and it's uniform from breech to the muzzle end of the slide. The slide thickness of the G21 starts off at breech being the same thickness as the G20C, but about three-quarters of an inch forward of the ejection port, the wall narrows to .171 inches. This is done because the .45 ACP isn't as powerful as the 10mm, so the slide had to be made lighter so the .45 could still cycle the slide.

The G41 takes this a step further: At about 1.5 inches forward of the ejection port, the G41 has the slide thickness cut to .111 inches, which is the same thickness as the 9mm G34. I found this to be interesting, though not entirely shocking. It's not a high-stress area of the slide. In fact, on the G34 the top portion of the slide at this position has actually been removed, forming a large port, like a sunroof on a car. But here's what I found to be really interesting: The thickest portion of the slide, from breech to the area 1.5 inches forward of the ejection port, is only .186 inches. This means that at its thickest point, the entire slide wall of the .45 G41 is thinner than the 9mm G34, which is .197 at its thickest point.

When I look at the G41, I see a shift in how Glock is positioning its .45 lineup. With advancements in metals and design, Glock is now able to chamber .45 ACP in slides with the same width as the G17 9mm, which is how wide the G41 and G36 are. With that, it will be interesting to see if some day, since Glock has released the Gen5, the company will move its entire .45 ACP lineup in that direction. The G21 and G30 will be that much better with a slimline slide, primarily better for carry. It's completely possible and seems like it would be the next logical step.

THE .45 ACP SUBCOMPACTS
THE G30

The G30 .45 ACP is the subcompact version of the G21. The original G30, released in October 1996, is 6.96 inches long, 4.8 inches in height and 1.27 inches in width. The sight radius is 5.91 inches, and it has a barrel 3.77 inches in length. It weighs 26.48 ounces unloaded, and 33.89 ounces loaded with the full 10-round magazine. The barrel height is the same 1.26 inches as most other Glock pistols, and it has the same 5.5-pound trigger pull found on all Glock pistols (with standard connector) and the same .49 inches of trigger travel. It will take the full-capacity G21 magazines, giving it an optional capacity of 13 rounds.

The G30SF has had the grip shortened by one-fourth inch, just like the G21SF. In fact, other than being a subcompact version, the G30SF is nearly identical to the G21SF, and the design method used to shorten it, a modified trigger mechanism housing, is the same. The G30SF is slightly shorter in length than the G30, by .08 of an inch; which is something one would not necessarily notice, much like the fact that it's .18 ounces lighter.

The G30 Gen4 is identical in specs to the G30SF, but it will come with all of the Gen4 updates, including the modular back straps. At 6.88 inches long, it's nearly an inch shorter than the 1911 Commander-size handgun and half an inch shorter in height, yet holds three

The G30 Gen4 makes for an outstanding carry gun if one is looking for a subcompact .45 ACP. Despite its compact size, it carries more rounds than a full-size 1911.

The G30SF (foreground) has the same dimensions as the G30 Gen4, but without the upgrades.

more rounds, for a total of 10. Even better, it can accept G21 full-capacity magazines for a total of 13 rounds, almost double that of a 1911. Despite being smaller than a 1911 Commander-sized pistol, it shoots better, with less felt recoil. I found it to be pleasant to shoot, with very manageable recoil and offering fast follow-up shots.

G30S

Forget what Glock marketing people are telling you about the G19X being the first crossover model, they're wrong. The G30S is the first crossover (using Glock's definition of a crossover: taking the frame of one model and the slide/barrel of another model and combining them). The G30S is a slimline G30, meaning Glock took a G30 frame and put a G36 slide on it. The G36 slide is roughly the same width as a G17 slide, which is 1.005

The G30S has junk in the trunk: a slim top and a large-frame bottom.

inches, as is the G30S I measured. Due to the decrease in slide mass and grip width from the standard G30, it does come in lighter at 22.95 ounces empty and 30.36 ounces loaded. The grip is the same G30, holds the same number of rounds and takes the G21 magazine.

The G30S is slightly longer than the G30. Because it has the slide of the G36, it also shares the same overall length at 6.96 inches. All the other measurements are the same as the G30, with a height of 4.80 inches and the same overall width (the grip on all Glocks surpass the width of the slide, so when you read the specifications, the width is referring to the overall width, not the slide width). One difference is the weight. The G30S uses a slim slide, so the weight has been decreased by 3.6 ounces to 22.95 ounces.

It's a nice carry option; the thinner slide makes it easier to conceal, with less printing and also lighter to carry. A few ounces do not sound like much, but if you carry it all day, every day, after a few years it will make a difference. Some say the slides on the large-frame

Comparing the G30S to a 1911. More rounds carried, smaller package, plus the option of using a 13-round magazine from a G21.

Glock pistols are hard to conceal because they're so wide, and the solution was to make the slide thinner. Here, it works. I'm sure that after the Glock engineers tested the G36 with the narrow slide, it played a big part in the design of the G41, which is also a slim slide (compared to the G21).

The G30S has the same grip as the G30, so it will also accept 13-round G21 magazines.

The entire G30 lineup is incredibly easy to shoot. They're comfortable in the hand, despite being a little large, and they all handle the recoil well. They're very shootable. In fact, as far as shootability goes, they're head-and-shoulders above a Commander-size 1911, and I would venture to say they even beat out the full-size 1911 Government Model. And I say that with enormous reverence for the great John Browning design.

G36

Americans love the .45 ACP unequivocally. We invented it. It carried us through two world wars, Korea, Vietnam and every other military action for most of the 20th century. And although we adopted the 9mm for military service in 1985, when push comes to shove, Marines and many special operations forces love to pull the .45 out of mothballs and put a whoopin' on whomever is sending hate and discontent our way. This is why the 1911 is still so popular.

However, the Glock G21 and other polymer, high-capacity .45s haven't caught on as well. Don't get me wrong, Glock sells a lot of them. But it doesn't dominate the market with the .45 the way you would think it would over the 9mm and .40 Glocks. Especially given how popular the cartridge is. There is still a good-size crowd that believes any gun with less than a "4" in front of the caliber isn't worth owning.

So, what gives? The problem is many high-capacity, double-stacked .45s (the G21 and G30 included) just have too big a grip for average-sized hands. Glock released the SF (Short

The G36. There's a lot to like about this compact package.

Framed, not Special Forces as some believe) version in 2007, which I think is a great idea, but it didn't catch on as well as many thought it would (let me qualify that: Glock still sold bucketloads of them, but they didn't take over the .45 market). There are still a lot of shooters out there who like the single-stack, narrow grip of the 1911. It fits in the hands of pretty much everyone and is comfortable to shoot. So, Glock responded: and the G36 was born.

When the G36 hit the market, it gave Glock shooters three different grip size options: the full size G21 for those with big hands (as well as those who just want a lot of rounds in the magazine and don't care how big the grip is); the G21SF, which is the same capacity, but with the back of the grip cut down so it isn't as long; and, of course, the G36.

The G36 isn't really a single-stack. Yes, it's touted as a single-stack, and the observation holes on the back of the magazine line up in a straight column, but it's too wide to be single-stack, and if you look closely the rounds alternate inside the mag. It makes little difference, however, in grip size, because the grip on the G36 is thinner than that of a 1911. With my trusty Hornady digital caliper, the G36 comes in at 1.119 inches in width, and my Government Model 1911 measures 1.31 inches. It comes down once again to the difference between a polymer frame and a metal frame. The metal frame requires grip panels to be affixed to the frame, whereas on a Glock the polymer is the grip.

When talking about grip, though, I would be remiss in discussing grip size, but not mentioning the length of the grip, fore to aft. The position on the grip where it's most important is the portion where the thumb, web of the hand, and middle finger come into contact with the handgun. This is where you enclose your hand around the gun. At this point, the G36 measures 2.257 inches fore to aft. It's 1.918 on the 1911 (with the grip safety engaged, since it's gripped with it engaged). So, while it is thinner, which is better for concealed carry, it's still not as easy to hold onto as the 1911 for someone with small hands.

The Glock 36 holds six rounds, which is one less than the government-size 1911, but the grip is substantially shorter on the Glock, offering better concealment. With the magazine inserted (the magazine adds .34 inches to the overall length of the grip) the Glock 36 is .74

The G36 size compared to a 1911 Government model. The two bores are lined up, but notice how much closer to the bore the hand will sit when gripping the G36 compared to the 1911.

inches shorter than the 1911. Compared to the G30, the G36 is technically shorter in height, but by .04 inches. Unless one has highly precise calipers for hands, I don't think the difference will be noticed. The one downside is that unlike other Glock subcompact offerings, the G36, being a slimline pistol, uses completely different magazines than the other .45 ACP models, the G21 and G30, so you cannot use the higher capacity magazines.

I found the G36 to be a positive shooting experience. It has excellent handling qualities. If you're accustomed to shooting a Commander-size 1911, you'll really enjoy this. The first thing you notice is felt recoil is less than with a Commander, because the polymer absorbs some of the felt recoil, whereas the metal frame on a 1911 transfers all the energy to the shooter. In a full-size 1911, I think the longer slide and heavier weight absorb some of that recoil, so it's mostly a wash. But in the Commander comparison there's a difference; the G36 has significantly less muzzle flip. When I conduct a rapid unload of a 1911, there's a rhythm to it. You ride the wave as the muzzle comes down, you acquire the sights, squeeze, then ride the wave down, again and repeat. With the G36, I can simply unload the magazine, the muzzle flip is negligible.

This is due to the inherent qualities of a striker-fired handgun compared to one that's hammer fired. Removing the hammer from the equation results in a lower bore axis (1.26 inches), which means the source of recoil is closer to your hand, thus creating less muzzle flip.

To illustrate the point, conduct a simple experiment using an extreme example. Hold a baseball bat tightly by the grip, arms straight out in front of you, with the tip of the bat pointing straight up. Have someone place their hands over yours and push gently toward you (make sure it's a trusted friend or family member doing the pushing. Don't use the neighbor whose window your kids busted out, playing baseball). The energy should push directly toward you. Now have them grab the bat just above your hands, but touching, and push again with the same amount of pressure. Most of the energy moves straight toward you, but some goes into flipping the tip of the bat toward you. Now have them grab toward the top of the bat and push. All the energy goes into flipping the tip of the bat toward you.

The G36 size compared to an HK USP .45 Compact. The grip height is pretty comparable, but the HK grip is a little taller. For that length you get two extra cartridges. Also note the G36 has the hand sitting much closer to the bore than does the hammer-fired HK.

The farther away the energy is from your hand, the more flipping it does. Though not that extreme, that's how the bore axis height works when shooting a handgun.

This is evident when I compare the G36 to my HK USP .45 Compact. Both are polymer guns, so that factor is negated. The HK is heavier, so that gives it the advantage in felt recoil. But the HK is hammer fired, and thus has a much higher bore axis. The HK, as a result, has much more muzzle flip. This makes it harder to control in rapid fire.

The G36 is one of only three models of Glock that is not offered in Gen4 (the other two being the G38 and G39). I suspect this is because it hasn't sold well enough to make it worthwhile, which is unfortunate. For someone who would be inclined to carry a Commander-size 1911 and wants a single-stack .45 but doesn't mind fewer rounds in the magazine, the G36 makes an excellent alternative. This wouldn't be my choice, however; I would rather carry a 9mm or a .40 with more rounds.

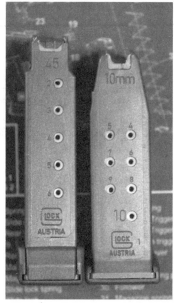

The G36 magazine (left) compared to the G29 (which is the 10mm version of the .45-caliber G30). The G36 magazine numbering makes it look like it's a single stack, but it's not quite.

The slide is almost to its most rearward point, and the empty case is about to exit the ejection port. Hardly any muzzle flip up to this point.

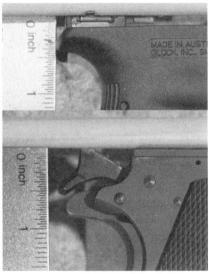

The G36 (top) has a significantly shorter bore axis (the wood dowel is the bore). This means your hand is closer to the bore, so there is less muzzle flip.

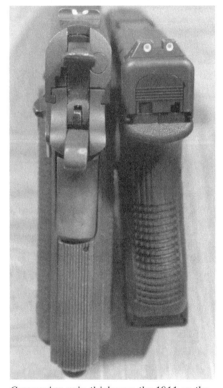

Comparing grip thickness: the 1911 on the left, G36 on the right.

I tested the G30SF, G30 Gen4, and G36 together, along with the G41, G21 Gen4 and G21SF. Shortly thereafter, I tested the G30S. I enjoyed testing them side by side, but that also meant the ammo had to be split seven ways. I had 200 rounds of American Eagle 230-grain FMJ, and 100 rounds of Federal Premium 230-grain Hydra-Shok JHP, along with 100 rounds of Winchester white box bulk ammo. It wasn't enough ammunition for detailed testing, but it was enough to get a good feel for each pistol. I don't need to tell

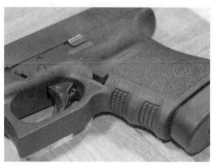

The G36 is one of only three Glock models not offered in the Gen4.

From this angle, there's a huge difference in bulk between the HK (left) and the G36.

you how it shot; you know how it shot: It's a Glock. I've done testing on other firearms and had some interesting results, but testing with a Glock is not that interesting. In fact, it's downright boring. Conducting the tests themselves aren't boring, mind you. It's a lot of fun to shoot any firearm. But the results are boring. Simply put, Glock pistols are boringly reliable. Empty a magazine. Change. Empty a magazine. Change. Empty a magazine *yawn*. Change. It makes reporting the results of testing and evaluation, well, not very exciting, but in the real world, boringly reliable is a great thing.

The Glock compact .45 offerings can be a bit confusing to keep straight if you're not familiar with them, so to summarize: The G30, as mentioned, is the subcompact version of the G21, much like the G26 is to the G17 in the 9mm world. There is a Gen3 version, a SF version (since it's a large frame Glock), and a Gen4 version. Then there is the G36, the single-stack .45. It has a slimmer grip and a slimmer slide that is the approximate width of the G19 slide. Lastly, we have the G30S, which is a G30 frame with a G36 slide, which gives it a wide grip and slim slide.

Is there a subcompact .45 in the lineup for me? Nope. I will not argue the .45 ACP as a round for everyone. In fact, (for now, anyway) I'm over the .45 as a carry cartridge. It's a great round, and I will always think of it as one of the best cartridges of all time. That's also not to say I will never buy another .45, because I'm sure I will. But I will buy as a collector, rather than one to carry. I'm all about round capacity. Frankly, if I'm going to carry a large-frame Glock, it's going to be a 10mm. The .45 has nothing on it. Otherwise, I might as well strap on a .40. It comes in a smaller package and holds more rounds, and performance-wise there's not a huge drop off from the .45 to the .40. If I can't get the job done with the .40 then I need to spend more time at the range.

CHAPTER 9:
THE G22 AND OTHER .40-CALIBER GLOCKS

G22

I have always been a law-and-order type of guy. In general, I'm for having rules (but not over-ruled, or nonsense rules or rules just for the sake of having rules). However, I have a little rebel streak. A bit of a rabble-rouser. If a current is going one way, I'm going to try to swim against it for a while, just for fun. So, when it came to the .40 S&W, law enforcement and .40 fanboys were making a big stink about its greatness, so of course I had to resist a little. Some of it was a bit of that caliber trap we fall into (if it's not a .45, it's not worthy).

For me it was the 10mm, not the .45 ACP, that made me snub my nose at the .40. I called it the .40 Short & Weak, or the 10mm's little sister. Some of it could have even been my black-and-white personality; for me there's no room for gray (It's either 9mm or .45 ACP, there is no "in the middle"), and the .40 is the gray to the black and white of the 9mm and .45.

But when writing the first edition of this book, I got a chance to get to know the .40. I could see what all the hoopla is about. It's a good round. The performance is very respectable, with performance approaching that of the .45, yet the magazine capacity is generally only about two rounds short of a 9mm. That's 15 rounds in the full-capacity G22 magazine.

However, since the first edition came out, the .40 S&W has really fallen out of favor as a cartridge. More studies have been done, including one by the FBI, and with modern 9mm

The entire family of .40 Glock pistols (left to right): the G27, G23, G22 and G35.

bullets there's a lot of evidence showing that the performance gained from the .40, compared to the 9mm, isn't worth the tradeoff. The tradeoff being high chamber pressure, extra wear and tear on the gun, and fewer rounds in the magazine. There's a big difference in shootability as well, the .40 has an aggressive report compared to the 9mm, and it has a "snappier" muzzle. Unless an agent/officer gets to train frequently with his or her duty gun, and the majority do not, it's not as easy to shoot. With more muzzle flip it's obvious that follow-up shots are not as fast, but even more alarming, the FBI found that accuracy really suffers with the .40. Not because it's less accurate, but because the majority of agents/officers don't shoot it enough to feel comfortable shooting it, due to how loud and snappy it is.

Of all the Glock offerings, the .40 Glock pistols have had the most growing pains. Back when the FBI made the decision to adopt the .40, it caught everyone off guard, except for Smith & Wesson, which was involved with the development of the cartridge. There was a belief that whatever the FBI filled its holsters with, other law-enforcement agencies would be quick to follow suit. That belief would turn out to be correct (and it's looking like it will be correct again, as the FBI has largely returned to the 9mm, and other law-enforcement departments are following suit).

9x19mm (left) is great, but the .40 S&W is better. When it comes to power, anyway. In other aspects, many are reconsidering if that slight bump in power is worth it.

To try to beat Smith & Wesson at its own game, Glock developed the G22 based on a model it already had, the G19. To be the first to market, Glock was taking a pistol designed to shoot the 9mm and chambering it for a cartridge that fired a bullet approximately 50 percent heavier, and at the same 35,000 pounds per square inch maximum SAAMI chamber pressure.

Other makers took longer to get their .40 pistols to market, as they developed a pistol for that cartridge. Glock took what it had, and made it work with the .40. However, Glock was forced to face a very real problem: that pesky Third Law of Motion laid out by Sir Isaac Newton, paraphrased, "For every action there is an equal and opposite reaction."

Since the .40 is larger than the 9mm, the slide will come back with more force, which will batter the pistol and give it a very short service life. So, engineers had to find a way to slow the speed of the slide.

One way is to add more mass to the object subjected to that opposite reaction, i.e. the slide. On the G22 versus the G17, the slides weigh 13.5 ounces and 12.6 ounces, respectively, a difference of less than 7 percent.

I'm not an engineer, and I know this is apples to oranges, but it doesn't seem like a 7-percent difference in the slide will cancel out the nearly 40-percent gain in bullet weight. There's not going to be any help from the weight of the barrel during that initial time af-

The G22 was a law enforcement favorite for years. It also found favor with contractors over in the sand box. Now, that status as "favorite" is in serious decline.

ter the primer ignites and the barrel and slide are locked. The G22 barrel is actually .75 ounces lighter, because remember, it's the same barrel, but with a larger hole cut through it, leaving less mass.

The easy solution? Add a more robust recoil spring. This creates a stronger counter force to the heavier bullet. In the Gen4 pistols, the G22 shares the same spring as the G31, G35 and G37 pistols, and the G23 shares the same spring as the G32 and G38 (the G38 is still the Gen3, at the time of this writing).

Another thing Glock did to shore up the pistol with the fast-moving slide was to add a third pin (in Glock armorer jargon, it's actually referred to as the "first pin," because when disassembling it's the first pin out, and during assembly it's the first pin back in), the locking block pin. It started with the G22, but eventually Glock filtered it down to all the models. Now with the Gen5 pistols, which just come in 9mm at present, the "first pin" has gone away and there are only two pins. (It will be interesting to see if Glock comes out with a Gen5 .357 SIG, or, if the .40 S&W becomes popular again, if the "first pin" be reintroduced down the road).

The other issue caused by fitting a .40 into a G17 is feeding. The cartridge is roughly the same length as the 9mm, yet the .40 is .045 inches larger in diameter. It doesn't sound like much, but it's almost a 13-percent difference. The .40 is wide for how long it is. To adjust, the length of the feed ramp needs to be longer than the G17, so the feed ramp extends farther into the chamber to assist with feeding, which creates the side effect of leaving more of the case head unsupported. This could potentially lead to case failure, which isn't good for the pistol or the shooter. This is entirely exclusive to reloaded or remanufactured ammunition, *not* from commercially manufactured ammo. Glock shuns reloaded ammo for all of its calibers, and it can void the warranty, but there is even more concern with the .40. In fact, most reloading manuals will now warn not to use reloaded ammo in chambers that leave the case unsupported, like the Glock.

A third problem the G22 has faced is adding a weapon light to the accessory rail, which could lead to feed problems in some guns. It wasn't all of them, and it wasn't even all the time. It was an odd thing, really. It was an issue that could develop over time in one handgun, while never occurring at all in another, and it could be a problem from the start with the one after that. For some of them, it might be with one particular kind of ammo, a different kind of ammo with another one. Some of the G22s even worked for years with no problem and one day suddenly started having problems.

The reason for the problem is that when a Glock is fired, the polymer frame flexes. When a G22 is fired, it flexes *a lot*. When a light is attached to the accessory rail and clamped down tight, it was hindering the flex, which led to problems when the gun cycled.

Fear not, however, as this has been completely fixed with the Gen4 G22. In fact, when they were designing it, this was one of the main areas of focus. So, it's really just an issue with third generation G22s, since second generation frames don't have an accessory rail.

I have a Glock GTL22 Light/ Laser combo mounted on my G22 and did a rapid unload on two full magazines with not even the faintest hint of a glitch. Since then I've continued to use a light on my G22, with no issues whatsoever. Perfect.

With a third generation G22, this could have been a problem. Not so with a G22 Gen4. All problems with tactical lights were addressed when it was developed.

Yes, the .40 Glocks have had some growing pains, but Glock saw the issue, took all of this to task, and came out with the Gen4 models. What I wrote earlier in this chapter about the G22 being built on the G17 platform (as well as the other .40 Glocks being built on 9mm Glock models), is no longer the case. Now it's been reversed, and the G22 is the base of the Gen4 platform, and the 9mm line is built off of it. It's a smart move by Glock, and one that mirrors the other handgun manufacturers that didn't rush a .40 to market. It's going to increase the reliability and longevity of the Glock .40s, and cut down on the number of issues shooters have with it. Not that those were big issues, the .40 Glocks are still Glocks. Names and reputations aren't built and given without earning them.

With everything that has been said in the past about Glock's .40 S&W issues, I do think that needs to be put in perspective. Right now, between 65 and 70 percent of police departments and other agencies here in the United States issue Glock handguns. From the information I had at the time of the first edition, roughly two-thirds of law-enforcement departments/agencies/offices issued a Glock in .40 caliber. I didn't have numbers on this, and Glock doesn't give them out, but that's well over 100,000 handguns, probably much more. And that's only what they were carrying at that time and didn't include the previous generations they had purchased. Of course, as I wrote earlier in this chapter, now things have changed and the .40 is losing market share with law enforcement. The number of departments/agencies now issuing the .40 is way down from two-thirds. I don't have the numbers for that now, and neither does Glock (or at least they're not sharing) but a Glock representative did tell me they are seeing an increasing number of agencies/departments switching to 9mm from the .40. And not just the 9mm, there's been a lot of interest in the MOS versions of the 9mm Glocks.

It's been more than 25 years since the Glock .40 pistols first become the law-enforcement pistol of choice. Given all of the Glock .40 pistols sold, it's a testament to the G22 how few problems it has had. And these numbers don't include the numbers of .40 Glocks that have

The G23 loses two rounds from the 9mm G19, but the .40 is a definite power upgrade.

been sold to private individuals, which is far more. As departments continue to drop the .40 in favor of 9mm, it's not likely to change how many of those departments choose Glock.

G23

The G23 is the compact-size Glock chambered in .40 S&W. It's nearly identical to the G19 in every regard except

The G23 doesn't have a significant increase in recoil from the G22. Here, a G23 with a G22 magazine gives even more to hold onto.

the barrel is forged for .40 instead of .355. There are some parts that are different, such as a stiffer recoil spring and an ejector with a different angle, but that's about it.

The brilliant thing about the G23 is that it doesn't lose much capacity from the G19. The G19 holds 15 rounds, the G23 holds 13. With the loss of only two rounds, but with a much more powerful round, that's a no-brainer. In most situations I'm a big believer in more rounds are better; however, if the loss in rounds is minimal and there's a substantial gain in power, then the tradeoff is worth it.

The tradeoff between the three 9mm pistols to the .40 pistols is around 10 to 15 percent. To me, that's worth it. To make an analogy, which would you rather have as a draft team: a team of 15 donkeys, or a team of 13 mules (with all other considerations such as food and housing being equal)? If you have some hard work to do, you would take the mules.

For someone who shoots a G22, shooting a G23 won't be much different. I didn't notice a huge increase in recoil from the G22 full-size frame. It's about like comparing the G19 to

The G26 9mm (gun is top, cartridge is top) is an outstanding combination, but for the same exact size handgun and a loss of only one round, the .40 S&W G27 is a no-brainer, if the shooter is comfortable with the recoil of the .40.

the G17; it's spunkier, but not at all more uncomfortable to shoot. For a shooter who hasn't fired a .40 S&W before, the G23 can be a little intimidating. Like all of the .40s, the G23 has a pretty sharp report, and it can take some getting used to. My wife is a novice shooter, and I have her stick primarily to the 9mm. I know shooting a .40 would turn her off shooting.

G27

The .40 version of the G26, dimensionally speaking, the G27 is identical in nearly every aspect, except the size of the bore down the barrel and the chamber the cartridge sits in. When I shoot the G27, I marvel at the brilliance of whoever thought to stick a .40 in such a small package. It's impressive.

The G27 loses only one round compared to the G26, but it's in .40 instead of 9mm. That's an acceptable loss in round count for the increase in power.

This G27 was made after the spring of 2014; the "MBS" is not present.

As my friends, and pretty much anyone who has ever been in a conversation with me about guns can attest, I often preach of the virtues of the 10mm. I might have mentioned it a time or two in this book as well (speaking from the British traditional sense of understatement). But considering how small the G27 is, this right here gives the G29 a run for the money.

The G27 has a very impressive round count. A standard G27 sub-compact magazine holds nine rounds, which is only a loss of one from the G26. In most people's book, that's a very acceptable loss, one I would take any day. The amount of power in the .40 coupled with the round count in the magazine makes this about the perfect concealed-carry gun, in my estimation.

While there isn't much difference in recoil between the G22 and G23, the G27 is a very noticeable increase in recoil. It's a lot of power coming out of such a little package, although it has more to do with the grip than anything. I can only fit two fingers on the grip, the last digit dangles below the magazine. It's not easy to hold on to, though it's manageable. I've only fired about a box of ammo through it, so I'm pretty sure with more range time one would become accustomed to it. Yes, it can be a bit wicked if you're used to shooting the nine mil, but not too terrible. It's nothing the average shooter couldn't learn to shoot effectively.

The sides of the magazine well have been cut away so the magazine sits as high as possible, making it shorter and thus easier to conceal.

The G35 is the .40 S&W version of the G34.

G35

The G35 was introduced in January 1998, concurrently with the G34. It is the .40 equivalent to the G34, and just like the other models of .40 S&W, they are nearly identical to the corresponding 9mm model. Both Gen4 models are 5.43 inches in height, 1.18 inches in width, and 8.74 inches long (the Gen3 models are both 8.81 inches long). The G35 is about 1.5 ounces heavier than the G34, coming in at 27.53 ounces. The sight radius is also the same on both, at 7.55 inches.

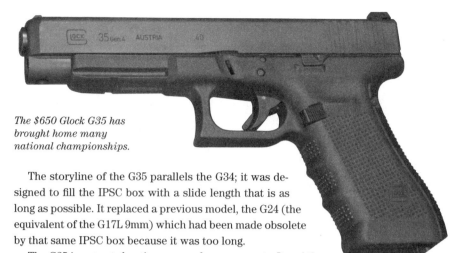

The $650 Glock G35 has brought home many national championships.

The storyline of the G35 parallels the G34; it was designed to fill the IPSC box with a slide length that is as long as possible. It replaced a previous model, the G24 (the equivalent of the G17L 9mm) which had been made obsolete by that same IPSC box because it was too long.

The G35 is a great-shooting gun, and very accurate. It and the G34 have won a lot of championships, and there's no doubt these two handguns will win more. Dave Sevigny of Team Glock used the G34 and G35 to win more than 15 national titles shooting United States Practical Shooting Association (USPSA) and International Defensive Pistol Association (IDPA) competitions. Keep in mind that some of these were done in divisions containing custom 1911s that cost thousands of dollars, and the G35 (and G34) cost about $650. It will shoot as accurately as the shooter can make it shoot. The G35 has become mostly a non-factor though, as few shooters use the .40 S&W for competition.

The G35 would make for an outstanding tactical gun (if the .40 is what you're looking for), just like the G34 and the G41. The problem is that it's too long for carry in most other capacities. It's too long to be carried concealed OWB, the barrel would stick out from under the shirt or vest, and if carried IWB, it would dig into the leg every time the wearer sat down.

As for a law-enforcement duty gun, it has the same issue; sitting in a squad car with this on your belt would get old in about five minutes. It would be far too uncomfortable.

For the person who has a drop-down thigh holster, however, the G35 would be a great choice. For the SWAT or SOF team member, the G35 would reign supreme, especially for all the reasons the G22 would: near-.45 ACP power, yet near-9mm magazine capacity. The

To make the G35 slide light enough to cycle reliably, an opening is cut into it.

The G35 has adjustable sights.

A hole is cut in the bottom of the elongated guide ring so the front sight can be removed.

only problem would be sorting out logistics for the team overseas. No one else in the world uses the .40 S&W, and it's not even that popular here in the U.S. anymore, but if you get a handle on that, you would be good to go. I offer this all with a grain of salt, because the 9mm has really taken over, given the dramatically improved bullets now designed for it. I think for the most part, people are going with the 9mm, and if something larger is desired, they go with the .45 ACP.

THE FUTURE OF THE .40 S&W CARTRIDGE

I have no idea what's going to happen to the .40 S&W cartridge. At the time of the first edition, I would not have predicted its drastic crash in popularity. I thought it was a good cartridge at the time, and still think it's decent. It just seems that as more time passes, the info that comes out about the .40 doesn't make it shine as much as once thought. It really looks like it's dying, at least at the time of this writing. It's most evident by the number of companies that are putting out new handgun offerings in .40, almost none come to mind. But, who knows what the future holds, and who knows what new information could come out that could change the opinions on the .40?

One thing that could save the .40 from death, the only area I have seen new products, is in PCCs. Pistol Caliber Carbines, that is. Several companies have released AR-style PCCs in .40 S&W, and companies like Ruger have released a non-AR PCC in .40. (More on PCCs in Chapter 20.)

What does this have to do with Glock? Well, the sheer domination of the .40 S&W market by Glock, especially in law-enforcement circles, has led to a gluttony of .40 caliber Glock magazines. Given that most of these companies have long made 9mm PCCs – and most of them using 9mm Glock magazines – it was a natural progression for these companies to release their .40 using Glock mags. It's a smart move on the part of these companies to make their PCCs compatible with Glock mags.

However, even if you don't plan on buying a Glock (or any handgun) in .40 because of the questions about the future of the caliber, it would be wise to snatch up some Glock .40 magazines; because you never know if you might want a PCC in .40.

CHAPTER 10:
THE .357 GLOCKS

When the revolver ruled in law enforcement, the .357 S&W Magnum was the law-enforcement cartridge of choice from its inception in 1934 until the 1980s, when law enforcement shifted to semi-automatics. Not every agency used it, but every officer wanted to use it. To this day, it's the Holy Grail in one-shot stops.

That's always been the dilemma with the semi-auto: It's hard to replicate that sort of stopping power with another cartridge, and you can't put a .357 Magnum into a semi-auto pistol. It's a rimmed cartridge, intended for revolvers, and you can't stack rimmed cartridges in a magazine reliably like you can rimless cartridges. There have been several companies that have produced semi-autos chambered in .357 Magnum, such as the Desert Eagle from Magnum Research, but that's a behemoth and not a practical self-defense weapon.

This is the concept behind the .357 SIG cartridge: Replicate the .357 Magnum and put it in a semi-auto. For the most part, it's right there with the .357 Magnum in velocity. The .357 SIG is screaming fast, it's accurate and it shoots flat, which makes it easy to shoot at longer distances. It is the first widely produced commercial cartridge with a shoulder since the 1960s.

Glock 22 .40 S&W next to a Glock 31 .357 SIG.

Developed jointly between SIG Sauer and Federal Ammunition, the .357 SIG is a .40 S&W case necked down to a 9mm (.955), though if you're a handloader you cannot make ammo using .40 cases. The .357 SIG case is slightly longer, .865 inches compared to the .40 S&W at .850 inches in length. So, if you want to reload, it's best to use your fired brass or buy brass specific to .357 SIG. Both cases are .424 inches in diameter, both are rimless and have a rim .055 inches thick with a .424-inch diameter.

A rimless case does have a rim, but by definition it's called rimless because the rim is the same diameter as the case. It does not protrude like the .45 Colt, nor is it rebated like the .45 G.A.P. From there the case is necked down from .423 to .381 inches and given a sharp 18-degree shoulder. The shoulder starts at .649 inches from the bottom of the cartridge, and ends at .715 inches, making it .066 inches long. The neck is .150 inches long.

Since the .40 case is used, and the feeding, firing, extraction and ejection are all centered on that .40 case, the three Glock pistols chambered in .357 are the same pistol used for the .40, the only exception being the cold hammer-forged barrel is for a .355 bullet instead of a .400 bullet. Every other part is the same, even the magazine. So, if you own a G22, G23 or G27 and want to own a .357 SIG, all you need is to change out the barrel to the equivalent-length barrel and you now own one. In fact, of all the caliber conversions you might have read about in publications and online, this is the only one Glock authorizes.

The .357 SIG (center) next to the .40 S&W parent cartridge (left) and the .357 S&W magnum (right).

This is the only difference between the Glock .357 and .40: the barrel.

More specifically, the only physical difference is the hole through the barrel (.357 SIG on left, .40 S&W on right).

It is named .357 to draw attention to the round it's trying to replicate, however the name is a bit misleading. The .357 S&W Magnum uses a .357-inch bullet, while the .357 SIG uses the same bullet as the 9x19 NATO, a .355-inch bullet. I think the marketing concept behind it was sound. Aside from trying to draw a correlation between it and the .357 Magnum, it was also important to not be "just another 9mm" among the plethora of 9mm cartridges already on the market, cartridges such as: 9x18 Ultra, 9mm Kurtz/9mm Browning

The .357 SIG (left) next to its parent cartridge, the .40 S&W.

(.380 ACP), 9mm Browning Long, 9x19mm Parabellum/9mm Luger/9mm NATO, 9x21mm, 9mm Largo, 9mm Steyr, 9mm Bayard/Bergman-Bayard, 9mm Mauser, 9mm Dillon, 9mm Winchester Magnum, 9x23mm Winchester and the 9mm Makarov.

This is only a partial list of common 9mm cartridges. If I were a marketing guy, and set out to name a new cartridge, I would definitely steer clear of a name involving anything 9mm.

The .357 SIG is limited by the magazine size and grip size, as well as the bullets offered in .355 (9x19mm). Bullets for the .357 SIG start at 88 grains, with the main bullet being the 124-grain. Recent loads have increased the bullet size to 147 grains. Contrast that with the .357 Magnum, which runs the gamut from 110-grain to 180-grain, with the most common being around 158 grains. Aside from this limitation, what you get in return is a cartridge with a very flat trajectory, making it a good long-range pistol. It's a fast-moving bullet and has excellent penetration.

Using the Winchester ballistics calculator, a 125-grain JHP with a 25-yard zero will have zero drop out to 35 yards, and at 50 yards there will be a 0.5-inch drop. Even reaching out to

All .357 SIG models are offered in Gen4 (pictured) as well as Gen3. Top to bottom: G31, G32 and G33.

100 yards, you're looking at a drop of only 4.39 inches. Compare that to a 9mm Luger with a 124-grain bullet: With a 25-yard zero the 9mm will have a drop of almost twice that of the .357, at 50 yards and at 100 yards.

On its website, Glock reports production of the G31, G32 and G33 began in 1998, although serial numbers show they actually began rolling out in August 1996 for the G31 and November 1996 for the G32 and G33. All three of these models are currently available in Gen3 and Gen4.

I've had a renewed interest in the .357 SIG since the first edition of this book. It's extremely accurate, it shoots fast and flat, and it can reach out a little farther than 9mm. And, apparently, I'm not the only one. I attended the NRAAM 2019 (National Rifle Association Annual Meeting), and one of the questions I asked the numerous gun companies that are making Pistol Caliber Carbines (PCCs) was: Are they coming out with anything in .357 SIG? I was told more than once they were getting fielded that question quite a bit. Which makes me wonder if perhaps the .357 SIG is making a comeback.

Ammunition for the .357 SIG can be hard to find on shelves, and most people will have to purchase online. I happen to live close to one of the largest sporting goods retailers

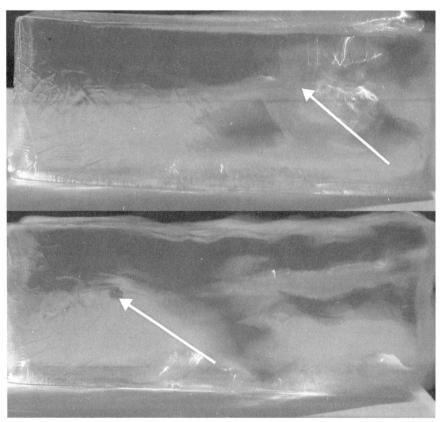

.357 SIG has excellent penetration. Just as it hits the Clear Ballistics FBI Block (top), and then it comes to rest (bottom).

Left to right: Unfired bullet, bullet fired from G31, fired from G32 and fired from G33.

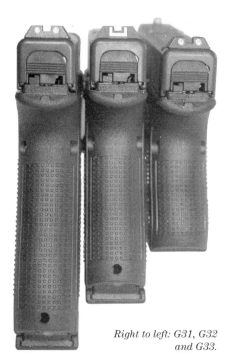

Right to left: G31, G32 and G33.

in the country, and it stocks .357 SIG. At the time the first edition of this book was written, the choice was limited to SIG Sauer Elite Performance 125-grain JHP. That was it. Times have changed, however, and as another sign the .357 SIG is making a comeback, this particular store now has more available on the shelves, including several loads from SIG ammo, Winchester, Hornady and Fiocchi.

I recently got my hands on some Federal Premium Tactical 125-grain HST and Speer Gold Dot 125-grain GDHP. I forgot how accurate this round can be. At the self-defense range of 10 yards, I put 10 rounds into a 2.24-inch group with the Federal HST, and a 2.13-inch group with the Speer GDHP.

G31

The G31, Glock's full-size .357 SIG, was introduced in 1996. It is essentially a clone of the G22, the only difference being the hole going through the barrel. It even weighs the same and has the same dimensions. It's like back in the day on a GM pick-up truck assembly line: One truck gets stamped "Chevrolet" the next one gets stamped "GMC." Here, one gets a .40 barrel, the next gets a .357 barrel and stamped. I don't know if that's really how Glock does it, but it makes for a good mental image.

The G31 holds 15 rounds of ammo, only two short of the 9mm G17, which gives the G31 a whole lot of mini rockets. Glock does make an extended-capacity magazine for the .40

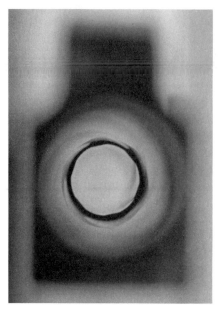

A look down a Glock .357 SIG barrel. Note the polygonal rifling.

The compact G32 is extremely accurate, as demonstrated by these two 10-shot groups, fired at 12 yards. The Federal HST and Speer Gold Dot loads are excellent self-defense loads.

that holds 22 rounds, and it will work with Glocks chambered in .357 SIG.

Of the three models, it is the easiest to shoot. The recoil is milder than the .40, but it has a little more snap to it, if that makes sense. You're sending off a smaller projectile, but you're sending it off at a faster rate. There is also a little more bark to the bite, as in muzzle blast. I enjoyed shooting it, and really liked the snappiness it had.

I tested the penetration on a Clear Ballistics 10-percent FBI Block, firing a SIG Sauer Elite Performance V-Crown 125-grain JHP. It hit the block fast and penetrated 11 3/4 inches.

G32

This one is a shortened G31, and is the same pistol as the G23, except for the barrel. It's the same compact category as the G19, with the same frame, which makes it a very handy size for a pistol.

For someone looking for a .357 SIG pistol, this the best choice for a one-pistol solution. It's small enough to conceal with a jacket or vest, yet almost a full-size pistol. It comes with a 13-round magazine, but can also use the 15-round G31 magazine. It uses all the same parts as the G23 and accepts the same accessories.

With the half-inch-shorter barrel, a slight increase in recoil and report is discernible, though nothing significant or to the point that will bother the average shooter. If you can handle the G23 .40 S&W, you can easily handle this.

It weighs in at an even 24 ounces unloaded, and is 7.28 inches in length and 4.99 inches in height. Out of the four-inch barrel the .357 penetrated 11 inches.

G33

The baby of the group, it's the subcompact cousin of the G27. It's 6.41 inches long and 4.18 inches in height. It uses a nine-round magazine, one less than the 9mm G26, but will accept mags from the G31, G32 and of course the .40 Glocks.

I've read other writers who report it's uncomfortable to shoot, and not fun, but I didn't think it was bad at all. It was controllable, and with the minimal muzzle rise it was fast to reacquire the target for subsequent shots. The recoil on my Walther PPK in .380 is far worse as far as comfort goes. Glock does a great job of handling the .357 SIG in this small package. Remember, the .357 SIG was designed to replicate the stopping power of a .357 Magnum, and I stress the word Magnum. This is a magnum cartridge being fired from a handgun that's much smaller than what the .357 Magnum was designed for.

When Smith & Wesson released the .357 Magnum cartridge to the public in 1935, the pistol released with it was also called the "S&W .357 Magnum." It weighed a little over 40 ounces, or about 2.5 pounds. The G33 weighs just under 22 ounces, about half the weight of the revolver. Despite that, recoil is very manageable.

A .357 Magnum in a comparable size is the Ruger LCR revolver, which has a capacity of five rounds, just over half that of the G33 with the nine-round magazine, except the G33 can be loaded with 13- and 15-round magazines. Plus, even with the nine-round magazine, reloading for the Glock takes only one to two seconds, while even with a speedloader the revolver takes three to five seconds. The G33 is also going to handle much nicer than any revolver of comparable size.

Still, if one chooses to carry a G33 every day, it will require practice to ensure the shooter is proficient enough to deploy it if need be. The G33 is not for inexperienced shooters. The .357 bullet left the 3.42-inch barrel like it was on fire and penetrated the FBI block to a depth of 11 3/8 inches.

CHAPTER 11:
THE .45 GAP GLOCKS

Americans love the .45. We invented it, we used it through two world wars, Korea, Vietnam and who knows how many other hostilities. We love it so much that it's still being used by some entities inside the military. With more than 100 years of loyal service, the .45 ACP is just hard to beat.

I enlisted in the Marine Corps in 1990, just after the Beretta M9 was phased in, so I never served with the .45, even though all the manuals we were issued in boot camp still referred to the 1911. The .45 ACP is so intertwined with American culture, and with the 1911, that when I call the issued weapon a ".45" everyone knew the gun I was talking about, even though it's actually called a 1911. The 1911 is the .45, and the .45 is the 1911.

Things change, however, including the requirements and tastes in fighting guns. As I mentioned previously when I covered the G21, seven- or eight-round capacity isn't what the military or law enforcement is looking for, and it's not the preference of many civilians, either. In order to increase the carry capacity of .45s, makers have had to increase the size of the handgun, and that's an issue engineers have had to contend with, balancing carry capacity with handgun size.

A great example of this is the Heckler & Koch Mark 23, the predecessor to the company's USP. It carries 12 rounds, but it's a monster. It weighs 2.5 pounds empty (about one-third the

Left to right, G39, G38, G37: the Glock .45 GAP.

The .45 GAP (left) compared to the .45 ACP. Both are 230 grains.

This shows just how controllable the Glock G37 is. In the height of recoil, as the slide is a blur from motion, there is very little motion in the author's hands and arms.

Ouch! These will leave a mark. Fired into FBI 10-percent block. Results from the G37 (left), G38 (middle) and G39 (right) are remarkably uniform.

weight of an M4 Carbine) and is 9.85 inches long by 5.9 inches tall by 1.54 inches wide. That's big, but that's what you get for an extra five rounds of .45. The Glock G21 manages to stuff one more round into a smaller package than the Mark 23, shaving off almost two inches off the length, one-half inch off the height, and almost .3 inches off the width (8.03 by 5.47 by 1.27 inches). Leave it to Glock engineers to squeak one more round out of something smaller. That's significantly smaller, but for the shooter with average-sized hands, it's still a big package.

Though the G21 and G30 sold well, sales of the large-frame .45 ACPs didn't approach the standard-frame models, the G17 and G22. The short-frame versions helped, but it was still a large grip. The trick would be to shrink the .45 to fit in a standard frame like the 9mm. It was done with the 10mm when it was shortened to the .40 S&W, so why not the .45?

This time it would be a little different. The intent was not a less-powerful cartridge in a smaller case like the .40 S&W. Instead, the goal was a cartridge that was equal in power, but in a shorter case. Enter, again, the engineers. Speer/CCI engineer Ernest Durham designed the cartridge in collaboration with Glock.

What he came up with is the .45 Glock Automatic Pistol (G.A.P.) pronounced as "gap." It is basically a .45 ACP bullet in a cartridge that is approximately the same length as a 9x19mm NATO (.760 inches verses .754 inches of the 9x19). They were able to equal the power of the .45 ACP due largely to the increased performance of modern powders, which weren't as efficient when John Browning invented the .45 ACP. Initially the .45 GAP was available in 185 grains and 200 grains, not the 230-grain bullet that is the meat and potatoes of the .45, but this would eventually change.

A surviving example of a .45 GLOCK case. That name was scrapped, and Glock decided to go with .45 GAP. (Photo from Shane Hicks.)

.45 GLOCK?

I found some photos of a cartridge case from Speer, marked ".45 Glock." I confirmed from a source at Glock who wished to remain anonymous, but the story is that when the .45 GAP was in development, it was a toss-up as to whether it was going to be called the .45 GAP or the .45 GLOCK. Glock had prototype cases made up that were stamped .45 GLOCK, and somewhere along the way the company decided to go with .45 GAP. These cases all were supposed to have been destroyed, yet some still managed to find their way to freedom.

To attain the performance of a 230-grain .45 ACP in a 185-grain .45 GAP, velocity had to be ramped up, which was done by increasing the chamber pressure. A standard .45 ACP has a chamber pressure of 21,000 pounds per square inch (psi), while the .45 GAP is set at 23,000 psi, the same as .45 ACP +P.

One thing to bear in mind, particularly if handloading the .45 GAP, is although the GAP is a shortened .45 ACP in stature, the case is not an actual .45 ACP case, there are some differences. The big difference between the two is that the GAP uses a small pistol primer, whereas the ACP uses a large pistol primer. According to Speer (Reloading Manual #14), using a cut-down ACP case can lead to excessive pressure. The GAP also differs in its internal taper and the height of the web, as well as having a slightly rebated rim.

A little background on rims is in order. All cartridges must have a rim in order to be extracted from the chamber. Back in the revolver era, cases were rimmed (the rim is larger in diameter than the case) so revolver extractors had something to hold on to in order to get the cases out of the cylinder. When the semi-autos came about, rimmed cartridges could not be stacked in the magazine, so rims were scaled back to be the same diameter as the case and were thus named "rimless."

This wasn't an issue with rifles of the era, because rimmed cartridges can be stacked in a rifle magazine. The curvature of a rifle magazine has no bearing on the operation of the rifle, since the rifleman doesn't hold onto the magazine to fire it. Not the case with handguns, where the magazine must be straight in order to fit into the grip.

Next in the evolution of rims is the rebated rim, where the rim is smaller in diameter than the case. This is most commonly found when you have a firearm platform with a particular cartridge, and designers want to chamber a larger cartridge in that platform, without changing the breechblock (in a handgun) or the bolt face (in a rifle). This is the case with the .45 GAP, where they wanted to load a .45-caliber bullet/case into the chamber of a handgun that uses the same breechblock used for 9mm and .40 S&W case diameters. The result isn't a drastic difference between case and rim. I have a Speer case which measures .472 inches just above the extractor groove, and the rim measures .469 inches, a difference of only .003 inches.

Probably the most extreme instances of rimless cartridges are the various large-bore cartridges designed for the AR15 platform, such as the .458 SOCOM, the .450 Bushmaster and the .50 Beowulf. Designers stuck .45- to .50-caliber cartridges in a rifle designed for a .223-caliber bullet.

The result is a massive case with rims so small it looks a bit silly. It's like taking the upper body of Dwayne "The Rock" Johnson and sticking it on the lower body of Taylor Swift. I have a Hornady .450 Bushmaster case, which measures .499 inches just above the extractor groove, and the rim measures .466 inches. That's a difference of .033 inches. Now contrast that with the .45 GAP, which is .003 inches.

Rimless cartridges can pose problems for the feed systems of a platform if that

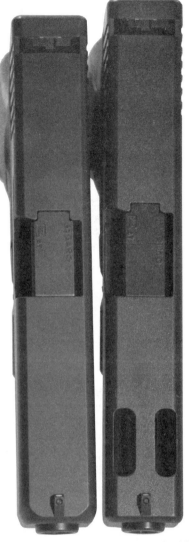

The G37 (left) has the same slide as the G20 (right) or G21 (not shown), but on a G19-sized frame.

system is not designed properly. To put it simply, the rebated rim is a smaller target for the feed rails to pick up. The number-one priority for Glock is always reliability, and if the engineers can't accomplish that, they wouldn't offer the model. For the .45 GAP, this meant a new extractor, ejector, recoil spring and magazine, as well as a heavier slide.

Glock introduced the complete .45 GAP line, the G37, G38 and G39 at the 2003 SHOT Show, with the G37 being the standard-size pistol, the G38 the compact and the G39 the subcompact.

The overall dimensions of the three .45 GAP pistols are nearly identical to their 9mm cousins, however, and this is a big however, the slide width of the .45 GAP pistols are slightly wider at about 1.14 inches (the G17 slide measures 1.005 inches). In fact, the .45 GAP slides are the same width as the large frame .45 ACP and 10mm lines. This doesn't change the overall width of 1.18 inches, that's still the same as the G17, but it's a big enough difference that the .45 GAP won't fit in holsters that are made for the G17 and other standard-frame Glocks.

Loading the .45 into a frame the same size as a 9mm does have a tradeoff, and that is lower capacity. The full size G37 holds only 10 rounds, while the full size G21 holds 13. That's one area I hear as the biggest criticism of the Glock .45 GAP Pistols: Capacity isn't that great. One thing that is important to remember, however, is the .45 GAP was intended to reduce the circumference of the handgun grip, not to increase capacity. The cartridge was shortened, but the diameter remains the same. The shorter cartridge results in a shorter grip length (fore to aft), but since the diameter is the same, the stagger of the rounds has to be lessened, resulting in fewer rounds. If the capacity were to remain the same as the G21, then the grip would be just as wide.

The G37 (left) compared to the G20 (the same size as the G21 .45 ACP). A standard-size Glock grip has a width of 1.209 inches, while the large-frame Glock, such as the G21, has a grip width of 1.295. The difference in grip size is visually subtle, but not so subtle in the hand.

Shooting the .45 GAP pistols is not any harsher than shooting the various other .45 ACP pistols on the market, despite the reduction in mass. I have a fair amount of experience with the .45. The first pistol I purchased when I turned 21 was a Government Model 1911. I've fired full-size 1911s, Commander-size 1911s, the XD, the XDS, the HK USP and Compact, as well as every model of .45 ACP Glock offers (Gen3 and Gen4). I will say this: If you've shot a .45 in any other pistol, then shooting the Glock .45 GAP will be mostly as you expect – very similar.

The Glock G37, G38 and G39 all shoot as well if not better than all their comparably sized counterparts. Due to the lower bore axis, muzzle flip is less with the Glock than the 1911s I've fired. I was able to control it better, which led to faster and more accurate rapid fire.

The shorter and narrower grip makes the .45 GAP pistols easier to control than the full size G21. I have pretty big mitts, and the large-size frames of the G21 and G20 fill my hands up pretty much to the max. I own the G20 and have more experience with it than the G21, and I don't have any problems

Ammo pickings were slim. I couldn't find any ammo on shelves. I bought these three boxes from a buddy who had them sitting around.

manipulating the controls or controlling it during firing. However, the G37's smaller grip does allow me to wrap my mitts even tighter, so it does afford more control.

I have never been one to shy away from trying new or different calibers, and some of my favorites aren't your garden variety. I love trying exotic and unique cartridges. But I can lump my various cartridges into two different categories: practical/useful, and novelty. My 10mm is useful, due to its sheer power. My 7.62 Nagant is fun to shoot, but a .30-caliber revolver is a novelty. My 9.3x62 is useful as a big-game hunting rifle and as a "the threat stops where it stands" rifle. My 7.62x45 Czech in my CZ Vz.52 rifle would be useful, and as a cartridge is superior to the 7.62x39 Soviet, but scarcity and high price make it a novelty.

So, where does the .45 GAP fit into all of this? I think it has, or at least had, the potential to be a very useful and excellent

For some people this is enough ammo in their magazine, as long as it's a .45.

cartridge. The concept is great (stick a .45 into a smaller frame) and the follow through with the caliber is even better. Not many shorter, or compact, or revised cartridges meet or exceed the original. Think about the .308 Winchester. It almost replicates the ballistics of the .30-06, but not quite. We say, yeah, but it's a smaller package, so a slight drop-off is OK. Think about the .357 SIG: It nearly meets the .357 Magnum in the light-grain bullets, but not quite, and it can't quite fit the heavier-grain bullets that the original .357 can. But the .45 GAP is right there with the ACP; it meets the performance.

The problem is that most of us who carry for self-defense, as well as law enforcement, want more rounds in the magazine. For most people today, 10 rounds are what the poor saps in magazine-capacity-restricted states carry, and not by choice. Which is why for a lot of people the .40 was so popular for a while: the performance isn't a big drop-off from the .45, yet it holds nearly as many rounds as a 9mm.

I think the worst enemy of the G37, G38 and G39 was the success the Glock .40s had for a while, the G22, G23 and G27. I own a G22, and it's the best .40 on the market. It's unfortunate, because I think the GAP is a good round, but if given the choice between a caliber that only a few companies offer and is expensive and hard to find, and a caliber that everyone makes and is all over the place, like the .40, most people will go with the .40.

I would love to see the .45 GAP catch on, and I have hopes for it in the future. I think it's a good cartridge.

At the time of this 2nd Edition writing, the G37, G38 and G39 .45 GAP pistols are only offered in Gen3. Which would lead one to believe sales are lackluster on these models, so Glock isn't making the investment to upgrade them at this time. I don't personally know anyone who owns one of the .45 GAP Glocks, though I have about a box and a half of ammo and no gun to shoot it through.

G37

If you're looking for a full-size handgun in .45, but you don't want the full-size grip of the G21, then the G37 should be a strong contender. At 10 rounds, the magazine holds three more cartridges than does a standard 1911 magazine. I'm always a fan of more. It's a great concept for a pistol; unfortunately, it has a G21-width slide on it, so it won't fit in the holster of your other standard-frame Glocks, like the G17. I know there is much more pressure in the .45 GAP than the .45 ACP, but it would have been nice if the engineers could

The G37 is a really sweet shooter. If you haven't shot one, you owe it to yourself.

Even the subcompact G39 is very controllable; two cases in the air and already back on target.

have gotten a standard G17-size slide to work. However, Glock engineers are some of the best in the business, and I'm sure they tried. So, if they couldn't do it, it probably can't be done at this time.

Spec-wise it has the same dimensions as a G17, except for the wider slide, and it's .08 inches taller in height and about 4 ounces heavier (due to the heavier slide). That comes out to 7.95 inches in length, 5.51 inches in height and 28.95 ounces unloaded. The overall width is the same at 1.18 inches since the widest part of both handguns is wider than the G37 slide.

G38

The compact version is still a nice handful and will net you eight rounds in the magazine, still one more than a standard 1911 magazine. Plus, with the G38 you have the option of loading a G37 10-round magazine. It's .08 inches longer in length (7.36 inches) than its G19 cousin, the same height (4.99 inches) and about three ounces heavier. The width on both is the same at 1.18 inches.

G39

The G39 is a lot of power in a little package, and it's a great choice if you're looking for a subcompact .45 that has a smaller grip than the G30. This is really where I lose interest in the .45 GAP, though. I can't bring myself to carry only six rounds of any caliber, unless perhaps it's a 10mm, or maybe a micro-compact 9mm. It's just not my cup of tea. Some people are perfectly fine with it, but here's where I start looking at other options. I will admit, however, that carrying the 10-round G37 magazine as a spare does ease that pain. It's .08 inches shorter in length (6.49 inches) than the G26 and comes in at just over 2 ounces heavier (24.19 ounces). The height on both is 4.17 inches.

CHAPTER 12:
THE G42

I debated whether to group the G42 into the Slimline chapter for the 2nd Edition, but decided to leave it with its own dedicated chapter. Because it deserves it. After the G17, the G42 is the second most important model Glock has designed. It's the first major design change since the Gen1 was introduced, with several changes that are complete overhauls from previous generations. Plus, it's the design that lead to the Gen5. It's also the first Glock that's made in the USA.

Prior to its release, speculation on the G42 abounded across the Internet, the anticipation of a slim, single-stack Glock in 9mm was almost too much to bear for Glockophiles. January 6, 2014 came, and we all learned it was a 9mm Kurtz (or as we Yanks call it, .380 ACP), not a 9mm Luger. Disappointed Glocksters swore they wouldn't buy the "useless .380." However, I've watched as, one by one, many of them have. In fact, for a long time, Glock couldn't keep them on store shelves, they sold out as soon as they came in. Many stores even had waiting lists. The truth is despite what the critics said, Americans have wanted a .380 Glock for a long time. Reasons for wanting a .380 Glock are many, but sometimes it boils down to: People want something they can't have, and for some time that was the G25 and G28, the .380 ACP Glocks. Except those were available only in markets other than the U.S. Due to import restrictions, Glock would never be able to import the G25 or G28 for civilian use. Glock users wanted a .380, and they've been asking for one for years. Glock finally delivered.

The G42: It just feels nice in the hand.

The G42 symbolizes something much larger than just being the smallest Glock made. It's the very first Glock to be made in the USA. Other Glock pistols have been assembled here, but the G42 is made here. It's the first one with "Made in USA" mark. The implications for this are huge, much more so than just finally having a .380 Glock. Glock now has production in the U.S. This means Glock can now offer pistols in the U.S. market they otherwise wouldn't have been able to offer here due to restrictions, guns like the aforementioned G25 and G28 (which, as of 2019, Glock still does not make here, and I cannot get a straight answer from Glock as to why they don't). It would also be nice to see a .22-caliber Glock. There are conversion kits, but people want the real thing, a genuine .22 Glock. Only time will tell if Glock will deliver. What I have been seeing, thanks to the magic that is social media – promoting open communications – is photos taken in foreign countries, such as Russia for example, with photos of G19s and such marked, "Made in USA."

At first, I didn't really want a G42. I have a micro-.380 that is so small a European could conceal it in his bikini briefs at the beach, and I figured I would just hold out until Glock finally released a single-stack 9mm. Then I held one, and I have to admit, it felt nice in the hand. It didn't take much convincing before I was sure I wanted one. It's bigger than other micro-.380s on the market; in fact, it's about the size of the micro-nines, except it's a Glock. That means it just feels right in your hand. It feels like you could pick it up and shoot 1,000 rounds without a failure. It feels like it will last a lifetime. I can't say that about the other .380s I've held. Plus, if your primary carry gun is a Glock, you'll be familiar with the controls, and there is much to be said about the importance of that.

I'm not one who believes you must pick one carry gun, and only one, and never use anything else. Nor am I one who believes that if you carry Brand-X, you must only carry Brand-X with those same exact controls and trigger pull. However, there is an advantage in carrying guns that have similar control types. For example, if your primary carry gun has a manual thumb safety, you should probably stick to that for the other guns you carry. If your primary carry gun does not have a manual thumb safety, it's probably best to stick with guns that don't have a manual safety. The reason is simple: If, in the face of danger, you draw your weapon thinking it has no safety but in fact it does, you've just cost yourself seconds. Seconds can cost you your life in a dangerous situation. The inverse is also true if you think you have a safety, but don't.

Some people take it a step further and believe any alternate carry gun you use should be the same exact thing as your primary carry gun. That's easy with a Glock pistol, because it is exactly the same from the front of the trigger guard and back. Draw a mental image and extend the front edge of the trigger guard up, dissecting the slide; everything behind that is the same, with the obvious exception of the length of the grip in the compact and subcompact models. Every model has the same controls and the same trigger, whether you have a G22, a G34 or a G26. The G42 continues that "same exact control" feature down to an ultra-compact .380. It's true, as I mentioned before, there are smaller .380 pistols out there, and even smaller 9mm pistols, but if you're looking for that familiarity with the rest of your Glocks, then the G42 is the way to go.

Glock pistols come in various sizes, and for the most part they are scaled-down (or up) versions of each other, with minor tweaks. That is, until the G42. Upon its release, many people thought it was just a miniature version of a Glock, but it's not, it has been redesigned from the ground up. The essential design is still the same, but holes and slots have been moved, and some of the parts that go into those holes and slots have changed. A couple of parts have completely changed, and one part that used to be one part is now a three-part assembly, though listed as one part. More on that later.

The G42 is different enough that when I went through the armorer's course in July 2014, approximately six months after it was released, the recommendation for armorers was that if a G42 was brought to us for repair or maintenance, we not work on it ourselves, but instead send it in to Glock. Back then, there just weren't enough spare parts in the supply chain. All parts that were made were going toward building new pistols to meet the demand for it. This is a big departure from the premise of Glock that I outlined in my "Parts Is Parts" chapter.

As I wrote earlier, a Glock from the breech back is essentially the same. The only exception to this is the G36 and G30S, the two slimline pistols. Now the G42 can be added to that list. All other Glocks decreased their size by trimming the front of the slide and the bottom of the grip (not physically trimming, but in the design process). The slimline models are different, because they use slides that are not as wide as standard Glocks, so it's not just a matter of trimming the front of the slide when designing it. Until Glock introduced the G43, the case of the G42 was completely unique, it was just an all-around smaller slide. Now it's not unique because there's a whole line of slimline 9mm pistols.

While many .380 designs are blowback operated, especially older designs like the Walther PP series, the G42 is a locked-breech design. While blowback relies on the mass of the slide and spring resistance, a locked-breech pistol keeps the breech locked, or closed, just long enough so pressure is reduced to a safe level. Once that pressure is safe, then the slide operates. Since a locked-breech design doesn't rely on slide mass, it can be designed smaller, and since it doesn't rely on spring tension, it is easier to rack the slide. The smaller size is the reason for the resurgence of the .380, in pistols such as the G42, Ruger LCP, Kel-Tec P3AT only and Smith & Wesson Bodyguard. Yes, locked-breech designs chambered in .380 have been around for years, in pistols such as the Colt Mustang, but modern polymer designs allow for the smaller and lighter pistols being offered today.

DIMENSIONS

The G42 is listed as 5.94 inches long, by 4.13 inches in height, by .94 inches wide (the grip width is .87 inches) and weighs 13.76 ounces unloaded, 17.29 ounces loaded. It has a sight radius of 4.92 inches and a 3.25-inch long barrel. It includes two six-round magazines, though aftermarket extended magazines are offered. One thing to make a mental note of when comparing the thickness of the G42 to other pistols on the market; most companies list the thickness of their slides, not the overall thickness. Glock lists the overall thickness, and it would appear that the .94 inches is thicker than some subcompact pistols from other companies. But to compare the slide thickness I measured the G42 slide to be .826 inches thick, which is quite a bit thinner than other pistols I have found.

To compare it to another popular Glock carry model, the G26 Gen4 is .47 inches longer, .04 inches taller, .24 inches wider, (grip thickness is .33 inches wider) and 7.95 ounces heavier. Just like on the G26, I can get only two fingers on the G42 grip to hold it, but it doesn't matter with the light recoil of the gun.

The G19 is 1.34 inches longer, .86 inches taller and 9.89 ounces heavier. The G17 is 2.01 inches longer, 1.3 inches taller and 11.3 ounces heavier. All are .24 inches thicker at the thickest part of the handgun. In real-world relation to each other, each smaller model of Glock is approximately one-half to three-fourths of an inch smaller than the next largest model category. The G42 carries on this trend, as it's roughly half an inch shorter in length

G42 laid on top of a G26.

G42 (bottom) beside a G26.

than the G26. However, it does not continue the trend in height, because there is only an .04-inch difference between it and the G26, because to make it any shorter Glock would have us holding it with one finger.

INTERNAL CHANGES

Internally, there are some differences that you mostly won't see unless you're a Glock armorer. Four key differences were pretty drastic at the time, but it's interesting because those four changes worked so well for Glock, that not only were they incorporated into the following 9mm slimline models like the G43, they were actually the basis for the Gen5 handguns. I did cover these in the Gen5 section of CHAPTER 4: IT'S A GENERATIONAL THING, but I'm going to briefly go over them again here.

The first key difference is the trigger spring. It's unlike any other Glock trigger spring, including the New York triggers. It almost resembles a miniature fire extinguisher. It disassembles into three parts: the bearing, spring and rod. Because of this change, the dropdown leg on the trigger bar cruciform wasn't needed, so that's now gone.

Another internal difference is the slide stop lever. Rather than the lever with the round hole in the front and the flat spring, it has a C-shape to the front with a compression spring

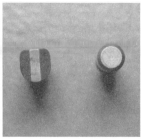

The G42 trigger spring (left) resembles a miniature fire extinguisher. The standard (pre-Gen5) trigger spring is on the right. This G42 trigger spring would be used in the G43 and then become the standard trigger spring for the Gen5 and follow-up 9mm slimline models.

G42 firing pin safety (left in both pictures) next to a Gen4 firing pin safety. This G42 firing pin safety would become the standard firing pin safety for all post-Gen4 models (G43, Gen5, G43X, etc.).

clamped into the C. This design would be used in the G43 and the following slimline 9mm pistols. This compression spring was then incorporated into the Gen5 slide stop lever. The Gen5 slide stop lever is based on this G42 design, except it was made ambidextrous.

The firing pin safety is also shaped completely different, and instead of being round and fitting into the hole any old way (round is round, there is no "correct way" to insert a round object into a round hole), it fits only one way.

Another key difference is the slide lock spring. Whereas it used to be a flat spring, it's now a coil spring. It doesn't really have an impact on performance, but it does affect disassembly – don't let it launch, you'll never find it.

The extractor is unique to the G42, but it still resembles the other model extractors, it's just not as wide.

The G42 is unique in that it is not really a Gen4 or a Gen3, nor is it exactly a Gen5, it is its own entity. The grip texture resembles the RTF (Rough Texture Frame) texture of a Gen4, but not as aggressive.

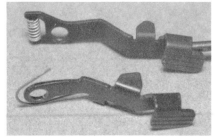

Slide stop lever of a G42 (top) compared to a Gen4 Glock slide stop lever (bottom). The coil-type spring would be used in the G43 and become the standard for post-Gen4 models (Gen5, G43X, etc.).

G42 extractor (top), G26 extractor (bottom).

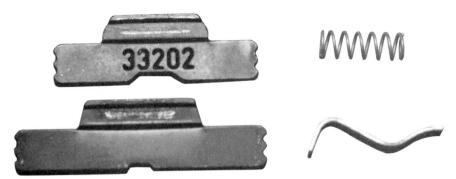

G42 slide lock (top) with coil spring, compared to the G26 slide lock with flat spring. This G42 coil spring became standard in post-Gen4 models.

The texture of the G42 (right) is not as aggressive as the standard RTF of a Gen4 (left).

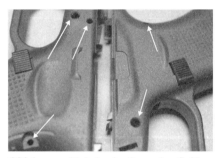

G26 frame with holes for three pins (left), G42 with two pins (right).

The mag catch release is also Gen4, as is the is the fact that it's ambidextrous. The guide ring on the slide is a Gen4, as is the recoil spring assembly. The magazine is also ambidextrous like a Gen4 magazine. The lack of finger grooves on the front grip strap, however, is not Gen4, but would become Gen5. It also has no accessory rail, which is just like all Glock subcompact models. It has only two takedown pins, unlike all Gen4 pistols that have three, which will become standard in the Gen5 9mm models. Stress-wise, there's really no need for that third pin for a .380 or 9mm, and size-wise, there's not a lot of extra space for things that aren't necessary.

A couple of minor differences include a narrower thumb rest and a completely different raised groove around the slide catch. This has absolutely no bearing on function. Another difference is the appearance of the bottom of the grip. It's still beveled on the inside, though only slightly, and it's not as pronounced on the outside of the grip bottom as it is in other models. So, all around the circumference of the grip bottom, it sits flush with the magazine base plate, with the exception of the rear, which extends about three-fourths of the way down the magazine base plate.

Let's compare the dimensions of the G42 to two other popular .380 pistols currently on the market: the Ruger LCP and the Smith & Wesson Bodyguard 380. In length, the G42 is .78 inches longer than the LCP, and .69 inches longer than the Bodyguard 380. It's approxi-

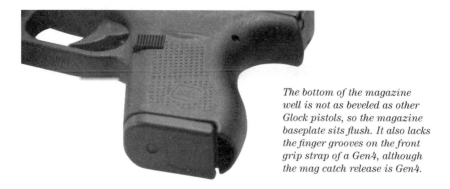

The bottom of the magazine well is not as beveled as other Glock pistols, so the magazine baseplate sits flush. It also lacks the finger grooves on the front grip strap of a Gen4, although the mag catch release is Gen4.

mately half an inch taller than the LCP, and one-third inch taller than the Bodyguard .380. The slide is essentially the same width, with the G42 being .076 inches thicker than both. Overall thickness has the G42 at approximately one-tenth of an inch thicker than both. All hold six rounds plus one.

Now that's all fine and dandy, except I don't think the LCP and Bodyguard are exactly what Glock was going for. I believe a better comparison for the G42 is the Ruger LC380. These two are nearly identical in size, but with the LC380 being slightly heavier, taller and holding one more round. The difference between these two versus the LCP and Bodyguard 380 are subtle, but you notice it at the range.

I think Glock went through a lot of effort to make this a nice-shooting .380, and in doing so sacrificed some size. I'm good with that. The bikini-brief .380 I mentioned before, the LCP, is tiny. But let's be honest, it can be wicked to shoot. I know a lot of .357 guys out there who would never admit that a little .380 can be harsh to shoot, but I will. I have large hands and that little pistol is hard to hold on to. And I love big-bore guns, so it's not like I can't handle recoil. It's not as harsh as a .454 Casull, but I can shoot my big Ruger GP100 in .357 all day. I can shoot my Glock 20 10mm all day. But a tiny .380 can be not so fun to shoot. That's why Ruger took the LC9 (9mm) and chambered it in .380 and called it the LC380. There's a consumer desire for it, and that's why the G42 is here. Many people want a more shootable .380.

SHOOTING THE G42

To say I've shot a few small-caliber defensive pistols here and there, would be an understatement. I've fired most of the models that are the current trend in .380s, as well as some European military surplus pistols, and the G42 shoots better than all of them.

Being a little bigger than the other modern .380s really helps it in the shootability department. I can barely hold on to the ti-

The G42 is the best shooting .380 pistol the author has ever fired.

niest .380s with my big meat hooks. And as for older .380s, most of them are blowback operated, which means the barrel is fixed, which doesn't do as much to cut down on recoil as the Glock. When I shoot a couple boxes through my Walther PPK, the web of my hand hurts. Not so with the G42. I can literally shoot this all day. I'm not exaggerating. It's that comfortable to shoot.

I've read more than one article from reputable online sources that, out of the gate, the G42 was having some feed issues. The issues were specific to the high power (+P) and light loads (under 90 grains), and it involved failure to feed (FTF), failure to eject (FTE) and stove pipes. I have confirmation from Glock that some changes have been made to the G42. Comparing my G42 made in summer 2014 to a first release G42, I see noticeable change to the slide lock lever, magazine and trigger mechanism housing. It's possible other changes could have been made. Either way, mine shot perfectly.

Federal was generous enough to send me 200 rounds of American Eagle 95-grain FMJ, which the G42 thanked me for. I also had on hand 100 rounds of Remington UMC 88-grain JHP and around 50 Blazer 95-grain FMJ steel-case rounds. Out of 350 rounds I had not one issue. The G42 shot perfectly without skipping a beat, just as a Glock should. Since testing the G42 for the first edition, I've put hundreds of additional rounds through it, and still no issues. I'm pretty choosey about carry ammo, especially for the.380, which some people consider too underpowered for self-defense. Three rounds I really like for carry include Federal HST, Black Hills Honey Badger and G2Research.

Another thing to like about the G42 is that it has actual sights. In contrast to many of the tiny .380s on the market that give you a tiny sliver of a sight that makes it hard to shoot accurately, the G42 has standard Glock sights with the U rear sight. No sight will ever make everyone happy, but these sights are leagues better than the other stuff I've seen on the market. Glock also makes night sights for the G42, as do several after-market companies.

So, why would one buy a G42 in .380 ACP, when there are other companies making 9mm pistols that are smaller? That's a good question. First, there will be a segment of people who pick it up and say, "Wow, this is nice. I want one." When the G42 was released, I had zero interest in buying another .380, especially one this big. Then I held it in my hands, and as I wrote earlier, I wanted one. I had to sit back and tell myself "It's only a .380, I don't need it." It's a very appealing pistol.

Second, there will be a segment of people who carry a Glock, either for duty or personal carry, and want a small backup that's also a Glock. That makes sense to me. Third, this gun's shootability. Rarely does one find a pistol this small, in any caliber, that shoots this comfortably. In regard to my first point, and as a testament to my third, it took me one trip to the range to know I would buy one. After the second trip to the range I knew I would buy one that day, and I did. That doesn't happen to me often, but it did when I shot the G42.

But the best reason to carry a G42, if you already carry and train with a Glock, is the trigger. When comparing the G42 trigger to other Glock models, it's exact. It has the same trigger manipulation as other Glocks, despite the size differences between the pistols. When you pull the trigger, it takes 5.5 pounds of pressure to move it .49 inches until it breaks. It has the same take-up, the same break and it feels the same. I'm a gun writer, so I shoot many different pistols and pull countless different triggers. But for many, the

Markings on barrel. The pentagon with the dot is the barrel proof. The "US" is made in the U.S. The Georgia state outline with the "P" in the center is the Georgia proof mark.

Marking on the frame. The Georgia state outline with a "P" in the center.

Glock is it. That's all they train with, and all they shoot. For them, the G42 is exactly what they need for a micro-compact carry or backup gun.

Also, the other controls compared with other Glock models are nearly identical in spatial relation to each other. The distance between the slide catch and magazine catch are nearly identical. The control group has been pushed rearward about five-eighths of an inch, so it's closer for your thumb to get to, but your thumb travels the same dis-

Slide marking. Made in Smyrna, Georgia.

tance to get from one to the other. This allows for muscle memory to do its work.

MARKINGS

The G42 has a new marking never before seen on a Glock. Since it's made in the USA, Smyrna, Georgia, to be specific, it has the Georgia state outline around a letter "P" stamped onto it. There has been discussion about what the letter "P" stands for, but by itself it doesn't really stand for anything per se, the Georgia outline and the letter P are all one symbol, and it stands for the Georgia Proof. It's stamped at three locations: the frame, slide and barrel. On the slide it's located on the right side, above the trigger guard, forward of the slide lock. On the frame it's located behind the ejector. On the barrel the marking is located on the barrel hood, after the Glock symbol and the "U.S." At the time of the G42's introduction, the U.S. marking was also new, since it was the first and only (at the time) Glock made entirely in the United States. Another marking along the right side of the frame, above the grip and behind the takedown pin, usually reads, "MADE IN

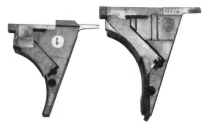

G42 trigger mechanism housing (left) vs. G26. Note the difference in the ejector (top right of housing).

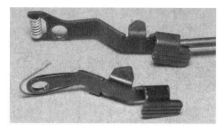

Slide-stop lever of a G42 (top) compared to conventional Glock slide-stop lever.

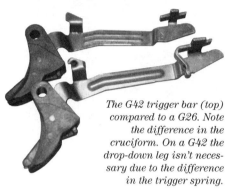

The G42 trigger bar (top) compared to a G26. Note the difference in the cruciform. On a G42 the drop-down leg isn't necessary due to the difference in the trigger spring.

The barbell-shaped slot in the trigger housing.

Though it's not necessary to do so, here is a disassembled G42 trigger spring assembly.

AUSTRIA" on the top line and "GLOCK, INC., SMYRNA, GA." on the bottom line. On the G42, the top line is marked, "MADE IN USA." This is the first time for this as well.

DETAILED DISASSEMBLY/ASSEMBLY (FOR G42, G43, G43X AND G48)

Detailed disassembly is nearly identical to all other Glock models and if you follow the same steps, you'll have the same result. There are a couple differences which I will note as I go through the steps.

First field strip just like any other Glock pistol, then grab the frame. Frame disassembly starts off differently from the Gen4 Glock models, which are all three-pin. The G42 is a two-pin, like earlier Gens, and like the Gen5. Remove the trigger pin left to right using constant, but not excessive, pressure. It has a groove that engages with the slide stop lever through which it sits, and it can be a little difficult to get out, especially on new models. You'll need to work the pin through the lever, and the best way to do so is to press down on the lever at the junction where the pin sits in it, or by grasping the lever and moving it back and forth until the pin moves. Once the pin is out, remove the trigger housing pin, left to right. Now use your armorer's tool to pry out the locking block and then lift out the slide stop lever.

Next, pull straight up on the extractor, lifting the trigger mechanism housing assembly out of the frame, just as you would any other Glock model.

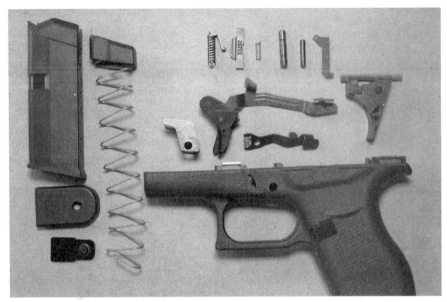

The frame completely disassembled, except for trigger spring, which counts as one part.

Holding the trigger mechanism housing in your left hand, and grasping the trigger bar in the right, rotate the trigger bar counterclockwise and the cruciform will rotate out of the drop safety slot.

Unlike other Glock models, the trigger bar is not connected to the trigger spring and will come right out. The trigger spring is one of the main differences between the G42 and other models, and its removal is completely different. The trigger spring is actually an assembly, comprised of a bearing, spring and rod.

After the trigger bar has been separated from the housing, remove the connector by pressing the armorer's tool punch through the hole on the opposite side, and push it

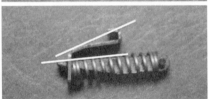

Trigger Spring Assembly: The angle of the spring rod top and the bearing should be approximately the same angle (top). The bottom picture shows one improperly installed.

out. Never remove the connector by grasping it and pulling it out. It can be bent, and damage the housing. To remove the trigger spring, first take a look at the front of the housing. You'll notice a slot that resembles a barbell. Inside the bottom groove, you'll see the end of the trigger spring rod. The objective is to push the notches on the trigger spring rod through the front of the housing, then slide it up the "bar" slot and out the top groove.

The trigger spring rod is in its seated position. To remove, press on the trigger spring rod (from the opposite end) until the rod clears the seat, push it up the slot, and out

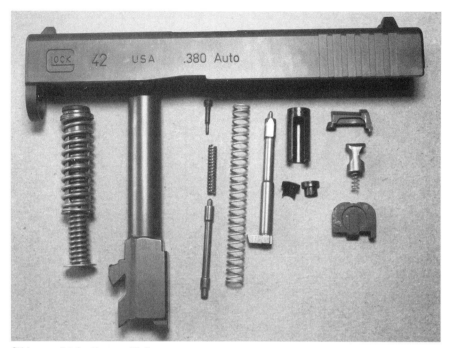

Slide completely disassembled.

through the top notch. To reassemble, do the opposite.

Do so by pressing down on the trigger spring bearing with the armorer's tool, then use your other thumb to push the end of the rod up the slot and through the top groove (keeping in mind there is spring tension, which always has the potential for something being launched). Once the trigger spring is out, though not necessary to do so, you can disassemble it by pressing the rod and spring while twisting the rod so the end can be pulled out of the slot in the bearing. Then the rod can be pulled out of the spring.

The G26 (left) EDP channel will be almost entirely covered by the slide plate cover when it's installed. With the G42, most of the channel is left uncovered by the slide plate cover.

Slide lock removal is the same, though the spring is a coil type, not a flat spring, as found in other Glock pistols.

When sliding out the slide lock, be careful to not damage the coil spring, or to allow it to launch. I like to leave my thumb over the spring when removing the slide lock, so if it does launch it doesn't go anywhere.

Magazine catch removal is done in the same manner as other ambidextrous models.

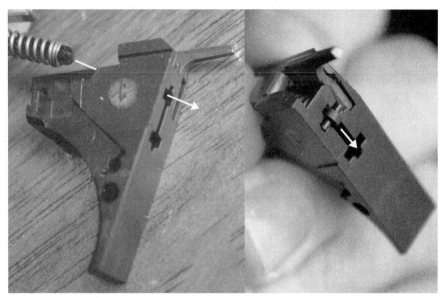

Slide the trigger spring bar end through the top slot (left), then down along slot and into seated position (right).

To disassemble the slide, use the same procedures as you would a standard Glock slide, it's an identical process. This doesn't have any bearing on disassembly, but one thing you'll notice is the extractor depressor plunger assembly (EDP) channel. It is positioned just a little differently than in the other Glock models due to the reduced size of the slide. With other Glock pistols, the slide cover plate almost entirely covers the EDP channel. Only a sliver is exposed. On the G42, the slide plate cover leaves approximately 70 percent of the EDP channel uncovered.

To assemble, you'll note special attention at the same places noted during disassembly. When reinstalling the slide-lock lever (with the groove facing up and to the rear as with all other models), insert it through the right side of the frame, pointed up at an angle so as to go up and over the coil spring. Use your thumb to press down on the lever, which presses down on the spring, and slide it through the left side of the frame. Next insert the connector into the trigger mechanism housing. Make sure it's fully seated and be careful to press only at the point where the connector inserts into the housing, otherwise you can bend the connector.

Grasp the trigger spring assembly, with the bearing oriented up, and insert it through the top "barbell" slot and slide it down until it snaps into place.

When assembling the trigger spring assembly, the first thing to note is the end of the rod that fits through the bearing (it resembles a digging spade). If you lay it on a table, it has a flat side and an angled side. After you insert it through the bearing and turn it, the flat side should be opposite the bearing. Once assembled, the spade end of the rod should have an angle that runs approximately parallel to the angle of the bearing.

Next, with the housing in your left hand and the trigger bar in your right, hook the front part of the cruciform into the upper lip of the trigger spring bearing, and twist the left part

It's like putting shapes into holes when you were a kid. The firing pin safety goes in only one way. This is the wrong way.

G42 magazine follower, G26 magazine follower.

into the drop safety slot. Pull up gently and slightly on the trigger bar until the end of the trigger bar snaps under the lip of the connector. To reinstall the trigger assembly, insert the housing straight down into its proper position in the frame, while at the same time, guiding the trigger into its slot. Make sure both are fully seated.

Insert the slide stop lever, coil forward, into its slot, then insert the locking block into position. To insert the trigger pin, everything is going to need to line up by pressing down on the slide stop and possibly the trigger bar. I found the best way to do this is to look through the trigger pin hole, from the left side. Insert the trigger pin on the right side, going left. Once inserted, take the square end of the armorer's tool, and use one of the corners to press on the pin to center it in the frame. Insert the trigger housing pin into the grip hole, from left to right, and center it using the same armorer's tool method.

Slide assembly doesn't differ much from a standard slide, with one difference. First, insert the firing pin safety into the hole, spring end down, making sure it is aligned correctly. This is the only difference. On a standard slide, the firing pin safety is cylindrical in shape going into a round hole, so you can insert it any which way, there is no right or wrong (as long as the spring end is down). The one in the G42 has more of an oblong shape, and must be seated correctly, with the rounded side pointed toward the stripper/feed rail, and the flat side toward the slide rail, running parallel.

Next press down on the firing pin safety while inserting the ejector. It should pop into place and not come out. Assemble the extractor depressor plunger assembly (EDP) as you would on any other Glock, and insert it into the EDP channel, metal end first (metal on metal, polymer on polymer). Assemble the firing pin assembly as you would a standard Glock and insert it into the firing pin channel. Press down on it as far as you can while sliding the slide plate cover into place and over the firing pin, until it stops at the EDP. Using your armorer's tool, press down on the EDP, while sliding the slide plate cover over it, and into position. It should snap in place.

Finish assembling the Glock slide to the frame. Do a function check and you're finished.

CHAPTER 13:
SLIMLINE 9MM

The U.S. concealed-carry market has been booming for many years now, and it shows no signs of stopping. As the concealed-carry market has become more and more popular, so have the micro-compact guns that fill the segment, and no caliber is as popular as the 9mm. It's a full-power load that is able to be packed into a small package, so it's no wonder why it's so popular.

The Glock Slimline 9mms have been very popular, ever since their introduction, starting with the first Slimline 9mm, the G43, in 2015. The G43 design is based off the G42, a .380 ACP caliber. There was a slimline pistol prior to that, the G36, but its design was based off the original Glock. As we covered in the G42 chapter, the G42 design (and thus the Slimline 9mm) is different from the traditional Glock design, incorporating significant design changes.

The G43 came out just as the first edition of this book was going to print, and the Slimline 9mm lineup has now expanded to include the G43X and G48.

G43

Prior to the introduction of the G43, shooters had been clamoring for a single-stack 9mm Glock for years. And when Glock finally gave them one, in the form of the G43, people were lining up on waiting lists to get their hands on it.

Glock took heat from a lot of fans after not releasing a single-stack 9mm at the 2015 SHOT show. Some took it a little too personally and filled the Internet forums with overdramatic vows never to buy another Glock. Further salt was thrown on the "wounds" of fans, by the other makers who have had single-stack 9mms on the market for several years now.

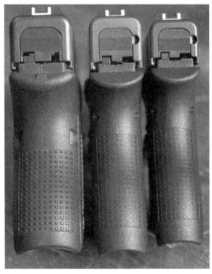

The G43 (middle) is larger than the G42 in .380 ACP (right) and the thin version of the 9mm G26 (left).

I believe Glock was simply taking a little extra time to make sure it got it right, after taking a hit when the G42 had some issues coming out of the gate (mostly malfunctions when using over-powered and under-powered ammunition). It was easily remedied with modifications to a few parts, but Glock isn't a company that takes well to having reliability issues. So, Glock took a little extra time with this one, and judging by my experience, as well as what I've seen from others, with the G43, they got it right.

It's nearly identical to the G42, just slightly larger; it's essentially a thin-frame G26. To compare it to other popular 9mm carry pistols, it's roughly the same size as the Smith & Wesson Shield and Ruger LC9, and slightly smaller than the Walther PPS. In other articles I've labeled pistols of this size as micro-nines, as other authors have done, but Glock calls it a slim-line subcompact. For the sake of this chapter, when comparing it to similar hand-guns, I'm going to refer to it a micro-nine.

The specs on the G43 are as follows, with G26 specs in parenthesis for comparison. Most of the differences are less than one-tenth of an inch. The length is 6.26 inches (6.49), height is 4.25 inches (4.17) and width is 1.02 inches (1.26). Keep in mind the published width is not slide width, which is 0.86 inch (1.04). The published width is measured at the widest part; the thumb shelf at the top of the grip (in the Gen5 G26, it's at the new, ambi-dextrous slide catch, which is even wider). It has a sight radius of 5.20 inches (5.39) and a barrel length of 3.39 inches (3.42). Unloaded, it weighs 17.95 ounces (21.71) with .49-inch trigger travel. The trigger pull is listed as 5.5 pounds, but I'll get into that in just a bit. It comes with two six-round magazines, one with an extended grip.

Glock put a lot of effort into making it as small as possible while still maintaining the typical shootability of a Glock. The result is a handgun slightly larger than other micro-nines on the market, but small enough that it can be concealed with most reasonable cloth-ing. I've fired most of the micro-nines, and those are a "hold-on-for-dear-life" endeavor, especially for those with medium-to-large hands. Not so with the G43. It's comfortable enough for a long day at the range. The G26 has been my primary carry gun for a while now, and the G43 has felt recoil that is only slightly more than the G26. The primary difference affecting recoil is the G26 has a wider grip so it fills your hand, offering greater control.

The difference in physical size between the G42 and G43 isn't much, but I have to quan-tify that because in the handgun world the difference between full-size and compact is of-ten less than one inch. Referencing Glock's published specifications and using my Hornady digital calipers to fill in the blanks, I've come up with the following: When compared to the G42, the G43 is 1/64 inch wider, .69 inches longer and .12 inches taller. The slide is 1/32 inch wider and it is 4.19 ounces heavier.

With most Glock models, when you compare the three size categories, standard, com-pact and subcompact, the differences in sizes are accounted for by "chopping" a bit off the front and the grip. As I've written elsewhere in the book, the difference in slide length for Glock is removed forward of the ejection port; everything behind it is the same. This isn't the case when comparing the G43 to the G42. The G43 is proportionally larger, so the G42 is a *shrunken* version of the G43, not a *cut* version.

It has the same grip texture as the G42, which has at its roots the Gen4 RTF, except less aggressive. It provides the perfect blend of good grip for control, but not enough that it scrapes flesh off when carrying. I've had a couple people voice to me their concern

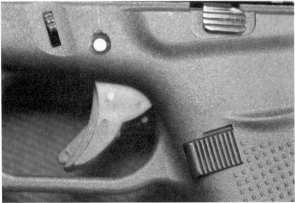

The controls of the G43 and other 9mm Glock models are nearly identical spatially, so transitioning from one to the other uses the same muscle memory. Here, a G19 compared to a G43. Which is which? You can't tell from the controls, but other clues give it away.

that it wasn't aggressive enough. Both had gotten their hands on one, but hadn't fired it yet. I didn't have any slippage at all, and it was incredibly easy to control.

The G43 has a short beavertail grip for a high and tight grip for optimal control, and a large magazine release for fast reloads. Also, like the other Gen4s it uses a captured dual-spring assembly. Like the G42, it's been made as snag-free as possible by not using an extended mag release or an accessory rail. The one Gen4 feature it doesn't have is the Modular Back strap system.

The controls are the same as any other Gen4 Glock, so transitioning between a full-size Glock to this one will be smooth as butter. If you took a picture of the control group of a G17 you could superimpose it onto a picture of the G43 control group, and it would line up pretty evenly, if not exactly. So, if your thumb is accustomed to the mag release being in one spot, your muscle memory will hit the mag release on the G43.

Same with the trigger and the slide catch. They are all the same. There's a big benefit to that. When you can work your duty/carry handgun like it's second nature, transitioning to a different size Glock is also second nature.

When Glock released the G42, it was unique; no other Glock model was like it. With the release of the G43, it's no longer unique. The G43 is just a larger version of the G42. To clarify the discussion of parts, I want to differentiate between two things. First, there is the official Glock part number. This is generally what is being referred to when Glock discusses parts commonality. The trigger mechanism housing with ejector is an example of this. They all pretty much look the same, but by Glock part number there are seven

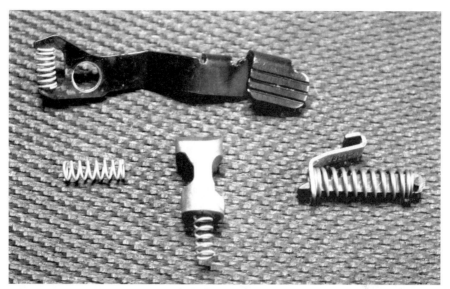

When considering component parts, the G43 (and G42) uses four parts that are different from the component parts of other models. (Clockwise, from the top) slide stop lever, trigger spring, firing pin safety and slide lock spring.

different ones. So not all Glock models list this part as being in common. Glock probably has a few hundred different parts, going by Glock part number. The barrel is another great example, every Glock has one, but there's a different Glock part number for every caliber and category, so there are more than 21 different barrels.

The second item to that discussion is the component part. There are only 35 component parts; 34 for the earlier models that don't have a locking block pin (third frame pin). Component parts are where we talk about the Glock design that makes the Glock so unique among firearms. By Glock design, that is, component parts, all Glocks are the same. They have the same basic parts.

That is, until the introduction of the G42, and now the G43. These two models have four component parts that are different from all the other Glock models, and I covered them in the G42 chapter: Slide stop lever, trigger spring, firing pin safety and slide lock spring. If you hold these four parts next to the same four parts of other Glock models, they look completely different. You could possibly include a fifth part, the locking block pin, since all Gen4 models of Glock include this pin, but the G42 and slimline 9mms do not. And now the Gen5 releases thus far have not included it either.

Getting back to Glock part numbers, the G42 and G43 have 12 parts in common: trigger mechanism housing with ejector, trigger spring assembly, connector, slide lock spring, firing pin safety spring, magazine catch spring, trigger housing pin, sights, spring cups, EDP (Extractor, Depressor, Plunger) spring and EDP bearing.

There are 15 parts that are different from the G42 and completely unique to the G43, and those are: slide, frame, barrel, locking block, trigger pin, slide stop lever, slide lock, trigger with trigger bar, magazine catch, firing pin, firing pin safety, EDP rod, extractor, slide plate

The G43, disassembled.

cover and recoil spring assembly. The magazine is also unique, as are the five parts that it is comprised of.

The spacer sleeve is one part that is not the same as the G42, but is the same part as other Glock models. The front sight is the same across all Glock models.

Another noticeable difference in the G43 is the barrel hood. Glocks typically have a straight barrel hood, there are a few exceptions, but none as drastic as the G43. With most models, running a finger over the top of the slide is smooth, and when going over the barrel hood/ejection port, not much of a bump is noticed. The front half of the barrel hood on a G43 is angled down, and when a finger is run over the top of the slide a significant bump is noticed where the front of the hood meets the slide. This helps it unlock a little easier during the firing process. When the slide is moving rearward, it will clear the hood faster.

When the G42 was introduced, some were happy to see it was made in the USA, and some preferred that an Austrian pistol stay in Austria. Whichever side of the fence you fall on, production of the G43 was solely in Austria, at least initially. Now production is in Austria and the U.S.

The G43 shoots excellent: I have fired the six most popular micro-nines on the market, and as far as shootability, I rank it as either first, or tied for first. It should be noted that if it is called a tie, the pistol it's tied with, the Walther PPS, is slightly larger. Some of the other micro-nines can be tough to hold on to with larger hands. When you fire one, it feels like it's going to jump out of your hands, but that's not the case with the G43. When firing, it feels very similar to the G26, with a barely discernible increase in recoil.

Accuracy was surprising for me. I mostly fired it at self-defense range (seven yards) and it grouped very well. The best group of the day was with Hornady Custom 147-grain XTP.

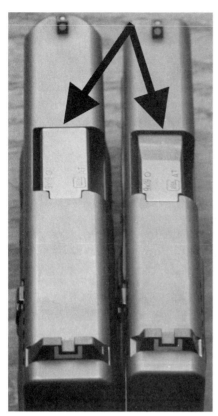

Best group of the day: Hornady Custom 147-grain XTP, six rounds, seven yards.

The barrel hood of the G26 (left) is straight, so it's even with the slide, whereas the G43 (right) has an angled front portion.

Six rounds grouped into a hole not much bigger than a quarter. I used a Caldwell pistol rest to test the accuracy of the handgun, not my own abilities. I also fired Hornady American Gunner 115-grain XTP and 124 XTP +P, American Eagle 115-grain FMJ, Federal Premium 124-grain HST JHP and 135-grain Hydra-Shok JHP Low Recoil, Winchester 147-grain HP and Buffalo Bore 124-grain JHP +P. With the exception to the two issues mentioned later in the chapter, all performed well and exhibited very good accuracy.

Even though my first range experience with the G43 was a very good one, it wasn't perfect. The most disappointing thing is the weight of trigger pull. Don't get me wrong, it's still a good trigger, it's just not the Glock 5.5-pound trigger I like. Glock has deemed the trigger-pull weight on every other model of Glock as safe. In fact, it's called a Safe Action Trigger. But on the G43, like the G42, Glock has determined it should have a slightly heavier trigger pull. The representative I talked to said it's around 6 pounds, but my Lyman scale averaged 8.1.

I'm a fan of the standard Glock trigger, so this is disappointing. It's still a clean pull, with a crisp break and excellent reset, but there's no reason it should be heavier. If the 5.5-pound trigger is safe on all other Glock pistols, then it would be safe on a G43. As is though, it's still one of the best triggers found on a micro-nine. I would rank it tied with the PPS, or perhaps slightly behind it. A standard Glock pull weight would have put it in first place alone.

Mine is an early model G43, and my understanding is Glock has since improved the trigger on the G43. I cannot confirm this firsthand, because the only stock-trigger G43 I've fired is my own, all the others I've fired have had aftermarket triggers put in.

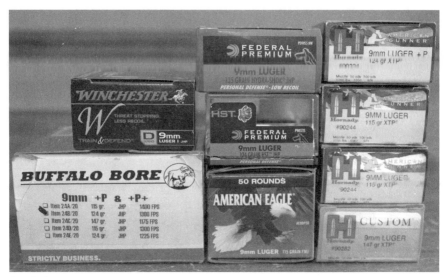

The G43 ate through all of this and had trouble with only two rounds out of 230.

The other issue I had with the G43 involved two malfunctions out of 230 rounds fired. The first, a failure to eject with round number 64, was Federal Premium 123-grain HST JHP. The second, a failure to feed with round number 223 was Hornady 147-grain XTP. Neither issue was with +P or underpowered ammo. Two rounds out of 230 isn't a lot, and compared to other handguns I've written about is still very good. But it's two more malfunctions than I had total for the other 25-plus Glocks I fired for the first edition of this book. I know some manufacturers state the first X-number of rounds are a break-in period, whether it be 300 rounds or 500. But that hasn't been my experience with Glock, and most of the other 25-plus Glocks were also new out-of-the-box specimens (except the Gen1 and Gen2 G17s, and the G20c and G26 from my own collection). In the four-plus years since the first edition, I've put well over 1,000 rounds through this G43 and it hasn't had any other malfunctions to this date.

I don't want the negative to take away from the G43, though. It's an excellent little Glock that will make a perfect carry gun for a lot of people. I think it's also going to find favor as a backup for a lot of our men and women in blue. This one has been a long time coming from Glock, and it didn't disappoint.

G48

I get to test a lot of guns, which often requires me to carry the gun for EDC, especially when the gun is designed to be a carry gun. However, my go-to carry gun is a Glock: The G19 when my attire permits, the G43 when my attire doesn't. I'm going to be honest, however, when it released it in 2018, SIG Sauer had me with the P365. Ten rounds in a micro-compact pistol that shoots like a larger pistol, it truly is a game-changer. And it did change the game, because now you see responses from other companies, including Glock. When Glock an-

The G48 is a single-stack, compact 9mm. Think of it as a Commander-size 9mm 1911.

nounced the G43X and G48, I was extremely happy. While the P365 is a fine gun, and has performed perfectly for me, my comfort level really is with the Glock. So, when the G48 (and G43X) were announced, I couldn't have been happier.

So, what is the G48? The best way to think of it, dimensionally speaking, is a "G19 Slim." The G19 Gen5 has an overall width of 1.322 inch (thanks to the addition of the ambi slide lock), a slide width of 1.00 inch and a grip width of 1.19 inch. The G48 has an overall width of 1.059 inch (the widest part is at the mag release), a slide width of 0.87 inch and a grip width of 1.03 inch. It's roughly 2/3 to 3/4 the width of the G19. The height is about the same, at 4.6 inches (no magazine inserted, and not including sights). The slide length is about the same at 6.79 inches for the G19 and 6.74 inches for the G48. As for weight, the G48 weighs 20.88 ounces and the G19 Gen5 weighs almost 4 ounces more, coming in at 24.25 ounces (both with empty magazine). The G48 is about 2.5 ounces heavier than the G43, which comes in at 18.25 ounces. So, there's not a lot of difference between them, about 1/8 pound.

The length of the barrel differs slightly, and this is an interesting bit of trivia. The G19 barrel is 4.008 inches long, while the G48 is slightly longer at 4.19 inches. "Why?" you might ask, is the G48 longer. This little tidbit was passed on to me by James Tarr, fellow gun writer, TV personality and competitive shooter. While at a match, shortly after the G48 was released, he was talking with two Canadian shooters, and it turns out Glock had our neighbors to the north in mind when designing the G48. Canadian law prohibits handguns with a barrel length of 105 mm or less. The G19 barrel measures 101.89 mm in length, which makes it just under the minimum, by about 3 mm. So, Glock went ahead and fixed that with the G48, giving it a barrel length of 106.2 mm, thus making it a non-restricted firearm in Canada. For those of us who are metric-impaired, that's a difference of 0.18 inches.

In order to fit 10 rounds of 9mm into the G48/G43X magazine, Glock had to make the magazine slightly wider than a G43 (which holds six rounds), which caused the frame grip to be a little larger as well. A G43 magazine is 0.68 inch in width, while the G48/G43X magazine is 0.79 inch, which falls about halfway between the G43 and the G19 magazine

The G48 will need its own specific holster, like this one from Wisco Holsters, however the G43X will be able to use holsters made for the G43.

(0.91 inch) in width. This means you won't be able to use G43 mags in your G48 or G43X. Factory six-round G43 magazines are of course, too short, but are also too narrow. If you own extended-round G43 magazines that are long enough, they'll be too narrow to work properly. This also means the 10-round G48/G43X magazines will be too wide to fit in the G43 mag well. The basic grip width (not including mag release or raised portions) of the G48/G43X is 1.02 inch, and the G43 is 0.93.

While we're on the subject of G43 things you can't use with the G48, most holsters will not work either, due to the longer slide on the G48. An open-bottom holster (to accommodate the longer slide) with adjustable retention, might work, but test it first.

If you look at the frame of the G48/G43X compared to the G43, you'll notice a subtle difference in appearance. On the G43, the area around the slide lock, and the same area on the opposite side, is raised, making it a little thicker than the rest of the frame/grip. The frame of the G48/G43X is thicker overall, than the G43, so it doesn't appear to have this raised area.

What is gained by the slimmer G48, over the G19? The answer is that it's a little easier to conceal. Football is a said to be a game of inches. Concealed carry often comes down to tenths of an inch. A great illustration of that was made just a couple paragraphs ago with regard to Canadian gun laws. A mere 0.18 inch makes one gun model legal to own and one gun prohibited. The difference in width between the Glock large frame (i.e., the G20, G21, G40, etc.) and the G19 is only about a tenth of an inch, but that tenth of an inch makes a big difference when carrying it concealed. The difference in width between the G19 and G48 is greater than that, at around 0.15 to 0.20 inch (depending on where you measure). It's a big difference when concealing it, especially when factoring in appendix carry. I've tried

A G43 mag is too small to fit into the mag well of a G48 or G43X.

The grip of the G43 (right) compared to the larger grip of the G43X.

A G48/G43X magazine will not fit in a G43 mag well. It's too big.

appendix carry with the G19, and it's too wide. The G43, on the other hand, works just fine for appendix carry, which means the G48 would be a good width, as well. As long as you can conceal the longer grip, and the longer slide isn't uncomfortable while sitting.

It's also easier to conceal when using off-body carry. I have bags and packs designed with Velcro for attaching a holster, and the G48 works exceedingly well with these bags. The narrower width means less bulge. A couple of my favorite bags for this include Grey Ghost Gear Wanderer Messenger Bag and Gypsy Backpack (greyghostgear.com) both of which allow you to carry all of your daily commuter gear/electronics, plus discreetly conceal a handgun without looking like you're armed; and Hill People Gear Runner Kit Bag (hillpeoplegear.com) that you wear on your chest, and is great for biking, hiking, canoeing and just about anything else. Another favorite off-body "conceal in plain sight" is the G-Outdoors Day Planner (goutdoorsproducts. com). It looks exactly like a generic day planner, but unzip it and there's room for a handgun, spare mags and more. Plus, it's lockable to keep curious hands from gaining access and revealing the contents.

The downside to the G48 (and G43X, as well), is that it holds the same number of rounds as the G26, however you don't have the option of using higher capacity magazines from the G19 and G17. You're stuck using only magazines for the G48/G43X (which use the same magazines). This has been the same drawback to the G43, it can't use magazines from higher capacity Glocks, so if you've been carrying the G43, then this is something you've already taking into consideration and decided it's OK. The G48 gives you a bump up in capacity of four rounds. I mentioned the G43 here, but just to reiterate, and clarify, the G48 and G43X DO NOT use the same magazine as the G43.

In summary, why would you choose the G48 for carry over a G19, if the grip length is the same, yet you have fewer rounds? Overall, it's more comfortable to carry, slimmer and lighter. It boils down to the thinner frame. In this aspect, it will not bulge under your shirt, so it's easier to conceal. It will also be easier to appendix carry, and more comfortable with any sort of IWB carry.

This Wanderer Messenger Bag from Grey Ghost Gear doesn't look like a carry bag, but it is. The G43X (shown) and G48 are a perfect fit, because they are slim so there's no bulge, but offer a full-size grip.

I think the G48 is going to sell by the truckload. Just the fact that it's a slimline G19 will make it popular. Glock owners have been asking for this for a long time. But I think people will discover it fits into another category of handguns as well. The G48 is Glock's answer to the 9mm Commander-size 1911, which has been wildly popular in recent years, with a lot of companies introducing them. One of the things people really like about the 1911 platform is how narrow the slide is; it's great for concealment. The slide is about 0.9 inch (I measured a Ruger SR1911 compact 9mm), compared to a G19 slide at 1.00 inch. The G48 comes in at 0.87 inch, so you a slightly narrower slide than the 1911, but with a grip that's 0.2 inch thinner and 0.6 inch shorter, with one extra round (most standard-capacity 9mm 1911 Commander magazines hold nine rounds). For weight, with empty magazines, the G48 is about 6.25 ounces lighter than the 9mm Commander-size 1911, which is a difference of about 25 percent.

As of July 2019, which happens to be a week before my deadline for this book, Glock has released a black-slide G48.

The G48 was tested with 24 different types of ammo and it ate all of them fine, with no hiccups, except for the SuperVel +P 115-grain JHP. It had a hard time cycling properly with it. No problems with other SuperVel loads or other +P loads.

G43X

You might wonder why I went out of numerical order and placed the G43X after the G48. It's because you really needed to get to know the G48 before the G43X, since the G43X is a hybrid of the G43 and G48, a crossover, which is designated with the "X." If you take the slide of the G43 and place it on the frame of the G48 (which is exactly what Glock did), you get the G43X. In fact, you can do it yourself. If you already own a G43, and buy a G48, combine the G43 slide and G48 frame and you have yourself a G43X.

By using the G48 frame, the G43X gives you 10 rounds, the same capacity as a G26 and SIG Sauer P365, but with a longer grip than those guns have.

The longer grip has pros and cons. The biggest con is that the taller grip is going to print easier than the G43 when you're carrying concealed. It won't be significantly easier than a G19 when it comes to concealing it because the grip is the same height. You might ask, "So why not carry a G19?" I'll answer that later.

There are four big things gained from equipping the G43X with the taller grip. First, the obvious one, higher capacity: 10 rounds of 9mm should solve most problems the armed citizen is going to encounter. A quick reload of another 10 rounds will generally solve the rest of those problems. Second, the longer grip ensures proper mag seating during reloads. Remember back in the "G19 and Other 9mm Glocks" chapter, when I mentioned me swapping from the G26 to the G19 as my primary carry? The same principle will apply to going from the G43 to the G43X (or G48). When gripping the G43, at least one finger will dangle below the mag well, as will the meaty portion of the bottom of your palm. When conducting a rapid reload, all of that can get in the way of inserting the magazine, and can get pinched when trying to seat the mag, causing the mag not to fully lock in. The taller grip of the G43X/G48 is the same height as the G19 grip, and won't cause that problem, ensuring for positive reloads.

The G43X is a crossover featuring the slide of the G43 and the frame of the G48

Take the slide from a G43 (second from right), mate it with a G48 frame (second from left), and you have the G43X (center, upright).

The third thing, a taller grip gives you a more secure grip when drawing from your holster. Try it yourself. Draw your (cleared) G43X (or G19, or any other handgun you can get your full grip on). You can get a nice, high grip on the gun easily, and when you draw, you're in full control. Now try it with a G43, or G26, or another handgun with a short grip. With lots of practice, you can get a high, solid grip on it, but the margin for error is a lot smaller. When the gun is drawn, the same level of control isn't there. The grip you have on the handgun doesn't always feel like it's the most solid grip you can get.

The fourth thing, the longer grip length also gives the G43X better control when shooting it, than does the G43. Getting your full hand on the gun makes it more comfortable to fire and allows the shooter to better control the recoil, which will make for faster, more accurate follow-up shots. Getting your full hand on the gun makes for a more secure grip, and oftentimes with smaller grips I see shooters constantly adjusting their grip on the gun, often between every shot. Do this: The next time you go to the range, record video of yourself shooting the gun. When you watch it, take notice of your hands. Are you constantly readjusting your grip? That's a bad habit, and I see it a lot. In fact, I sometimes do it, especially when shooting short-grip guns. With a full grip, however, I rarely ever do it.

Another plus, holsters that work with the G43 should all work with the G43X. The only dimensional difference between the two is the grip thickness, but holsters don't cover that part of the gun typically, so if you already have a holster for a G43, it should work fine.

The dimensions of the G43X, compared to the G43 and G48 (in parentheses, respectively), are 6.5 (6.26, 7.28) inches overall length, a barrel length of 3.41 (3.41, 4.17) inches, a height (with magazine) of 5.04 (4.25, 5.04) inches, and an overall width of 1.1 (1.06, 1.1) inch. You might notice a couple of differences between the G43 and G43X where you thought there wouldn't be. The reason for the difference in overall length, despite the G43X having the same slide as the G43, the grip of the G43X is taller in height, which means the

The G43X/G48 magazine (left in each of the four images) compared to the G43 mag. In order to fit 10 rounds of 9mm in the G43X/G48 mag, Glock had to make it wider and taller.

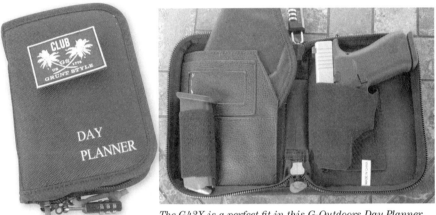

The G43X is a perfect fit in this G-Outdoors Day Planner. The short length helps it fit where a longer slide/barrel won't, but it still holds 10 rounds.

back of the grip extends farther back than the G43, making the overall length longer. Many people make a mental image of overall width being a measurement of the slide width, but that's generally not the case. Often, it's either the slide stop (especially if ambidextrous), mag release or a point on the grip. In this case, the G43X has a wider grip to start with, than does the G43, so any measurement is naturally going to be wider.

Do you want to know how much an approximate 1.2 inch of Glock polymer grip weighs? About half an ounce. That's the difference in weight between the G43X (18.75 ounces) and the G43 (18.25 ounces).

In summary, why would you choose a G43X over a G48? If you're looking for a carry gun that's the width of the G43, but with more rounds, and the G48 slide is too long to be comfortable while sitting, the G43X is the answer. It's about perfect for appendix carry, and any other sort of IWB carry. It offers everything a micro-nine has to offer, but with a full-size grip, it's easier to get your hands on it to draw from your holster and easier to control while firing.

As of July 2019, the G43X now comes in a black-slide version.

CHAPTER 14:
SPECIALTY GLOCKS AND GLOCKS YOU CAN'T HAVE

SPECIALTY GLOCKS

Throughout its history, Glock has manufactured several models of specialty Glocks; some offered to consumers, and some offered only to specific entities. Some specialty models are still available, while others have been discontinued. Some have been offered, then discontinued, then offered, then discontinued once again. It's an important thing to note: If an item has been discontinued, that doesn't mean it will never be produced again. If the numbers are right, Glock will most likely gladly oblige. For example, a new government entity decides tomorrow it wants to place an order for 10,000 G20s in lime-green polymer with compensators. Guess what? Glock is making compensated Glocks again.

COMPENSATED GLOCK

The compensated Glock has a ported barrel and slide and is designated by a "C" after the name. For many manufacturers, a "C" after the name of a pistol indicated it was a compact model, which led to some confusion when looking through the Glock catalog and in stores.

The purpose of a compensated pistol is to redirect gasses up, which helps keep the muzzle down. This improves the speed and accuracy of follow-up shots, as it keeps your sights

Compensated Glock barrel (bottom) next to a standard barrel.

You can't confuse this one with a standard Glock. You can't tell from the B&W photo, but this 17T is bright blue. (instagram.com/robb_manning #robb_manning.glock.book)

closer to the target during recoil. There is debate as to how effective this is in a handgun, but what isn't debatable are the cool pictures that can be found online of V-shaped flames shooting out the ports of a compensated Glock. My first Glock pistol was a 20C.

All standard and compact models through the G32 have come with a compensator at one point or another. The long-slide, subcompact and slimline models have not. According to Glock, compensated models have been offered in G17C, G19C, G20C, G21C, G22C, G23C, G31C and G32C. Glock has since discontinued the compensated models, though you never know when another run could pop up.

PRACTICE MODEL

Practice models come in models designated 17P, 22P, 19P, 23P and 26P, where the number coincides with the number used in the "G" models. It's designated with a red frame. Practice models are identical to their live-fire cousins in weight, dimensions, feel and handling. As it should be, it's a real complete Glock, with a few modifications. For one, the barrel and bore are not drilled out, it's one solid piece. There's no way to load a round into it even if you wanted.

Then Glock went and drilled through the barrel, perpendicular to the bore axis. When you pull back on the slide, you'll see the holes on the side - they look like a compensator has been machined into it. Then, when the action is closed, a hole has been drilled through the top of where the bore should be, showing that this is not an operational barrel. To further make sure it's safe the firing pin hole hasn't been drilled through the breech face, and the firing pin lacks the tip, even if there were a hole to go through.

What is it for? You can practice dry-firing, loading a magazine, sight alignment, trigger squeeze, everything you can do with a regular Glock, except load a cartridge into it. It's perfect, because you can use it for training and not worry that there could accidentally be a live round in the chamber.

It's great for classroom work where someone might need to point a gun at someone else, it's great for instructors to use and not worry about where it's being pointed. Officers can use it to practice weapons handling during arrests, covering suspects, etc. The applications are limitless. Well, not quite limitless. Applications can only involve police departments or military units, civilians can't have one. Glock keeps tighter control on these than they do their regular handguns. They are available only to law enforcement.

RESET MODEL

Comes in models 17R and 19R. It automatically resets the trigger without charging the slide (repeat strike), making it perfect for use with shooting simulators. The laser-impulse generator can be mounted on the accessory rail or integrated in the barrel. When the trigger is pulled, the firing pin strikes as it would in a regular Glock, triggering the impulse. Designated with a light red frame. Available only to law enforcement.

TRAINING MODEL

Models available include 17T FX, 17T UTM, 19T FX, 19T UTM and 26T FX. It comes with a blue frame. These models are designed for force-on-force training. Think paintball gun. It comes in two different cartridges, each with a paint variant and a plastic projectile variant. On the inside, it's mostly the same as other Glocks, except it's blowback operated, like a .22 pistol. They have the same look and feel, and the same weight. The controls are the same, and even the magazines load and operate the same way.

Force-on-force training is a very effective tool, because one side is going against a living, breathing, thinking opponent who is also trying to beat the other team. That kind of training can't be beat. I would have loved this kind of training gun in the Marines. For us, it was in imagined rifle lifted up in imaginary fire as we yelled, "bang, bang, bang." The best we had were blanks with a red BFA (Blank Firing Adaptor) attached to the end of our M16A2s. That just equates to people putting dozens of imagined rounds into each other. It looks more like a Hollywood shootout where the bad guys shoot full mags right at the hero and he doesn't get hit. But to have a paint-marking gun like this would have been most excellent. Visually it shows everyone who got hit, and it also serves as a physical reminder. These little things leave welts.

The plastic projectile ammunition isn't for force-on-force training, but for training in locations where live ammo cannot be used. Situations such as air marshals training on real airplanes, or a hostage rescue teams training in a real office building. The training can be done without worrying about a stray bullet going through a wall and killing someone in the next building, or doing damage to property (such as the airplane).

The 9FX cartridge is just like a standard cartridge, with a primer and propellant that sends the paint-filled plastic pellet on its way. The UTM uses compressed air in a self-contained cartridge to propel the paint. For paint marking or plastic projectiles. Available only to law enforcement.

The Cutaway Glock gives you full view of all the internal operations, including the safety features. It's as cool as it sounds. Now available in Gen5.

CUTAWAY MODEL

The Cutaway is currently available in the G17 Gen4, G19 Gen4, G22 Gen3 and G23 Gen3. These are often found at trade shows, presentations and Glock training courses. Openings are cut strategically throughout the pistol to show all working parts. I first handled one at the Glock armorer's course, and it's a great reference to see the Glock in ways you would never otherwise get to see. Plus, it's really cool to look at. Previous models available include the G17 Gen3, G19 Gen3, G20, and G21.

For this book, Glock shipped me a G17, and without the watchful eye of an armorer's course instructor, I was able to look at it a lot closer, and actually get to take it apart and study it. I've even been able to show it to some novice shooters in my family who were unclear on how exactly how a Glock works, how the safeties function and now they understand. It's very useful. Available only to law enforcement.

GLOCKS YOU CAN'T HAVE

G18

Introduced in 1987. You might have noticed that after the G17 I skipped a model number and went right to the G19. A newcomer to the Glock might question why I did this, but those familiar with the Glock know why. Glock aficionados have drooled over this one ever since it was first announced. It's the fully automatic G18.

The G18 has attained an almost mythical status among the Glock faithful. Picture in your mind the Glock 17. Maybe you own one, maybe you don't, but now imagine it could rattle off 1,200 rounds per minute. It takes one round .05 seconds to fire. That is a rate of 20 rounds per second (keep in mind there are only 33 rounds in a Glock extended magazine). Wow.

The G18 is the handgun on everyone's gun bucket list. A fully automatic 9mm handgun.

While the G18 is based on the G17, there are eight unique parts, plus a different frame. Gaston Glock knows human nature, and he knows the nature of the gun owner. He knew if he made the G18 an exact copy of the G17 plus the go-faster part or parts, then parts would be swapped and/or replicated. So, he made it in such a manner that even if you had G18 parts, you couldn't just add them to a G17. They wouldn't fit.

The G18 shoots at a cyclic rate of 1,200 to 1,400 rounds per minute. That's fast. I think back to my Marine days when my issued weapon was an M249 Squad Automatic Weapon (SAW). It had two settings: fast and faster. At the fast setting it fired 800 rounds per minute. On faster it fired 1,000 rounds per minute. That's really fast, and we were taught only to set it at that high rate of fire when it became gunked up and sluggish at the standard setting. I have fired it at the 1,000-rounds-per-minute setting, and I can tell you, it's ripping fast. Almost like a chainsaw, which makes the name fitting. It's hard to imagine holding something in your hand that shoots faster than that and is way smaller and lighter. I haven't fired one, but with my experience with full-auto weapons, I can't picture the G18 being something you could control, at least not without a lot of training and hands-on time.

One of the issues found in the development of the G18 is that at a cyclic rate of fire that high, there is a lot of friction that generates a lot of heat. Adjustments were made to the frame to allow for cooling as the slide cycles. When looking at a G18, it looks like Glock just took a G17, machined in a space for the selector lever, then reassembled the now-modified G17. This isn't the case, and there are a few key differences, of which Glock is hush-hush about. But the end result is that you can't simply take a G18 slide and mount it to a G17 frame, it won't fit.

Another popular topic is the Drop-In Auto Sear, commonly referred to as a DIAS. The DIAS replaces the slide plate on a standard G17 and comes in a full-auto version and a select-fire version. It's a felony to have one, unless you have the appropriate NFA paperwork, licensing, stamps, etc., but it is far cheaper than purchasing the rare G18 for transfer.

If this is something you can legally get (with paperwork), the next question to be answered is, should you? That is an easy one. NO. Sure, full auto is fun, but this is one that should be passed up. A G17 frame is just not made for full auto and running one at 1,200 rounds per minute is going to cause a lot of heat, and that's a problem.

A G18 has raised slide rails to allow for a larger gap between the frame and the slide, which allows for heat dissipation. If you put a DIAS (or other full-auto replicating device) on a non-G18 Glock, the heat created will compromise the polymer frame. At the least it will lead to sporadic operation and function failures, and at the worst could lead to a catastrophic failure. It's just not worth it.

The G24 is the predecessor of the G35. This one is a compensated model.

G24

The G24 is the .40-caliber equivalent to the G17L. It was introduced six years after the G17L, in 1994, had a great run in competitive shooting, then died off two months after the G17L in June 1999. It suffered the same fate as the G17L — the IPSC Box — and was replaced by the G35, which is the .40 version of the G34. The G24 was never very popular and was a victim of terrible timing on the part of Glock. It was introduced just as the competition world became obsessed with the .38 Super and 25-round magazines, so it wasn't met with much fanfare. Then just as the competition world was moving back to the likes of the G24, out came the IPSC box. Glock introduced the G35, and the G24 went out with a whimper. Not a lot of them were sold. The G35, on the other hand, was quite popular, until the .40 S&W fell out of favor.

G25 AND G28

Not a lot of information can be found on the G25 and G28, because they aren't imported into the United States. Both are blowback operated and chambered in .380 ACP. The G25 is the compact-size equivalent to the G19 (which is big for a .380), and the G28 is the sub-compact equivalent to the G26.

The G28 is a subcompact .380, but you'll never see it on this side of the pond, unless you're law enforcement.

The Glock website reports these are law-enforcement only, and supposedly it is something law-enforcement agencies can get their hands on. However, I cannot picture these being hot sellers inside the U.S. law-enforcement market, when we have access to all the other calibers Glock has, but in smaller packages. Who would issue their officers a G19 size handgun in a .380? I hope no one. Since it's blowback operated, it doesn't meet the minimum point requirement for import into the U.S., for civilians.

The G25 and G28 are offered because some countries do not allow arms of military calibers. The 9mm is off limits, and apparently the .45 ACP and .40 S&W are more for American tastes. One would think the .357 SIG would be offered in these countries as a viable option. Nope, they want a .380.

Now that Glock production facilities have been set up inside the U.S., it's entirely possible these two models could be made here and offered to the civilian populace. It would be extremely surprising if that ever happened, especially now with the G42 model being available. Even though it's completely not practical, as a collector, it would still be fun to own a G25 or G28.

Occasionally, G25 and G28 Glocks do show up on Internet auction websites. It's rare, and they're not cheap, being a collector's item. Despite the restrictions on importation, it's not illegal to own one. Once they're here, they're here. I do know at least one collector who has one of each.

For a look at the interesting magazine that's used for these two models, see Chapter 15.

Glock 46 left-side view.
(Photo by Glock.)

G46

The G46 was designed to fill a contract with the German state of Saxony-Anhalt for its 6,000-plus officers. Rumors about this one were around the Internet for a while, but a U.S.-based gun magazine published photos taken from a German-language magazine with an article and photos of the G46. It's very unique, because instead of the modified Browning cam-locking system used by the majority of modern handguns, it uses a rotary barrel design.

One of the key features is that it won't require the trigger to be pulled for disassembly, and there's a knob where the slide cover plate is normally, that is twisted for firing pin removal. The left side of the pistol has what looks like a small safety lever on the frame, but it's unclear if this is a safety, or decocker, or both.

I have been able to confirm only limited information on the G46 at the time of this writing. It's my understanding that changes have been made since the initial article was written. Glock will not confirm details about this pistol at this time and has provided only limited photos. As of this time, the G46 will not be available in the German or European commercial market, nor will it be available in the U.S.

G47

The G47 was designed to fill a contract for the U.S. Customs and Border Protection agency (CBP) and was announced along with versions of the G26 Gen5, G19 Gen5 MOS FS. The

Glock 46 right-side view.
(Photo by Glock.)

G47 is basically the G45, but with a G17 size barrel. Whoa, wait a minute. You might be wondering, the G45 is essentially a G17 frame with a G19 Barrel, so if a G47 is a G45 with a G17 barrel, isn't it just a G17? If you're wondering that, you're not alone, I was asking myself the same question. Except keep in mind, the G45 frame isn't exactly a G17 grip, it has a shorter dust cover to accommodate the G19 slide. Given the shorter dustcover, a standard G17 slide wouldn't work, so a special slide with an extended recoil spring hole (a.k.a. "nose ring"), like that found on a G34, is used for the G47. Which means the G47 can be described as a G17 with a shorter dustcover.

Seems kind of silly to me. I'm not sure why that would be something an agency would have a custom order for. As of this writing, Glock is still holding details about the contract as confidential information. I do think it looks neat, kind of like a shorter-barreled G34, but I don't base my carry-gun needs off looks.

I don't know if Glock will offer this on the commercial market in the future, but as of this writing, they do not and don't have plans to do so.

There are photos on the Internet showing the G47, but they're not official photos. At the time of this writing, Glock has not confirmed information about the G47 and contract, nor will it provide official photos. Because there could be changes made before the gun actually hits the hands of CBP agents, I do not want to include faulty information or incorrect photos, so my information on it is limited, and I have no photos at this time.

CHAPTER 15:
MAGAZINES AND ACCESSORIES

C heap plastic crap. That's what we would have called it 30 years ago. And for the most part, 30 years ago stuff made out of plastic was pretty much crap. Much has changed in 30 years, most notably the strength of plastic, as well as our opinion on plastic. In the gun world, Glock is the reason why our opinion on plastic has changed. Glock is the godfather of polymer pistols and is still the best at it. There are other companies that do a great job of making polymer and have made great progress, but none have yet to catch Glock.

But Glock isn't just about polymer handguns, it makes other polymer products equally well. The Glock line of accessories all are based on the same driving principles as its handguns. Simple. Tough. Works well. Priced right (note: I didn't use the word "cheap," I used "priced right." They are offered at a reasonable price, and for the quality you get, it's a very good deal).

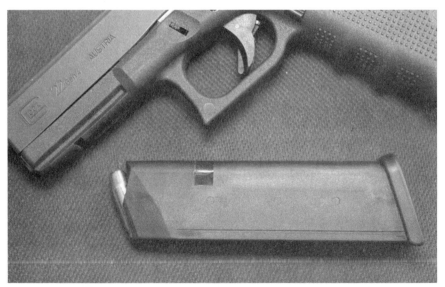

Glock magazines are about as fine as you can get. They're extremely tough and reliable.

In most books about gun companies, the chapter about accessories isn't as important as the chapters about the actual firearms, like they're almost an afterthought. With Glock, however, when you're talking about accessories, you're talking about how the company got started. When Gaston founded the Glock company in 1963, it wasn't to produce firearms. Some of the things he made were a knife/bayonet for the Austrian army, the Feldmesser 78; an entrenching tool (feldspaten); and grenade casings (the plastic shell that the fragments and explosives are housed in). He also made plastic and metal items, such as shower rods, for the civilian market.

MAGAZINES

One thing I often hear or read is that Glock magazines aren't forward compatible, specifically that previous generation magazines won't work in Gen4 Glocks. This isn't entirely accurate; in fact, it's only the case approximately 10 percent of the time, because 10 per-

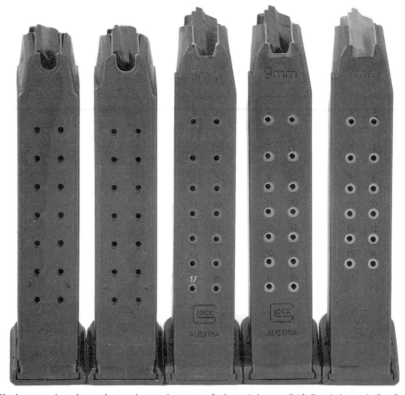

Glock magazines have changed over the years. Left to right are G17 Gen1 through Gen5. All will work in all generations of that same caliber, with the exception that Gen1 through Gen3 mags won't work with a Gen4 or Gen5 handgun that has had the magazine catch reversed to the right-hand side for a left-handed shooter. (Note: The G17 Gen5 mag on the right is from a restricted state and takes only 15 rounds.)

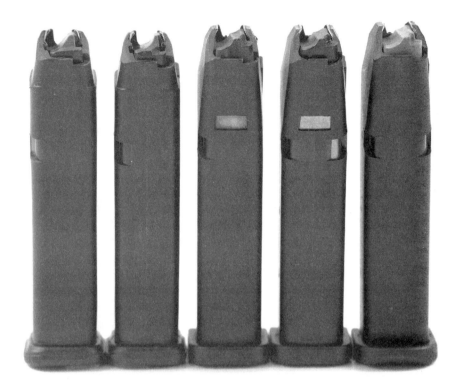

cent of people are left-handed, and therefore will switch the Glock magazine catch to the right side (the side for left-handed shooters). Of course, I don't know what percentage of left-handed shooters are right-eye dominant and won't switch the mag catch, or how what additional percentage of right-handed shooters are left-eye dominant and will switch. The gist, however, is the old magazines are only affected when the ambidextrous magazine catch is switched.

If you have an older Glock there are no worries if you do lose or break a magazine, because new magazines will work. When you have a rock-solid workhorse like a Glock, the last thing you want is to have it phased out due to not being able to feed it ammunition because of magazine incompatibility.

You won't be in that situation with an old Glock. My G17 Gen1 and Gen2 work just as well as my Gen3, Gen4 and Gen5 Glocks, and thanks to backward compatible magazines I can keep using them. If those magazines break or get lost, I'll always be able to buy new ones that will work in it. On the flip side, I can grab those old magazines and they'll work in my new Gen4 G17, as long as I don't flip the magazine release. The only exception to that is you can't use Gen5 magazines in the G19X, but not because the magazine won't fit, per se, but because the Gen5 magazine baseplate is blocked by the G19X's magwell finger tab.

There are essentially three main size categories of magazines, standard, compact, and subcompact, plus some additional sizes that could be classified as oddball. The standard-size magazines come with the standard-frame models, such as the G17, G22 and G34, and also come in a large frame size for the large-frame handguns (10mm and .45 ACP) like the

Glock Slimline magazines (left to right): G36, G42, G43, G43X/G48.

The G42 magazine is its own entity. No other Glock magazine is like it.

G20 and G21. The standard-size magazines also work in the compact and subcompact pistols of the same caliber. A G17 magazine, for example, can work with a G19 and/or G26 handgun. The 9mm magazine in this category holds 17 rounds.

Compact-size magazines come with the compact-frame handguns, such as the G19 and G23, and also work with the subcompact framed pistols of the same caliber, but not the standard-frame pistols. For example, a G19 magazine would be too short to work in a G17, but it works in a G26. The 9mm magazine in this category holds 15 rounds. There is no large-frame compact handgun (10mm and .45 ACP) equivalent.

The third category is the subcompact magazines, which are for the subcompact handguns like the G26 and G27. These do not work in any of the compact or standard-frame models of the same caliber. For example, a G26 magazine would be too short to work in a G19 or G17. The 9mm magazine in this category holds 10 rounds. The large-frame handguns (10mm and .45 ACP) do have a subcompact version, for the G29 and G30.

Next are the oddballs. I first have to mention the Slimline magazines. I'm including them in oddballs, because for the most part, each magazine works only in one specific model. At the time of the first edition of this book, the only oddball magazines were the G36 in the .45 ACP, the G42 mag in .380 ACP and the brand new G43 in 9mm (which was released after the book was submitted to printer). Now the Slimline lineup has grown a bit, and includes the G43X and G48, which both use the same magazine. Both of these are Slimline 9mm, like the G43, however they do not use the same magazine as the G43 and are not cross-compatible. A G43 magazine will not work in a G43X or G48, and the G43X/

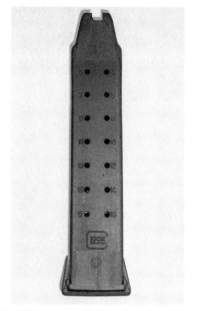
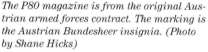

The P80 magazine is from the original Austrian armed forces contract. The marking is the Austrian Bundesheer insignia. (Photo by Shane Hicks)

A close-up of the P80 Austrian Bundesheer insignia. (Photo by Shane Hicks)

G48 magazine will not work in the G43. The reason for the different size magazine is because the target goal of the G43X and G48 was 10-round capacity, and apparently Glock could not make it happen with the G43 magazine under the parameters it set. In order to hit that goal, Glock had to make the magazine a little wider (and subsequently, the pistol grip had to be widened as well).

Next is the high-capacity magazine that holds 33 rounds of 9mm (and the .40 S&W equivalent that holds 22 rounds). It works in all the 9mm pistols, except Slimline pistols, and looks especially lethal in the G26 (tongue in cheek). The next one, which is mostly forgotten in most states, is the infamous 10-round magazine. These were brought on by the 1994 Assault Weapons Ban, which restricted magazine capacity to 10 rounds. This ban expired in 2004, and gone were the 10-round magazines, except in states which kept the ban, such as Massachusetts and California. Those states still use the 10-round magazine. The rest of us can find them online; they do make great magazines for GSSF competitions. Since the first edition was written, more restrictive laws have been written in some states, and for example, some states limit pistol magazine capacity to 15 rounds. And so Glock has had to respond to those consumers by making 15-round magazines for the G17.

Once you get outside the realm of these magazines, you start to get into some real oddball territory. Rare magazines, magazines only found outside the U.S. and one-off magazines. I had a great discussion with a Glock collector, and he opened my eyes to some Glock things I didn't even know existed. What's probably the Holy Grail of Glock magazines, the P80 magazine, will set you back about $600, or more. It has an upside-down triangle inside

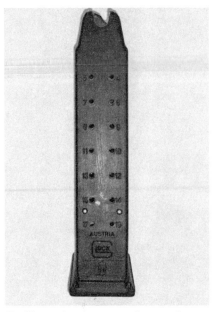

The Norwegian Army was the second contract Glock was awarded. Here's a magazine from that contract. Note the Norwegian Army Shield at the bottom. (Photo by Shane Hicks)

No, that's not an acorn; it's the shield of the Norwegian Army. (Photo by Shane Hicks)

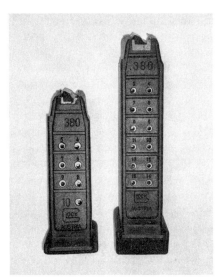

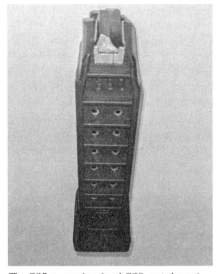

The Glock G28 (left) and G25 "ladder" magazines are very rare inside the U.S., but can be found on gun-auction websites. (Photo by Shane Hicks)

The G25 magazine (and G28, not shown) has a back that resembles a ladder. (Photo by Shane Hicks)

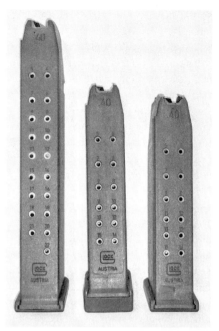

Looks like a G19X Dark Earth mag, smells like a G19X mag, but closer inspection reveals it's not. The ".40" gives it away. This is a Delta Force contract magazine.

The three mag types that are part of the Delta Force .40 S&W contract (left to right): 22 round, 15-round-plus extended baseplate and 15 round. (Photo by Shane Hicks)

of a circle – the Austrian Bundesheer insignia – and pre-dates the G17 Gen1. Another super-rare Glock magazine is from the Norwegian contract, and also fetches $500-plus. It has the Norwegian shield on it. Two other magazines that are also pretty rare, and I've been told fetch around $200 to $300, though I've never seen them in online auctions, are the G25 and G28 "ladder magazines." To make 9mm Glock mags fit the .380 bullet, the back wall of the magazine sleeve was moved forward for the shorter round, but ribs, or ladders, were left in place so it would still fit in a standard 9mm sized mag well. Another unique magazine that's a lot easier to find, looks a lot like the G19X Dark Earth colored magazine. Nearly identical, to be exact, except for the ".40" marked on the back. It's from a Delta Force contract for the G23. It came in three types: 15 round, 15-round-plus extended baseplate and a 22 round. I found the 15-round-plus extended baseplate online for $50.

MAGAZINE CHANGES

Note: One thing to keep in mind with Glock magazines, the generations I have listed below are not necessarily concrete correlations between generations of Glock handguns. For the most part, there is a correlation, but not always. Just like Glock handguns, Glock magazines often "evolve" over time, and don't necessarily have a specific date in which one generation ceases and another begins. From what I have seen, this is most often the case as one magazine generation nears the end of its run, you'll see some "evolution," and then as the new generation becomes official, those evolutions/changes are incorporated into that new generation and then you'll see more of a direct correlation between mag generations and handgun generations. One example is the cutout of exposed metal above the mag catch notches. You'll find magazines that by all other criteria are Gen3, but they don't have that metal notch. I've also seen magazines that are Gen5, but don't have the orange follower.

GEN1

The first magazine was not fully metal lined, and didn't have a disassembly hole in the floor plate. The shoulder had a prominent ledge, which would disappear by the third generation. The very first magazines did not drop free, which is something European makers prefer. You had to press the mag catch button and pull the magazine out with the other hand. The premise is that since the shooter already has his or her hand on the magazine, he or she might as well keep it and stow it away.

However, American shooters prefer the mag to drop free and get out of the way. As the first mag is dropping, the shooter already has the next magazine ready for reload. I've seen videos of some shooters who have the next magazine loaded before the first one even has time to hit the ground. To answer the call, Glock stopped making drop-free mags.

The Gen1 magazine was rounded at the top where the slide picks up the cartridge, and the follower had two legs with a hole on the right side for the magazine spring to rest in. The floor plate had no hole for disassembly.

The shoulder of a first generation magazine had a prominent ledge.

GEN2

The Glock armorer's book doesn't break out a second generation of magazine, but enough changes have been made that it should. At the least, you should know it's out there. For one, the floor plate now has a hole to assist in disassembly. It's still not easy, but it's better than it was. To go with the hole, an insert was added that had a nub that locked into the hole. The shoulder ledge on the left side of the magazine now also has an angle added to it, toward the rear of the side. The follower also changed and now has a hole that goes through the whole follower base, where the magazine spring connects with it. This magazine was also not fully lined.

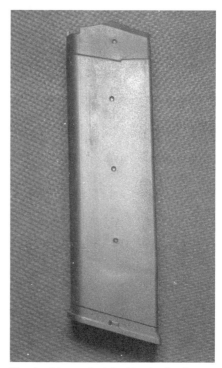

The Gen2 magazine still has the prominent ledge for a shoulder. The floor plate now has a hole for ease of disassembly, and the follower now has a hole on the right side for the magazine spring to connect to.

The shoulder on the left side of a Gen2 magazine has an added angle that the Gen1 magazine did not have.

GEN3

Just like in the Gen3 handguns, the Gen3 magazines have had the most changes since the previous generation. The magazine went through a pretty major overhaul. First, the magazine sleeve went through some changes, most noticeable a notch added to the front of the magazine, just above the magazine catch notch, exposing the metal liner. It also had the shoulder near the top smoothed out, so it's no longer a ledge.

The Gen3 magazine has had the shoulder smoothed out so there is no ledge.

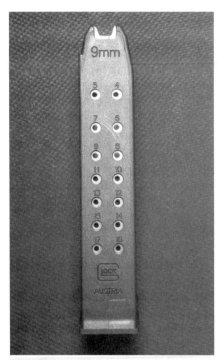

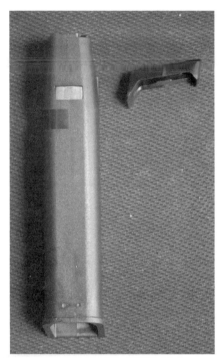

The Gen3 magazine has larger cartridge view holes, a caliber marking at the top, and the exposed metal at the cartridge feed slot is now squared off instead of round.

The Gen3 mag follower is completely different, and there is now a notch above the mag catch notch.

On the back of the magazine sleeve, at the top where the cartridge is picked up out of the magazine, the exposed metal liner is squared off instead of rounded. Also, the cartridge-view holes are larger, with more metal liner exposed. The caliber is now marked prominently at the top back of the magazine. Internally, the magazine spring has changed, as has the insert. The follower also went through a big change and is completely different. The magazine tube is now fully lined.

GEN4
There's one major difference between the Gen3 and Gen4 magazine, and that is the mag catch slot cut on right side of mag, for left-hand shooters. This makes the magazine ambi-

The Gen4 magazine sleeve is now ambidextrous.

dextrous. It's a big step forward, and it's good to see Glock make the step. Aside from that, there's no other difference between magazines.

GEN5

The Gen5 magazines have seen the most changes since the Gen3 magazine came about. Most noticeably, it now has an orange follower. It makes it easier to see when the mag is empty, but can also be spotted through the capacity-indicator view holes on the back of the magazine. The baseplate has also changed, it's now longer in the front with an oval shape, instead of squared off. It works alongside the mag well half-moon notch on the Gen5 to allow for stuck mags to be ripped from the pistol easier. I didn't even know that was a problem with Glock magazines. But since it was something Glock did to appease the FBI, I guess apparently the FBI had concerns. I've had rare situations where a round isn't entirely stripped from the magazine, and to clear the handgun I've had to take the mag out, and it was a little harder than usual, but not that big an issue. And it wasn't with a Glock pistol, which I've never had issues with. The other change in the Gen5 is to the magazine tube itself – it no longer has the notch of exposed metal above the magazine catch notch that was incorporated into the Gen3 and Gen4 mag tube. The exposed metal in the mag catch itself is also no longer present.

Some of these changes could filter down through all new production models. If you buy a new production of a Gen3 or Gen4 model, you could possibly see some of these mags with Gen5 changes. I'm not sure if you'll see the baseplate in non-Gen5 models, but as supplies of Gen4 magazine tubes and followers dwindle, it's feasible to think you'll see Gen5 versions ship with Gen3 and/or Gen4 pistols. I'm also not sure when or if you'll see Gen5 orange followers in non-9mm magazines (calibers are marked on the follower). In the G32 I just mentioned, that's .357 SIG, of which there is no Gen5 in that caliber, so I'm not sure if Glock will make an orange follower marked as such.

Previous generations of ambidextrous magazines (Gen4) will work with Gen5 pistols regardless of if the mag catch is set up for right- or left-hand shooters, but Gen3 and earlier magazines will only work with Gen5 pistols if it's set up for right-hand shooters, because those magazines are not ambidextrous.

The Gen5 magazine no longer has the Gen4 cutout notch of exposed metal above the mag catch, or the exposed metal in the mag catch, plus it has a new baseplate and a new orange follower.

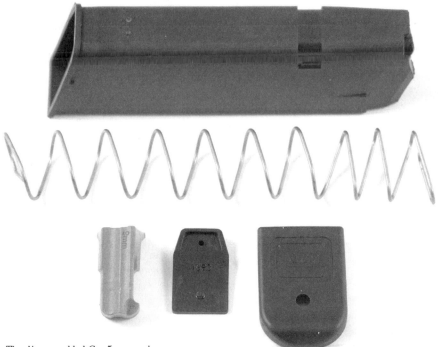

The disassembled Gen5 magazine.

GLOCK MAGAZINE LOADERS

Glock magazine loaders have gone through a few changes over the years, primarily cosmetic. The original loaders were very basic, with a Glock logo on top, and a smooth, non-textured side. My G17 Gen2 from 1992 has the same mag loader. I have a gap in Glocks from that one, until my next Glock I bought which had a born-on date of 2010, so I'm not sure of the loader styles between those dates.

Of the different loaders I've seen, I have found absolutely no rhyme or reason as to what loader comes with what Glock. It's not by generation, because you can have a Glock Gen4 made in 2009, and a Gen3 made in 2018, both with the same style of loader. More likely it's by when the specific Glock was made, but even that isn't always the case. The noticeable changes between various loaders are the texture on the side, if there's a model number and where it's located, and which side is marked.

I have a G22 Gen4 from 2010 that the loader is textured with Gen3 pistol texture, is marked on the right side and with a scan code. I have a G26 Gen4 from 2013 that has a similar texture but smaller, marked on the left side and has a model number 483-3. My G19 Gen5 FS is exactly like the one from the 2010 G26, but the other, non-FS G19 Gen5 I have is like that one, but marked on the left side. My G19X, from 2018, has the same loader as the one from 2010 (which is proof that there's no method to the madness). My G43X and

G48 mag loaders are textured like the pistol grips they came with, marked on the left side, with the model number 47814, marked near the bottom, separate from the logo. These are physically different from the rest because they have four ribs on the inside, two on each side, to go with the narrower magazine. They don't work with magazines from standard or large-frame Glocks. My G42 and G43 pistols did not come with a mag loader.

I have two large-frame Glocks, which come with a larger loader. My newer G40 Gen4 from 2015 came with a loader that's a larger version of the one mentioned above from

Four different loaders (L to R): G22 Gen4, G26 Gen4, G19 Gen5, G48.

The original Gen1 G17 came with a crude magazine loader, no texture, just a Glock logo on the top.

For some inexplicable reason, Glock marked the right side of the magazine loader that came with the author's large-frame Glock G20C in 2012 (left), but in 2015 the company marked the left side, which is customary on all the standard-frame-sized Glock loaders he has seen, on the loader that came with the G40 Gen4 (right).

2010, marked with the model number 5173. My older G20C Gen3 loader is almost identical, except marked on the right side.

My only guess is that there are massive bins, and when Glock makes runs of mag loaders, everything gets dumped into the bin, regardless of what style loader it is, and when the gun is packaged to ship to retailers, it's random what loader ships with the pistol (unless it's large frame or Slimline, they get their own bin).

ACCESSORIES

GLOCK ENTRENCHING TOOL

Known in the Austrian army as Feldspaten, the E-Tool is a very different design than the one issued to me while I was in the Marines, and for that matter I haven't seen anything like it issued to any other country. The handle telescopes out in two sections that you twist to lock. Fold open the shovel and twist the handle to lock it into the spade position, or a 90-degree angle for hacking stuff. The polymer handle fills your hand nicely.

I've dug, I've hacked, I've chopped and this is one tough E-Tool. I've bent a few of the all-metal E-Tools issued to us, and I've even broken one. But I haven't hurt this one yet. I have one in my ATV, and I love it so much I got another to keep in my truck. I'd like to get another one just to keep in my bugout bag. It's a great tool to have around.

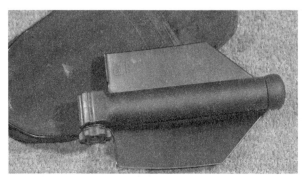

The Glock E-Tool folds into a nice little package. Turn the knob to open, turn it again to close.

Though it's not a substitute for an actual branch saw, it works well in the field for clearing shooting lanes. It's a great addition to have in the E-Tool.

The E-Tool fully extended with the saw.

GLOCK FIELD KNIVES: MODEL 78 AND MODEL 81

There are two models of Field Knives, or Feldmesser, in the Austria Army: the Model 78 and Model 81. Both are available in four colors: battlefield green, black, gray and sand. They were developed with the direct input of Austrian Army Rangers. The Model 78 is a standard 6.5-inch field knife with a clip-point blade made of spring steel with a Rockwell hardness of 50 to 55, and a black, non-reflective phosphate treatment. The blade is 3/16 inch thick and is solid. It has a non-slip polymer handle and is super tough, just like Glock pistols. The guard keeps your hand away from the blade and doubles as a bottle opener, of which I can vouch for. Just be watchful of what you do with the blade when you open that bottle. It's very sharp. The total length is 11.4 inches.

It's also balanced for throwing, and I'm a big fan of any knife you can throw. Not because I am an 1980s movie action hero, but because I just like throwing stuff. I really like the design of the kydex sheath. The knife can go in either way, for mounting on your right or left side, and the lock is simple, yet very secure.

The Model 81 is the same, except with a saw on the back of the knife, which Glock refers to as a root saw. The saw is an interesting design. The serrations are crosscut, forming an X, instead of typical serrations that run perpendicular to the blade. With it, I can saw through a two-inch sapling in no time at all. This knife would make an outstanding survival knife.

The edge on a Glock field knife is very good. Out of the box it's sharp, and it holds its edge well. It's not for knife snobs, but a good working knife. The knife itself is very durable. It's a slender knife, made for fighting, but very solid. I used my Model 78 to cut down a three-inch tree, and did it in no time. For how much this thing costs, I don't think you can find a better knife. It's not as heavy duty as a K-Bar, but it's darn close. If a K-Bar is 50/50 fighting/utility knife, I would say the Glock Knife is 70/30 fighting/utility knife. I've done plenty of hacking of small branches and it's still as solid as when it was new in box. The tang runs through the length of the handle, however the last several inches open up into a cavity to insert an adaptor that turns it into a bayonet, which is the issue bayonet for the Austrian Army.

It's very solid metal, and you're not going to get any blade wobble. When I'm up in my Northwoods cabin, I always have mine with me. In fact, I bought one and liked it so much I've bought one of each color. I've used it like a hatchet to cut saplings and I've used it like a machete to clear brush. I'd like to say I've gutted a deer with it, but I haven't been so lucky the last few seasons.

Model 78 (bottom) and Model 81. Both are the same, except the 81 has a saw on the blade back.

We've seen this before. The texture looks a little on the familiar side, too.

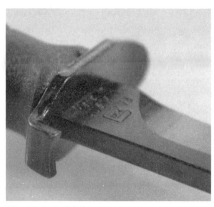

The blade is 3/16 inch and heavy duty. The bottle opener works well, too.

The model 81.

Remove the cap, insert the bayonet adaptor into the rear cavity, and the Feldmesser 78/81 becomes a bayonet.

The saw found on the model 81 has a unique and effective design. Soft woods will clog it up though, so keep the teeth clean while cutting.

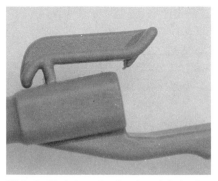

Slide the blade into the sheath and the latch locks securely onto the guard. It's extremely secure.

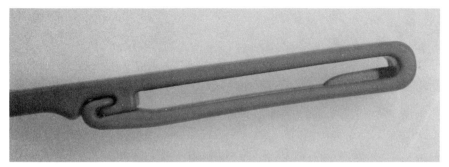

The belt attachment is ingenious and very secure.

GLOCK TACTICAL LIGHTS: GTL-10 AND GTL-22

I don't know how many people know this, but Glock makes tactical weapon lights, too. Two models to be exact, and they are made quite well, using the ultra-tough Glock polymer. One is a tactical light only, and one is a light/laser combo. The GTL-10 tactical light uses a Xenon bulb, has a 70-lumen focusable beam, and weighs three ounces with batteries. The GTL-22 light/laser combo uses the same light, but adds a laser. You can zero the laser to your handgun for accuracy. It can be set to four modes: off, light only, laser only or light and laser. The batteries seem to last, I change batteries on all of my lights and lasers once per year whether they need new batteries or not, and my GTL-22 always still turns on when it's time to change them. It can also be mounted on rifle accessory rails. I will mount mine on my AR on occasion.

Did I mention that it's tough? A lot of companies talk of the durability of their products, and how well they stand up to the elements. I can tell you firsthand how well the GTL 22 stands up to the elements, and not by my intention. I mounted my new, hot-out-of-the-box GTL 22 onto my new, hot-out-of-the-box G34. The problem was it didn't completely lock into place, but it felt firm enough. I was up at my cabin, shooting some gun video for my YouTube channel. I was shooting through my last magazine, with the GTL 22 mounted, but not turned on. I was testing how it affected the already minimal recoil. The slide locked to the rear, so with the gun pointed down range I dropped the magazine and racked the slide a couple times and peered over the top into the chamber for a safety check. I placed the Glock in my range bag and loaded it in my truck for home. Later that night, upon taking the G34 out of the range bag, I noticed the GTL 22 was missing. It wasn't so much a "noticed" as it was an, "Oh, crap!" moment. I frantically felt around the range bag, but nothing.

I pulled out the video camera and watched the video clip of the G34. Sure enough, two rounds before the end of the magazine the light rolled off the front. I noted the spot in the yard where I was standing in the video. Unfortunately, I knew it would be two weeks before I was up to my cabin again. I was kicking myself, and hoping the light would be OK. My land sits about two miles from the Wisconsin river, and the part of the land on which my cabin sits is not much higher than the river water level, so it stays pretty moist most of the year. And 2014 was wetter than most, due to the melt-off of the unusually large amount of snow for northern Wisconsin coupled with the unusually wet spring. Puddles were everywhere and what wasn't a puddle felt like a wet, spongy bog. During the two-week period

Did you know that Glock makes tactical lights and a laser?

A great combo — The G17 Gen4 and a GTL 22.

the GTL 22 lay there neglected in the elements, the area was subjected to no less than three serious thunderstorms and an almost daily shower.

Upon returning to the cabin, the grass was longer and the surface just as wet. I was concerned I wouldn't find it. The worry was unfounded. After less than a minute of searching, I retrieved the GTL 22, half submerged in a puddle of muck. I wiped it off and it looked no worse for wear. After doing a quick function check, it was working perfectly. In fact, after wiping it down later that evening, it looks just like it did when I pulled it from the box.

Some say the 70-lumen light isn't bright enough, but I found it to be more than adequate. Is it time for them to upgrade to an LED light of higher lumens? Sure. But until then, this one still works great. I really like the adjustable light; I found that having a room-filling light is great for home defense, which is better for me than a focused beam. In that scenario, the light is plenty bright enough for a long hallway, it doesn't need to reach out to 50 yards. And since the light isn't a focused beam, but fills the room, you don't have to point your firearm at a person to identify him or her, which you absolutely do not want to do when you have family in the house.

HOLSTERS

Glock makes two simple yet effective holsters. They aren't my first choice in a carry holster, yet they are very serviceable, and are cheap enough that you can have them around, just in case you might need a holster. The first is a duty holster, and it covers the entire handgun except the grip. It also comes with a retention strap to prevent gun snatchings. It fits all the standard-size Glocks of standard frame and slide, which are the G17, G22 and G31. It has a slide-through belt slot and two drain holes in the bottom. It comes in left- or right-hand models, and it costs about $21 on the Glock website.

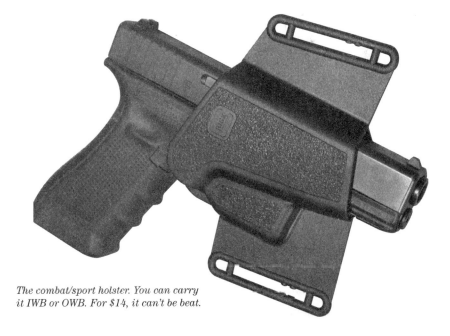

The combat/sport holster. You can carry it IWB or OWB. For $14, it can't be beat.

The duty holster. It's a great, cost-effective choice.

The other model is the sport/combat holster, which Glock sells for $14. This one covers from about halfway up the magazine catch button down to just in front of the trigger guard. This one is an open-bottom holster which gives you the option of holstering the subcompact and compact frames, as well as the full-size models. It comes in two models, one for the standard-frame models, and one for the large-frame models (which also hold the .45 GAP models). One or the other holster fits all models of Glock except the G36, G42 and the Slimline 9mm. It has belt slots on both ends of the holster, with cutouts so you can cut it to fit your belt. It also allows for Outside the Waistband (OWB) or Inside the Waistband (IWB) carry.

Glock also makes several models of mag pouches, which it sells for $12. Glock makes a small and large for standard- and large-frame magazines, plus one model for G42 mags and one model for G43 mags. Nothing yet for G43X/G48 mags.

GLOCK CO2 AIR GUN

Glock has an officially licensed CO2 air gun made by Umarex. I was happy to see it. I look at replica air guns as a good training aid. It's a good-looking replica, with a metal slide, however the follow-through wasn't so good. A Glock competitor has a line of CO2 air guns with the same look and feel of its firearms, they have a very similar set up for controls and even reciprocating slides/actions. These make for great train-

The Glock CO2 air gun by Umarex. It's a good BB gun, but it could be made to be more realistic for training with a reciprocating slide.

The Glock CO2 airgun looks like a G19 Gen3. Note the cross-bolt safety on the trigger.

ing tools, because you rack the slide the same and the controls are located where they should be.

The Glock CO2 air gun doesn't have any of that, and I was disappointed. The mag release is properly located and works, but the slide doesn't reciprocate, and the slide catch doesn't work. It has a cross-bolt safety on the trigger, which I understand having a safety, from a safety aspect, since younger kids could be using it, however I

The easy-load magazine holds 16 BBs. The backstrap panel comes off and the CO2 cartridge is inserted, then tightened using the bolt in the photo.

don't like the location. In order to take the safety off, it requires the shooter to put his finger inside the trigger guard space and fiddle with the trigger, which forces the shooter to violate one of the golden rules of gun safety. Not a good thing to teach young kids. It's kind of quirky though because it moves to the left for safe, and right for fire, which means you can't use the trigger finger to take it off safe if you are right-handed, you must use your left hand, or rotate the thumb of your right hand. Plus, the safety doesn't have a positive engagement on or off, it relies on friction (very little friction), and so it can easily work its way on or off during shooting.

It has a lower price point than the other brand, but I'd pay more for a more realistic working replica air gun. However, aside from the negatives, it's a good airgun that's built well with a solid feel. It has a similar heft to a loaded Glock. The removable magazine has an easy-load feature and holds 16 rounds of .177 BBs. It shoots at 410 fps.

You can find all kinds of Glock memorabilia on the Glock website or on auction sites.

MISCELLANEOUS STUFF

Those who love the Glock, really love the Glock. To some, the Glock just looks like a non-descript brick, but to others, it's the image of the modern-day handgun. Its image is as recognizable as an AK47 or an AR15. Those who love the Glock, love to collect Glock stuff. While a few things, such as coffee mugs and patches, can be found on the Glock website, there's a lot of fun stuff that can be found on various auction websites such as eBay.

You can find keychains, pictures, crystal paperweights, press passes to historic events and much, much more. Probably one of my favorite things I've seen is a 1-to-5 scale working, non-firing, replica of a Glock. The slide functions, the magazine comes out and the trigger pulls. I haven't gotten my hands on one yet, but I want one.

CHAPTER 16:
MAINTENANCE/DISASSEMBLY (WITH GEN5 UPDATES)

C leaning and maintenance on my Glock have been two of the things I have struggled with the most. It's the simplest weapon maintenance there is, which is why it has been a hard conversion for me. For the duration of my entire Marine Corps infantry career, every Friday we would march ourselves down to the armory and check out our weapon for maintenance. For the first couple years, my issue weapon was an M16A2. The next few years it was an M249 Squad Automatic Weapon (SAW) and M9 Beretta. After that it was just an M9.

A big part of that was slathering so much CLP in and on the weapon that trying to hold it was like trying to grab an oiled-up piglet at a state fair. One weapon got as much CLP as what the entire Austrian Army uses on all their Glocks. The amount used was dependent on the unit and the armorer, though. While at Twentynine Palms, California, (which in case you haven't been there, is a bone-dry desert) we didn't use as much. Sand sticks to CLP. But while in the sub-tropic of Okinawa, Japan, our armorer told us if he didn't see a puddle of CLP on the floor beneath our rifle when he came in Monday morning, he would call us back in, and for good reason. Most weapons needed it.

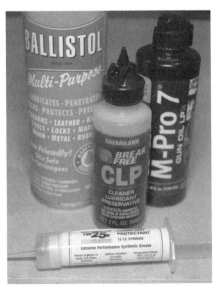

Some different products that work great with Glock. You'll only need about seven drops.

I remember when we went on a short cruise from Okinawa to South Korea on the USS Dubuque, we slathered on the CLP until it was dripping off, then loaded the weapons into the Conex box. Upon reaching our destination, we stood in line to receive our weapons. As the armorer handed each of us our weapons, just about every surface that wasn't plastic or alloy, had a faint hint of orange rust on it. This, despite all the CLP we put on it.

None of that is a concern with Glock pistols, and at first it was hard for me to

THE 4-IN-1 TOOL FOR GLOCK

It doesn't take a lot of tools to work on a Glock. For most tasks, the Glock tool is all you'll need. But for armorer work, you'll need the Glock tool (or punch), needle-nose pliers and small flat-blade screwdriver. Throw in the front sight tool and the tool for adjustable rear sights and now you're up to five tools. Real Avid has you covered for four of those tools in the 4-in-1 Tool For Glock. It has a 3mm pin punch, flat-blade screwdriver, .050-inch Allen wrench for adjustable rear sights and 3/16-inch hex nut driver for front sight removal. All packed into one neat Swiss-Army-type handle. Each tool is auto-opening – press each button

The Real Avid 4-in-1 Tool For Glock is a handy gadget to have around for just about any Glock maintenance that could pop up.

and that tool opens like a switchblade – and it locks open, so it won't slip. It's small and compact and will set you back about $25. As of this writing, it's new for 2019.

---

grasp that. My tendency was to use a lot of CLP. But I have learned the error of my ways, and now I clean it properly. Some people say you should only clean your Glock every thousand rounds or so. Some people say you shouldn't clean your Glock until you notice a degradation in function. I'm not buying into that one, and probably won't ever. I have seen police trade-ins for sale that look like they haven't been cleaned since being put into service.

DISASSEMBLY

Before maintenance can be done, the pistol must first be disassembled. Disassembly is so simple, I don't want to insult anyone's intelligence by including it in this book, but I feel it would be incomplete if I didn't.

First, make safe: Remove the magazine, lock the slide to the rear and visually and

Some of the different products the author uses for his Glocks.

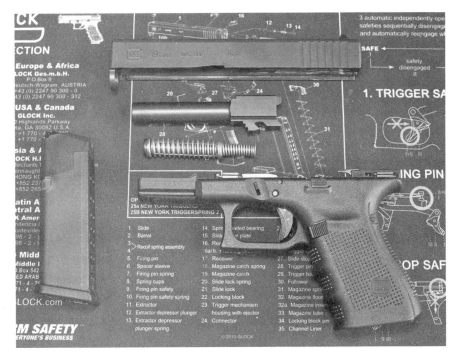

Field-disassembled Glock Gen4.

The disassembly grip.

physically check the chamber to ensure it is empty. Next, point the gun in a safe direction and pull the trigger. Using the disassembly grip (grasp the pistol so your four fingers are over the slide, and the thumb rests behind the grip, where the web of your hand would be in a firing grip), pull the slide back about 1/8 inch (the barrel hood will drop out of the ejection port, coming out of battery), and with your other hand, pull down the slide lock on both sides.

Grab the slide and pull it forward and off the frame. Push the recoil spring assembly forward with the thumb, and lift out. Grab the barrel by the locking cam, push it slightly forward, then lift out. Be careful not to drop the slide, while it's as tough as it gets when fully assembled, there are three points on the slide that can be damaged when disassembled. If you drop the slide and it lands on the guide ring it can bend, or if it lands on the rear slide rails, those can be damaged. Either one will convert your slide into an expensive paperweight. Fortunately, the Gen5 has a more robust guide ring to help prevent damage, but you still don't want to drop it.

Your Glock is now disassembled as far as a non-certified Glock armorer can get it. Disassembly past this point will void the warranty. One other thing to note: In my early days of Glock ownership, to disassemble I would grasp the slide, pull back on it, pull down on the slide lock then pull the trigger. The recoil spring is under slight pressure, and using this method can eject the slide off the frame, which could cause the slide to hit the floor and potentially damage it (the guide ring at the front of the slide can get bent, rendering the slide inoperable). It is best to use the recommended method, as you will be in control of the slide during the entire procedure.

REASSEMBLY

Just as simple as disassembly, but there is one detail to pay attention to. First, take the barrel by the bottom lug and insert it into the slide. Place the recoil spring/guide rod assembly small end into the guide ring, large end seated into the half-moon cut of the barrel lug. This is the important detail: Make sure the large end is fully seated, and the guide rod is perfectly centered on the barrel. If you don't, you'll feel resistance putting the slide on the frame, and once it's assembled and you pull the slide back, it won't go back properly, and the slide will get kind of stuck, and it can be a little difficult to disassemble. Yes, I've done it.

Next, line up the slide grooves with the frame rails and push the slide onto the frame.

CLEANING

The gear needed for cleaning includes a nylon AP (All Purpose) brush, bore brush, rod, patches, a rag and a good cleaner/lubricant/protectant. There are a lot of really good products out there that can be used for cleaning, lubricating and protecting. I've seen a lot of tests, using a metal sheet with the various products applied to it, then sprayed with a saltwater solution. Based on this, the best protectant out there remains BreakFree CLP. Others come close, but none are better. There are better cleaners, there are better lubricants, but if you want something that does all three, it's still the best. Never use a Nitrate-based solvent such as Hoppe's #9 on a Glock, it's not good for nickel plating.

Use a dry nylon brush to scrub all the surfaces. The inside of the slide will need extra attention, but stay away from solvents as much as possible. You shouldn't need them anyway.

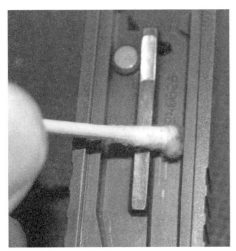
Follow the nylon brush with wood cotton swabs until they come out clean.

As for other solvents, you'll only need them for the bore. Except in rare situations, you won't need it for anything else. If you do need to use solvent, make sure when you are done you completely remove the solvent, so the surface is dry, and NEVER get solvent inside the firing pin channel. To use solvent on the slide, hold it so that the rear of the slide is pointed up, so no solvent drips enters the firing pin channel. Solvent or lubricant attracts dirt, and if dirt builds up inside the firing pin channel it can impeded proper function of the handgun.

For general maintenance, the best method is to use a dry nylon brush and go over all the surfaces until all fouling has been loosened, then wipe it down with a rag to get it off. I finish up with wood cotton swabs to get in the nooks and crannies. Make sure to get under the extractor hook and the slide grooves (if your Glock is new, there will be a reddish-bronze paste in the slide grooves. Don't remove this, it's a high-temperature lubricant Glock applies at the factory. It needs to be worked in.

DETAILED MAINTENANCE

BARREL
Punch the bore using the proper bore brush, giving it two to four passes, depending on how dirty it is. Push patches through until they come out clean. With the dry nylon brush, clean the feed ramp until all fouling is gone. Also scrub the lug area. When done, wipe all surfaces down with the rag, making sure it's completely dry and free of all residue.

SLIDE
(Note: There is a copper colored substance that is factory-applied to the inside of the slide. Do not remove; allow it to work its way into the slide as it naturally wears away). With the nylon AP brush, go over the entire inside of the slide, until all fouling is loosened. Extra focus should be given to the breech face, under the extractor hook, slide grooves and the ejection port. Wipe it with a rag to pick up the loosened fouling and finish up using cotton swabs to get the detail areas. Makes sure it's completely dry.

FRAME
With a dry nylon AP brush, start by going over the inside surface of the frame, looking for fouling as you go. Focus on the metal rails and the area where the locking block, lock-

ing block pin, trigger bar and slide stop all converge at the frame. Also make sure to hit the area to the rear of the trigger assembly where the cruciform and ejector are located. Pull a rag up through the grip, then use it to wipe down what you can reach. Use cotton swabs for all of the hard-to-reach places and once again make sure it's completely dry.

RECOIL SPRING

Scrub between the coils with the Nylon brush, then wipe down with rag. Inspect the spring and guide rod for any obvious wear. Make sure it's (drum roll) completely dry.

MAGAZINES

Try to keep your magazines as dry and free from debris as possible.

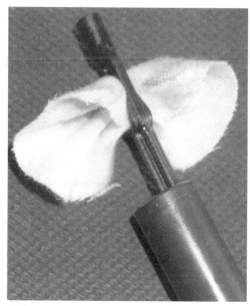

Make sure to punch the bore.

Unless you notice issues with function, it's not necessary to disassemble magazines, in fact Glock recommends that you don't. If you don't disassemble it, just wipe it dry with a rag, and clean the follower area with a cotton swab. Sometimes I'll push down on the follower with the nylon brush and give the inside a quick clean with a cotton swab. However, if you shoot pretty frequently, follow the advice I was given at the armorer's course: Disassemble and clean your magazines about once per year.

If you find it necessary to disassemble the magazine, insert the Glock armorer's tool (or a pin punch) into the hole in the floor plate and push in as far as possible. Never use a wood cotton swab. It's not strong enough and will break off. Once it's broken off inside the magazine, it is really hard to get out. It can prevent the floor plate from being pushed in to disassemble the magazine to remove it. I speak from experience.

Once the armorer's tool is pushed in as far as it will go, use it to pry the floor plate slightly forward. Use your thumb to cover the floor plate and press down to control the compressed magazine spring. Remove the armorer's tool, then the floor plate, and ease the thumb out to release spring tension. Remove the spring, insert and follower. A rag should get out all the debris and residue. Stubborn areas can be scrubbed with the nylon brush. Before you reassemble, make sure it's completely dry so as not to attract debris.

Honestly, the armorer's tool disassembly method kind of sucks. It works, but it's not that great. I always feel like I'm going to break something or mess up the magazine spring. There's a couple of solutions to Glock magazine take-down.

One is a simple tool from TangoDown that kind of looks similar to the tool used to open ammo "spam" cans. Insert the tool nipple into the floor plate hole as far as it will go, place the leverage bar on the side of the mag, then hold the mag and tool in your hand

When you buy a new Glock, you'll find a copper-colored substance along the inside of the slide; leave it, it will eventually wear away.

The Real Avid Smart Mag Tool For Glock is excellent for disassembling Glock mags and it also is great for stripping cartridges out of a loaded mag.

like you would hold a metal nutcracker, and squeeze – like a nutcracker – and the floor plate snaps open. It doesn't open all the way, but opens far enough to "break the seal."

The second tool is called the Smart Mag Tool For Glock, it comes from Real Avid and is multi-function. To remove the mag floor plate, hold the tool on a solid surface (I found it works best if you place it at the edge of a table in case you need more leverage to break the seal on the mag floor plate), insert the floor plate hole onto the tool's nipple as far as it goes (the front of the magazine should be facing down), and press down on the magazine to pop the

The TangoDown Glock mag disassembly tool is simple, but far more effective at taking down the Glock magazine than using the armorer's tool.

floor plate out. While you're applying pressure downward on the magazine, make sure also to maintain pressure so the nipple stays inside the floor plate hole, otherwise it will pop out. Once the floor plate is popped, there's a recess on top of the tool with a second nipple. Set the magazine in this recess and push it backward onto the little shelf. This completely removes the floor plate without having the magazine insert and spring fly out. It's a pretty nifty idea, and you can do this in reverse to assemble the mag as well. One last thing about this Real Avid tool, flip it upside down and there's a mag unloader, as well.

LUBRICATION

Unlike other firearms, especially pre-Glock and non-polymer designs which require a light coating of lubricant/protectant, the Glock needs very little. Buy a high-quality oil or grease product. Since so little is used it will last you a long time. For the most part, specific points are being lubed, so I prefer a syringe-style applicator. Glock recommends seven drops at specific points, but my instructor at the armorer's course uses less than four.

The most important location is a drop placed under the connector hook (right next to the rear right frame rail). This makes for a smoother trigger pull and prevents damage to the trigger bar and connector. Next place one drop on each of the two slide rail grooves and

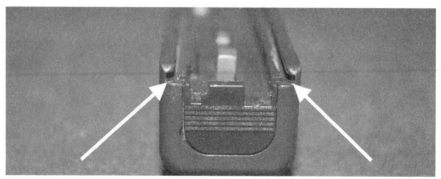

Place one drop of lubricant on each slide groove. Hold that end up and let it run down through the slide grooves. When you reassemble the pistol, work the action a couple times to distribute it along the slide groove and rails.

Place a drop where the barrel hood contacts the slide, and spread it around.

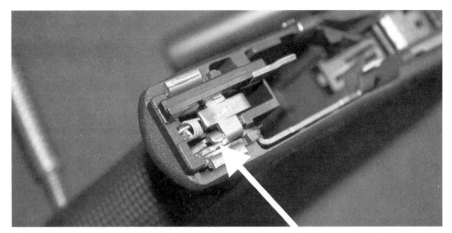

The most important drop is placed under the connector hook. The lubricant will travel down the connector to where the connector meets the trigger bar. This makes trigger pull smoother and prevents damage to these two parts.

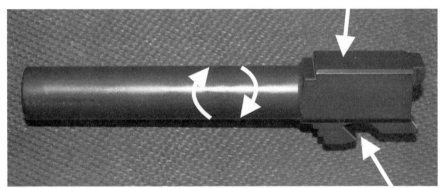

Lightly lubricate all around the barrel, barrel hood and barrel lug. One drop should cover the whole thing, but you might need an extra one for the barrel lug.

allow the drops to run the length of the grooves (once assembled and the action worked, the drops will spread to where they need to go).

Glock recommends you place a drop on the inside of the slide where the barrel hood contacts the slide, but use very little since the barrel hood also gets a drop. Place one drop each at the barrel lug, barrel hood and, using your finger, spread a drop around the outside of the barrel.

One important point to stress: You never want to leave any lubrication or solvent in the magazine or firing pin channel. It's a magnet for debris. Another serious point, but a rather funny one if you think about someone actually doing this, concerns the hole on the underside of the slide, right behind the breech face. This is not an oil-fill port. Don't inject oil into it until oil is flowing from all other holes. In the popular vernacular among today's youth, LOL.

DETAILED DISASSEMBLY/ASSEMBLY

Warning: This if for informational purposes only. Detailed disassembly/assembly should only be done by certified armorers. When done by an uncertified person, it can void your warranty by Glock.

DISASSEMBLY

There are some differences in the way a Gen1 through Gen4 Glock is disassembled, and the Gen5. The Gen5 disassembly is similar to that of the G42 and 9mm Slimline models, but it differs slightly, since there's no ambidextrous slide stop lever. It differs from Gen3 and Gen4 models in that it only has two pins, something it has in common with Gen1 and most Gen2s. (The locking block pin – aka "first pin" – was added across the whole lineup starting with the Gen3, however, some models, such as the G22, had them prior to that).

Start with a field-disassembled pistol. To disassemble the slide, hold the slide muzzle end down, resting on a table or firm, flat surface. Insert the armorer's tool punch between the spacer firing pin lug and the spacer sleeve and push down on the spacer sleeve. Use the thumb on your opposite hand to cover the slide cover plate, sliding it out from its position. Make sure to keep your thumb covering the space vacated by the slide cover plate, as you slide it out because everything under it is under spring tension.

The slide cover plate on newer pistols can be hard to remove and might require extra effort. If it still won't budge, a small flat-head screwdriver can be positioned between the slide and slide cover plate to lever it off, but do so cautiously so as not to damage the plate. Pull out the extractor depressor plunger assembly by grasping the plunger or spring. It's comprised of three parts: the extractor depressor plunger, extractor depressor spring and spring-loaded bearing. Other parts of the armorer's manual refer to these parts as "rod, spring and bearing." Unless you're replacing worn parts, it's not necessary to disassemble the three parts, although it is done by simply pulling them apart.

Using the firing pin lug, pull out the firing pin assembly. To disassemble the firing pin assembly, it's easiest to use the slide to assist you in disassembly, so use it as a base and set it on a hard surface on its end, muzzle down. Take the firing pin assembly and insert the firing pin spacer sleeve into the firing pin channel, making sure the lug is to the side, so it does not go into the channel. Pinching the firing pin spring between your thumb and forefinger, pull down as far as you can, and grab the two spring cup halves with your other hand (they are small and easily lost). Gradually ease up on the spring until the tension is released, then pull it off the firing pin. Remove the firing pin spacer sleeve. It's not necessary to disassemble the firing pin assembly unless you're replacing parts. Also, if one half of the spring cup is damaged or lost, it's important to replace both, since they break in and wear together, and you don't want one brand new and the other one well-worn. It's difficult to replace only one anyway, since they come as a pair.

To remove the extractor, turn it down so it is facing your work surface and press the firing pin safety. The extractor will fall out. Then turn the slide over and the firing pin safety will fall out. Don't intentionally remove the spring from the firing pin safety, but should it come out, press either end of the spring into position in the firing pin safety. Compress the spring fully and give it a quarter turn. You should be able to hold it upside down by the spring and the firing pin safety should stay attached. If it doesn't, get a new one.

To disassemble the frame, first look if you have three pins or two. If you have three pins, always start with the locking block pin, or as the instructor at the armorer's course called it, the first pin. It's the first pin out, and the first pin to be inserted back in during assembly. It's a steel pin,

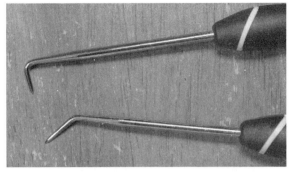

The secret to getting out the magazine catch: a dental pick-type tool to move and lift the spring out of the slot.

and like all the other pins, should be removed left to right, and reinserted right to left. The pins are not directional, so it doesn't matter which way the pin is flipped, it just needs to be inserted right to left. After the locking block pin is removed (or if you only have two pins to start with), remove the trigger mechanism housing pin (rear grip pin), then the trigger pin. (If that one is tough to get started, you might have to wiggle the slide lock to get that one out with Slimline and Gen5 models, press down on the slide stop lever near the trigger pin for easy removal of pin). After that pin is out, if you have a Gen4 or previous Gen, simply lift the slide stop lever out of the frame. (If you have a Gen5, this step and the next one are reversed).

Next, place the armorer's tool pin punch under the locking block lip and pry out until you can grasp it with your fingers. For the Gen5, remove the locking block first, then remove the slide stop lever. For all Glocks, the next step is to lift straight up on the ejector so the trigger mechanism housing assembly will slide out, followed by the trigger bar and trigger. Now, holding the trigger mechanism housing in your left hand and the trigger in your right, push the trigger away from you, rotating the cruciform out of the drop safety slot. For Gen4 and previous Gens, the trigger bar will still be attached to the housing by way of the trigger spring. Work the trigger spring off of the trigger bar, then turn the spring over and take it off the housing. For Gen5, the trigger bar is not attached by the trigger spring and just pulls free.

To remove the connector, look on the opposite side of the housing and there is a slot with a round hole in the middle. Insert the armorer's tool punch into that hole and push out the connector. Do not remove the connector by grabbing it and pulling it out, the connector can become bent, and if that happens it will need to be replaced. Older models do not have that hole on the opposite side for easy connector removal. For those, carefully insert a small flat-head screwdriver under the connector and slide it toward the part that goes into the housing. Get as close as possible to that point before trying to pry, otherwise the connector once again can become damaged.

The Gen5 trigger spring was taken directly from the G42 design and is removed and disassembled the same way. The trigger spring is actually an assembly, comprised of a bearing, spring and rod. To remove the trigger spring, first take a look at the front of the housing. You'll notice a slot that resembles a barbell; my armorer's course instructor called this, "toggle holes." Inside the bottom toggle hole, you'll see the end of the trigger spring rod. The objective is to push the notches on the trigger spring rod through the front of the housing, then slide it up the slot and out the top toggle hole. Easier said than done, here's how to do it:

The trigger spring rod is in its seated position. To remove, using a Glock tool, press the trigger spring bearing down and toward the front until the rod clears the toggle hole. Then use your thumb to push it up the slot, and out through the top toggle hole, maintaining pressure so the firing pin spring assembly doesn't launch. The trigger spring is sold as one part, comes as one part and works as one part. There's no need to disassemble it. If you feel the need, you can disassemble it by pressing the rod and spring while twisting the rod so the end lines up with the slot in the bearing, then removing. Then remove the spring from the rod.

Slide lock removal has changed in the Gen5, because the slide lock spring was a flat spring in previous generations, but in Gen5 it's been changed to the G42-design coil spring. To remove Gen4 and previous Gens, lay the frame on its side and, using the armorer's tool, press down on the flat slide lock spring. The slide lock should just fall out, but if it doesn't, jiggle it. Using the armorer's tool or needle-nose pliers, remove the slide lock spring, being careful not to bend it. For Gen5 – beware, the slide lock spring likes to launch – push the slide lock down halfway, then push sideways just slightly. You might need a small flat-head screwdriver. You don't have to push it sideways very far, just enough for the spring to clear the notch in the slide lock. From here, turn the whole frame upside down (so if the spring launches it won't go far) and finish pushing the slide lock to the side until it falls out, then remove the slide lock spring.

To remove the magazine catch, hold the frame so you can see into the magazine well. Pinch both sides of the magazine catch to prevent it from moving. Taking a small screwdriver (or better yet, a dental pick-type tool), push the magazine catch spring up and toward the U-shaped cut in the magazine catch. In the previous armorer's course, we were told not to remove the magazine catch spring, because when reinserted it can easily be pushed through the frame wall, damaging your firearm. The updated course I attended just recently, they've changed this, and now recommend removing the spring first, then the mag catch will slide out easier. Apparently, trying to wrestle the catch out with the spring still in place could cause damage to the spring, frame and/or catch. To remove the magazine catch spring, use needle-nose pliers and gently pull straight out of the frame. Then, as mentioned, the mag catch will just slide out of the frame.

Make sure the lip of the slide lock is up and pointed to the rear.

ASSEMBLY

To reassemble the Glock pistol, insert the magazine catch into position with the catch on the left side for right-handed users, and the right side for left-handed users. Using needle-nose pliers, insert the mag catch spring into the hole, then use the flat-head screwdriver to gently press it down until completely seated. The spring can be bent if too much force is used, so use caution, and stop pushing as soon as you feel resistance. Use the flat-head screwdriver to lift the magazine catch spring back into the U-shaped notch in the magazine catch. Before you go any farther, it might be a good idea to insert an empty magazine into the well to confirm the magazine catch does in fact hold the magazine in place, then press the catch to make sure it properly releases it.

Insert the slide lock spring into position, then press down on it with the armorer's tool while inserting the slide lock over the spring and into position. Ensure the slide lock lip is facing up, and to the rear. You should be able to read the item number printed on it, if it's facing the correct direction. If not properly positioned, the slide could disengage from the frame when the trigger is pulled.

Insert the connector into its slot, using care to press right at the position of the slot. Use the armorer's tool pin punch to press at that spot for best results. Pressing higher up on the connector can cause it to bend, and once it's damaged it would need to be replaced. Make sure it's fully seated in position.

In Gen4 and previous Gens, to install the coil trigger spring, hold it in front of you so the top hook and bottom hook form an "S" shape. Hook the top end of the "S" through the hole located on the bottom arm of the trigger bar, and the bottom end of the "S" through the hole on the top of the trigger mechanism. Push the trigger bar away from you so you can insert the left cruciform arm into the drop safety slot, then pull the trigger bar toward you, which twists the cruciform arm into position.

For Gen5, you'll need to reassemble the trigger spring assembly and install it into the housing. Slide the spring onto the slotted end of the rod. Then align the slot on the rod with the slot on the bearing and insert by pushing in and twisting 90 degrees. Notice on the rod that one side is straight and the other is cut at an angle. To make sure it's installed correctly, the angle of that cut should be roughly parallel to the angle of the bearing. Another way to think about it: The angled side of the rod should point toward the bearing. To install the trigger spring into the housing, hold the trigger spring by the bearing, and push the rod end into the top toggle hole so it pro-trudes out the other side. Slide it down and into the bottom toggle hole and it will snap in place. Next, grab the trigger bar and twist the trigger away from you so you can insert the front cruci-form arm underneath the upper lip of the bearing, while at the same time insert the left cruciform arm into the drop safety slot, then pull the trigger bar toward you, which twists the cruciform arm into position. It is IMPERATIVE to make sure the cruciform arm is underneath the bearing lip, because, if not, the trigger won't reset properly. If you don't know to do this, it's a detail that's easy to miss. I did. When the Gen5 first came out and I disassembled it to see the changes, and when I put it together, I didn't notice that little detail at first, until I noticed it wasn't working cor-rectly. Now the Gen5 is ready to proceed where we left off with the other generations.

Now, for all Gens, take the entire trigger assembly and insert the trigger into its slot in the frame, while at the same time inserting the trigger mechanism housing into the frame. It should slide smoothly into place; press to ensure it's completely seated.

For Gen5 pistols, place the ambidextrous slide stop lever into place, then slide the locking block into its position. One of the benefits to the new style of slide stop levers is you don't have to worry about if it's in the correct position or if the spring is in correctly. Just lay it in its position and it's good to go. For Gen4 and previous, slide the locking block into place, then insert the locking block pin, right to left. Whenever inserting a pin, use one of the corners of the square end of the armorer's tool to finish pressing the pin into place, this will center the pin in the frame. This pin must be inserted first, because the slide stop lever actually uses the locking block pin to create tension on its spring.

Next (for all Gens), insert the trigger mechanism housing pin (grip pin) into its hole and press into place, making sure it's centered in the frame using the method mentioned above (Note: The Gen4 and Gen5 come with two trigger mechanism housing pins: one short pin for use without a backstrap, and one long pin for use with a backstrap).

For Gen4 and previous (Gen5 has already done this step), insert the slide stop lever, spring up and forward, into the left-most slot. The spring will slip in just under the locking block pin. I have seen this inserted after the locking block pin, and what will generally happen is the spring won't be positioned under the locking block pin, so it has insufficient tension to keep the slide stop lever down in position, so it will want to pop up every time the slide is cycled, causing the slide to lock back.

For all Gens, at this point I like to look through the trigger pin hole from the left to ensure everything is lined up, as I insert the trigger pin. You will usually have to wiggle the slide stop lever back and forth to get the pin in place. Once in place, make sure the pin is centered in the frame. The frame is now assembled.

To reassemble the slide, first place the firing pin safety into its hole. With Gen1-4, the firing pin safety is round and goes into a round hole. With Gen5, it's not a circle, but shaped like the face of a shovel – one side is straight, the other side is oval/rounded. When installing the firing pin safety and spring, make sure the oval/rounded side is next to the stripper/feed rail and the flat side is parallel with the slide. Next, insert the extractor into its slot, while at the same time pressing on the firing pin safety. Both pieces should lock into place. Next, insert the extractor depressor plunger assembly into the slide, metal end first. One important thing to remember when assembling the Glock pistol is always keep polymer on polymer and metal on metal. In the instance of the extractor depressor plunger assembly, the metal end goes in first and makes contact with the extractor, also made of metal. The spring-loaded bearing end, made of polymer, goes in last and makes contact with the polymer slide cover plate.

To reassemble the firing pin assembly, insert the firing pin into the firing pin spacer sleeve. The firing pin lug should slide all the way forward in the spacer sleeve slot. Slide the firing pin spring onto the firing pin. Using the slide as you did during disassembly, slide the firing pin spacer sleeve into the firing pin channel. Pull the spring down as far as you can with one hand, then insert the spring cup narrow end down. Slowly ease up on the spring, allowing the end of the spring to slip over the narrow end of the spring cup, and move into its position.

Turn the firing pin assembly around and insert it into the firing pin channel, so the lug moves into the slot. Start the slide cover plate into its slot and hold it in place while pushing down on the firing pin spacer sleeve. Push the slide cover plate over the firing pin spacer sleeve until it rests against the spring-loaded bearing.

Now use the armorer's tool punch and press down on the spring-loaded bearing while at the same time pushing the slide plate cover into position. Ease the punch out as you move the slide cover plate over the bearing, then push the plate into position until it snaps in place. The Glock is now in the field-stripped state. Finish with assembly and it is complete.

Note: For special instructions on G42 detailed disassembly/assembly, please refer to Chapter 12 on the G42. Special instructions for G43, G43X and G48, please refer to Chapter 13 on Slimline 9mm models.

FIELD INSPECTION

A field inspection is how a Glock armorer can tell if all systems are working properly. It's also a great way for a Glock owner to check the operation of his handgun without paying for a professional to check it. It can be done every time the pistol is disassembled for maintenance, but should definitely be done after a full armorer's disassembly and/or if parts have been replaced. It is also a great tool when buying a used Glock.

FULLY ASSEMBLED GLOCK (ENSURE GLOCK IS UNLOADED FIRST)

1. SLIDE LOCK

Pull down on both sides of the slide lock lever at the same time, it should not pull down.

Using the disassembly grip, move the slide back approximately 1/8 inch and pull down on both sides of the slide lock lever and release. It should pull down, then snap back when released.

With the slide lock lever engaged (locked into home position), point the pistol in a safe direction, push forward on the slide with your thumb and pull the trigger. The slide should stay in place and not move forward.

2. TRIGGER SAFETY

Rack the slide so the trigger is fully forward and it's ready to shoot. Point the pistol in a safe direction and pull back on both sides of the trigger, without touching the trigger safety. The trigger should only move slightly, you should see the trigger safety engage, and the firing pin should not fall.

Point the pistol in a safe direction and pull the trigger back, depressing the trigger safety. The trigger should move freely to the rear and the firing pin should fall.

3. RECOIL SPRING/GUIDE ROD ASSEMBLY

Point the unloaded pistol up at a 45-degree

Springs should be replaced when a field inspection (or regular usage) reveals them to be weak.

angle. Pull the trigger and hold it back. Pull the slide to the rear and slowly ride it forward (with trigger still held back). The recoil spring should be strong enough to push the slide completely forward and into battery. Glocks are known for their reliability and functioning under non-ideal conditions. This check confirms that it will chamber a cartridge despite poor ammunition condition or a dirty pistol.

4. MAGAZINE SPRING

The magazine spring should be strong enough to feed every round, then lock the slide back. With an empty magazine inserted, pull the slide to the rear. It should lock back every time. This check also verifies condition of the follower and the slide stop lever (and the attached spring).

5. FIRING PIN SAFETY RELEASE

When the trigger is pulled it should move the firing pin safety out of the way, so the firing pin is free to strike the primer. Point the gun in a safe direction, pull the trigger and hold it to the rear. Shake the pistol back and forth (front to rear); you should hear the firing pin rattle forward and back.

FIELD-STRIPPED GLOCK

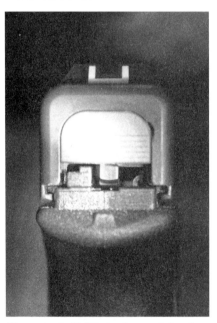

The orange half-slide in place and showing good engagement.

SLIDE

1. FIRING PIN/FIRING PIN SAFETY ENGAGEMENT

Pull back on the firing pin lug using your finger, then ease it forward. It should rest on the firing pin safety, but not move forward of it. Push on the back of the lug and attempt to move it forward of the firing pin safety; it should not move. Continuing to press the lug forward. Press down on the firing pin safety and it should move freely forward.

2. FIRING PIN FREE MOVEMENT

Press the firing pin safety and shake the slide back and forth. The firing pin should rattle as it moves freely.

FRAME

1. SLIDE STOP LEVER TENSION

Pull the slide stop lever up, then release. It should snap down with force.

2. DROP SAFETY

Pull the trigger forward (or push forward on the vertical extension of the trigger bar). Press down on the cruciform portion of the trigger bar, it should not move down, so the drop safety works. Now press forward on the vertical extension of the trigger bar and pull the trigger. The cruciform should move back and down (note: Pressing the vertical extension forward while pulling the trigger releases the tension on the trigger safety. If you pull the trigger without pulling the vertical extension forward, it can create unnecessary wear on the trigger safety.)

Ensure proper engagement between the firing pin lug and the face of the rearward-facing leg of the trigger bar cruciform. First, the slide cover must be replaced with an orange half-slide cover plate, then reassemble the Glock. The engagement can be viewed through the missing half of the slide cover plate. A minimum of two-thirds of the surface area of the previously mentioned cruciform face must be covered by the firing pin lug. This isn't an area of wear, so if there is two-thirds engagement it is good to go, it won't get worse.

SCHEDULED REPLACEMENT PARTS

Glocks have a deserved reputation as being as tough as it gets when it comes to firearms. Glocks have had things done to them we wouldn't do to the weapon of our worst enemies, and they still come out shooting. A Glock can even have certain key parts break, and, if run properly, still function as if nothing was wrong.

Despite that, a Glock is still a machine, and a precision machine at that. By definition a machine has moving parts, and where there are moving parts, there is friction. And of course, friction causes wear. Yes, despite its toughness, a Glock pistol will eventually have parts wear that will require replacement. If not replaced, those parts will eventually fail, and break. I've seen Glock detractors point to this as a fault with Glock, as if their brand of choice was impervious to physics.

Tough doesn't mean there isn't going to be maintenance. Most consider tanks such as an M1 Abrams to be as tough as it gets and nearly indestructible. Being a former Anti-Tank TOW missile man, I've spent significant time on and around the tank ramp, and you would be amazed at how much maintenance goes into one of those, and how often they break down.

Glock pistols used in a service capacity or those used by high volume shooters (i.e., competitive shooters) should be disassembled and inspected by a certified Glock armorer at least annually. Most users who do not fit in either of these categories won't need inspections and can conduct a field inspection that will suffice. If it passes a field test, it's not broken. If it's not broken, don't fix it.

SPRINGS

The one spring that will need replacing, and one that any owner can check, is the recoil spring. If it's an all-metal dual-spring, it needs to be replaced every 5,000 rounds. Any previous polymer single-spring model will need to be replaced every 2,500 rounds. This is what Glock recommends, but if you do a field test and the recoil spring is still strong, it's fine. If it's borderline, replace it.

All springs potentially need to be replaced at some point. These include (in addition to the recoil spring):

1. Firing pin spring
2. Firing pin safety spring
3. Trigger spring
4. Extractor depressor plunger spring
5. Slide lock spring
6. Magazine catch spring
7. Slide stop lever spring (integral with slide stop lever, one part)
8. Magazine spring

FIRING PIN/FIRING PIN SAFETY

There is metal-on-metal contact between the firing pin and the firing pin safety, which is an area where wear can occur.

EXTRACTORS

The tip should be checked for wear and should not be damaged. Check for chips. If feed or extraction problems occur, first check for dirt and debris underneath the extractor.

MAGAZINES

1. Check for damage to the front or side cut of the magazine. Damage can cause the magazine catch to malfunction.
2. Check for damage to the magazine lips.
3. Make sure the follower is in good condition. Damage can lead to failure to feed (FTF) and slide stop lever failure.

Keep the wrists locked to ensure proper cycling of the slide. In this picture of the author shooting the .45 GAP, the pistol is blurry from recoil, yet the hand and wrist did not move.

DIAGNOSTICS

If you're having an issue with your
Glock, and there isn't an obvious
breakage, it's time to go into di-
agnostics mode. There are two
main culprits to any Glock issue,
and it's best to eliminate them first.
The vast majority of "Failure to …,"
whether it's failure to fire, extract, eject,
feed or failure of the slide to lock back after
the last round, are caused by shooting with an
unlocked wrist. Be sure to lock your wrist. It used
to be called "limp-wristing" but some people get of-
fended by that, so the more politically correct term is
"unlocked wrist." If you're having problems telling if you
have a wrist problem, video record yourself shooting. Or
hand your Glock to an experienced shooter and see if he or
she has the same "Failure to…."

*The most common cause of
stovepipes like this one is
a wrist that isn't locked.*

Once you've checked that off the list and you're sure your Glock
isn't being fired with unlocked wrists, the second most common
cause of issues is ammunition. Try different brands or a different
weight of bullet. If you shoot a different brand and the problem
goes away, it was your ammunition. In the first edition, I was pretty firm about not shooting ammo from the former Soviet Bloc countries out of my Glock and other Western-made firearms. In general, I
still feel that way, because a lot of that ammo comes from operations with
some poor quality control. I've found some of the makers to be pretty good, but
the problem is, a lot of the makers are putting out ammo with some very sporadic results. You really have to know what you're looking for, because if you don't, you just don't
know what you're going to get.

There are, however, a couple of exceptions to that rule. The Czechs make good stuff,
whether firearms or ammunition. I've fired a lot of Sellier & Bellot (S&B) and have never had
any problems. S&B has been making ammunition for a long time: 2015 marked its 190th year.
Another exception is Serbian manufacturer Prvi Partizan (PPU). I have fired a lot of PPU
as well and have never had any issues with it. I've found both the S&B and PPU to be very
reliable, reasonably accurate and priced well. I have to add WOLF ammo to that list too. I've
found the ammo from WOLF to be reliable, and especially the Gold line of brass ammo. I'm
still leery of shooting steel case ammo, but the WOLF brass case ammo has been working
well for me. This is getting a little off subject for this Glock book, but I shot WOLF Gold line
of 5.56 ammo, and not only was it reliable, I got some good accuracy out of it. It's made in
Taiwan for the Taiwan military, whose T91 rifle is based off the AR-15/M16.

If your wrist isn't the problem and you're having the same issue with different types of
ammo, it's time to delve a little deeper.

FAILURE TO EXTRACT (FTE)

Extractor worn or broken
Dirt under extraction claw
Dirty chamber
Defective ammunition

FAILURE TO EJECT (FTE) OR ERRATIC EJECTION, INCLUDING STOVEPIPES

Damaged ejector
Dirty chamber
Too little lubrication
Dirty gun
Underpowered ammunition

FAILURE TO FEED (FTF)

Magazine not fully seated
Dirty magazine
Bad magazine spring
Dirty chamber
Tight extractor
Damaged magazine (magazine sides or lips deformed)
Weak recoil spring

FAILURE TO FIRE (FTF, USUALLY DUE TO SLIDE BEING OUT OF BATTERY)

Deformed cartridge
Weak recoil spring
Damaged recoil spring tube
Excessive dirt where slide, frame and barrel interact
Obstructed chamber
Underpowered ammunition

SLIDE FAILS TO LOCK OPEN ON LAST ROUND

Magazine follower damaged
Magazine sides damaged
Dirty magazine
Weak magazine spring
Worn slide stop lever notch
Dirty pistol
Too little lubrication
Trigger pin not properly centered
Slide stop lever worn or damaged
Improper grip
Underpowered ammunition

NO PRIMER STRIKE

Broken or worn firing pin tip

Spring cup inverted

Obstructed firing pin channel (check for presence of solvent or lubricant)

LIGHT, CENTERED PRIMER STRIKE

Hard primer

Obstructed firing pin channel

LIGHT, OFF-CENTER PRIMER STRIKE

Weak recoil spring

Tight extractor

Slide lock reversed or not beveled

Dirty pistol

INCONSISTENT TRIGGER PULL, OR WILL NOT RELEASE

Connector loose or improperly positioned in housing

Dirty pistol

Trigger bar is damaged

Wrong trigger bar

Connector needs lubrication

TRIGGER SAFETY FAILS TO RETURN TO ENGAGED (FORWARD) POSITION

Damaged trigger bar

FIRING PIN SAFETY FAILS

Damaged or worn firing pin safety

LOCKS OPEN WHEN NOT SUPPOSED TO

Damaged slide stop lever

Reverse tension on slide stop lever (improperly installed)

Improper hand placement during firing.

GLOCK GEN5 PARTS, BY NUMBER:

1. Slide

2. Barrel

3. Recoil Spring Assembly

4. Firing Pin Assembly

5. Spacer Sleeve

6. Firing Pin Spring

7. Spring Cups

8. Firing Pin Safety

9. Firing Pin Safety Spring

10. Extractor

11. Extractor Depressor Plunger

12. Extractor Depressor Plunger Spring

13. Spring Loaded Bearing

14. Slide Cover Plate

15. Rear Sight

16. Front Sight and Front Sight Screw

17. Frame

18. Magazine Catch Spring

19. Magazine Catch

20. Slide Lock Spring

21. Slide Lock

22. Locking Block

23. Trigger Mechanism Housing with Ejector

24. Connector

25. Trigger Spring

26. Trigger with Trigger Bar

27. Slide Stop Lever

28. Trigger Pin

29. Trigger Housing Pin

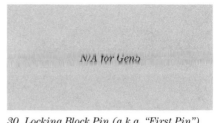

30. Locking Block Pin (a.k.a. "First Pin")

31. Magazine Tube

32. Follower

33. Magazine Spring

34. Magazine Insert

35. Magazine Floor Plate

CHAPTER 17:
THE GLOCK SHOOTING
SPORTS FOUNDATION

Whether you're a competition shooter, law enforcement or just a Glock enthusiast, if you buy one or more Glocks per year, it really pays to join the Glock Shooting Sports Foundation (GSSF). I made the mistake of thinking you had to shoot matches to get into the GSSF, and I regret not finding out the facts sooner. The truth is anyone can join. When you join you get some swag: a hat, pin, patch, a quarterly Glock Report subscription and access to the Glock armorer's course.

GSSF swag.

Where the value really comes in, however, is if you join for two years or more. Do that, and you get a coupon for the purchase of one blue-label Glock pistol per year. A blue-label Glock is $100 to $150 off the price of a yellow- or white-label Glock. A GSSF membership costs $35, and $25 to renew, which means the membership more than pays for itself if you're going to be buying a Glock, or multiple Glocks.

Three different Glock Gen4 labels.

Some of you might be wondering about the different Glock labels. Glocks come in boxes with three different labels, and there is no difference between the pistols contained within; the only difference is in what comes with it, or whom it's for.

The red label Glocks are for commercial sale with full-capacity magazines. White labels are for commercial sales with 10-round magazines in states with 10-round limits, such as California, but also found in pistols where the standard magazine capacity is 10 rounds or fewer, such as subcompacts like the G26. Blue-label boxes are reserved for those who serve: law enforcement, military, fire rescue, first responders and any of those who are retired. Blue-label boxes are also for those employed by state-certified security companies, judges, correction officers, commercial pilots, etc. That blue label has also been extended to GSSF members, which is awesome.

The first thing I did when I got my coupon was purchase a G34. There are no local police shops that carry Glocks, so I had to order it over the phone from the next closest police shop and have it shipped.

All the benefits are great, especially the armorer's course and the marked-down pistol, but the basis for the GSSF, and the reason it was founded, is competition. It's now time to put that shiny new Glock to use. Or, go with an old Glock, it doesn't matter.

Why shoot in a GSSF match? Three reasons: improve your skill set, learn to perform under stress and weapon familiarization. All three are important if you ever need your Glock to defend yourself or your family. You can, of course, get these three things by going through the police academy or joining the military. In lieu of that, however, you can get a solid foundation by shooting GSSF matches. Even if you are a cop or military, there is still much to be gained from shooting competitions.

IMPROVE YOUR SKILL SET

The only way to improve anything is through practice. Football greats like Aaron Rodgers and Brett Favre didn't become great because they were lucky. Sure, they were born gifted with athletic genetics. But they put in many hours to become that great. Hour upon hour of throwing, strength and agility training, and studying film. If you put into shooting the

The Glock in competition. (Photo by Ryan Wiedenmeier)

number of focused hours great athletes put into training for their sport, I can guarantee you will improve your shooting performance. Going out and plinking isn't going to cut it; you have to have focused and deliberate training. In order to have focus, you have to have a goal and training for a specific GSSF event will give you that focus.

LEARN TO PERFORM UNDER STRESS

Cops train to shoot under stress because someday they might need to draw their weapon and engage a threat. In this situation, they must be able to effectively engage that target even while under stress. In those moments of stress, you get kind of a tunnel vision where everything seems surreal, your body goes into automatic mode and you operate based on muscle memory. Military personnel are trained to operate under the stress of combat.

While I've never been a cop and can't speak on that from personal experience, I *can* attest that military engagements can be stressful. Both law enforcement and military can be subjected to life-changing stress so violent that it's rightly labeled as traumatic. While no training can ever replicate that, I do know the military gives it a good try. In the Marine Corps, we call this stress "drill instructors." There's nothing like trying to hit a 12-inch target at 500 meters with a drill instructor yelling as loud as he can from a distance so close you can see each hair follicle on his face.

In a unit, a lot of the stress is self-imposed. Everyone knows what is at stake, and what the consequences to you and your comrades are if you're not good at what you do. Everyone wants to train hard and do well when it comes to putting rounds on target. Plus, no one wants to look like an idiot in front of his or her buddies and superiors.

Is the stress at a GSSF competition equivalent to law enforcement or military training? Not in a million years, but it is not meant to be. In fact, GSSF is meant to be relatively relaxed and low-stress compared to other competitions, such as IDPA and IPSC. But it does give you some stress, enough to serve a function.

WEAPON FAMILIARIZATION

This one is a no-brainer; all those hours you spent improving your skill set (i.e., training), you became very familiar with your Glock. When you put a lot of rounds through it, you confirm what Glock owners already know. You own one reliable piece of hardware. That builds trust. Putting rounds through the bullseye over and over again, that builds confidence. All the repetition makes it so you could load and manipulate the weapon in your sleep. After all this, your Glock becomes an extension of yourself. When something becomes second nature, you can't ask for much more.

But the best reason for shooting a GSSF? A chance to win a free Glock. Do well, and you'll go home with one.

To compete in a GSSF match, you'll need a Glock (no other brands allowed), a minimum of four magazines (but 10 is better), factory ammunition (110 rounds plus extra, just in case), a holster, hearing protection, shooting glasses and you must be a GSSF member. It consists of three courses of fire: Glock'M, Glock the Plates and 5 to Glock. The most you'll shoot in one course is four strings of fire, so you'll want at a minimum four magazines. You will definitely not want to reload between your strings of fire. You have a total of 10 strings in a match, so with 10 magazines you can do all your loading first and not have to worry about it.

GLOCK'M

This consists of four NRA D-1 targets and three steel pepper poppers. It has three strings of fire, and each string of fire requires one 10 round magazine plus one in the chamber. Shoot two shots and two shots only, at the four D-1 targets, in order, and in the process knock over one pepper popper. The pepper poppers are center of the setup, with two D-1 targets to the left and two to the right. Most shooters shoot the pepper popper after engaging the first two targets, then continue on with the right two targets, which is a left-to-right sweep of the setup. I have seen shooters engage the pepper popper last. If you miss the pep-

At a GSSF match, you'll need a holster — not to draw from, but to transport your Glock around the course.

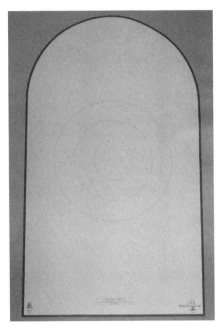

An NRA D-1 Target (a.k.a. Bianchi Cup Target). The rings are visible at this distance, but they won't be as visible at GSSF distances. Make sure to know where they are on the target.

per popper, you can shoot extra shots until it goes down or you run out of rounds (the most you'll have is three shots). There are 27 scored rounds.

GLOCK THE PLATES

Glock the Plates consists of six eight-inch steel plates positioned 10 yards away. Load 10 plus one in the chamber. Engage them in any order, through four strings of fire. Of course, the logical method is in order, left to right. The key is not to move on until the plate falls. If you miss, it's faster to keep your sights in place and shoot a follow-up shot, or even a third, than it is to continue on and have to bring your sights back on the target you missed. A plate must fall to be scored, and a miss adds 10 seconds to your time. Misses are only counted at the end of the string (it won't count against you if you miss one target, move on, then after all the other targets are down you come back and hit the one you initially missed). There are 24 scored rounds.

5 TO GLOCK

The 5 to Glock competition consists of five NRA D-1 targets positioned in one of eight different layouts. For this course, you'll need 10 rounds in the mag, but no "plus one" in the chamber. Fire two shots at each target through three strings, for a total of 10. Each layout will require its own tactic, which you'll have to determine beforehand. Some layouts will be left to right, some right to left, some close to far, others far to near. One even staggers the targets, so you have to jump from target to target, which doesn't allow for smooth transitions going from one target to the next. There are 30 scored rounds.

SCORING

Scoring is straightforward: You're scored on the time it takes you to complete the string, and with paper targets penalties are assessed the farther away you hit from the center. Hits inside the A or B ring are what you're looking for without incurring any time penalty. Hits inside the C ring will cost you one additional second, hits inside the D ring cost you three seconds and misses will cost you 10 seconds. It's advisable not to miss. Even if it takes an extra second or two for you to make a more accurate shot, those extra seconds are better than the three or 10 seconds you incur for a poor shot. On steel targets it's hit or miss. The target is either standing or it's not. If you hit the target, but it doesn't fall, it's still standing. If it's standing, you incur a 10-second penalty. Again, best not to miss.

Each string is approached with a maximum of 11 rounds; 10 rounds in the magazine and one in the chamber. This is a good opportunity to use those 10-round magazines you might have lying around, and if you don't have any you might want to consider buying some. They cost a little less to buy, and it will save wear and tear on your full-capacity magazines. I've found used ones online for less than $20. Of course, you'll always find the occasional seller who's trying to become rich one magazine at a time and is selling them for more than a new one.

The G34 in competition. (Photo by Ryan Wiedenmeier)

Any Glock model is welcome at a GSSF shoot. If you take it you can shoot it, but not all divisions are open to all Glocks. When you register, you'll have to look at what divisions are open to your model. The biggest limiting factors are the Glocks that come with magazines of less than 10 rounds, such as the G42, G36, G29 and G39. With the release of the G42, the GSSF started a new "Pocket Glock" division exclusively for the G42.

GSSF matches are designed to be a laid-back competition

Whatever Glock you own, or whichever one you prefer, you can shoot it at a GSSF competition. Or you can shoot them all.

that's accessible to anyone, be it a seasoned pro or newbies at their first competition. It is, above all, a competition where people go to have fun and enjoy the sport. All you need is a Glock, and it doesn't matter which Glock model you own, there's a category for all of them, whether you want to shoot the G26 you carry every day, or your G34. The fact is, you can bring both and shoot both.

Another great thing about the GSSF competition: You'll find a Glock armorer there, and he or she will repair or replace any worn or broken part your Glock might have. If you have an older Glock and want to upgrade the parts, take it. If you have a Glock with which you're having problems, take it.

CHAPTER 18:
GLOCK ARMORER'S COURSE

There are two Glock armorer's courses: the one-day basic course and the three-day advanced course. Back when it started, anyone could take the course, then Glock changed that policy to law-enforcement/Glock-retailer only. Now, however, Glock has opened it up to Glock Shooting Sports Foundation (GSSF) members, which means anyone who can legally handle firearms can go through it, as long as you are a paying, card-holding member of the GSSF. Not all classes given at all locations are open to everyone, some are restricted to LE or military only, but most are unrestricted.

The basic armorer's course costs have increased to $250, from $195, but it's still well worth it. When I took it the first time, I thought the only thing I would learn was a full, part-by-part takedown. I thought I knew just about everything there is to know. Silly me, I should have known better. The complete disassembly/assembly was only part of what I learned. I also learned more about the company and the operation of the pistol than I ever thought I could. The certification last three years, and I took the course again in 2019 to get recertified. I'm glad I did, because there have been some changes with the new Gen5 models, and it was good to get updated.

Both times, the instructor was outstanding, and even as he went over things I already knew, his sense of humor and demeanor kept us all paying attention. It was a great class that dispelled a lot of rumors and Internet lore. In the morning we learned how to do a complete disassembly/reassembly, with a step-by-step walk through. We then did timed drills to put a little pressure on us. It culminated in the challenge: complete disassembly/reassembly five times in 20 minutes. Good fun. I love stuff like that. After a catered lunch, we came back and learned about parts commonality between models, and between Gen4 and previous generations, and then we learned about the Gen5 and slimline models and how they differ from Gen4.

The Glock Armorer's Tool. Ninety-nine percent of all disassembly that requires a tool is done with this. For magazine catch removal, you'll need a flathead screwdriver or dental pick.

Overall the course is a great one. A lot of information was learned, the test was simple (you'll be mad if you get one wrong) and there's not a better way to spend a day than talking about Glock pistols and hearing cop stories. Best yet, I can now order parts directly from Glock.

They teach you what parts are going to wear out and how often you should replace them. For example, the part that wears out most often but gets replaced least often is the recoil spring assembly. On the current

Finish the course and earn this certificate.

dual springs, you're looking at every 5,000 rounds, on the older springs every 2,500 is when you should get it replaced.

We also learned how to troubleshoot the Glock if there are issues. Some of this information is geared more toward the department/unit armorer, but is still good information to know in order to keep your personal Glock running optimally.

We got in-depth discussion of how the three Glock safeties work, with excellent digital moving graphics showing the whole firing process, as well as three separate graphics showing each safety up close. The graphics were really good, and since a lot of people are a little fuzzy on exactly how the safeties work, especially the drop safety, it was very helpful. Also helpful was the hands-on time with the cutaway Glock.

One thing I found particularly helpful, especially for someone who purchases used Glocks, was the discussions of telltale signs of customizations and "improvements" made by Bubba's Basement Gunsmith Shop, and the problems such modifications can cause.

To be honest, I'm not much into customization. I tend to buy stuff because I like the way it is when I buy it, otherwise I wouldn't buy it. This includes guns. If I didn't like the way a Glock feels or performs, I would buy something else. I am a little biased against customization, and I tend to agree with Glock on its position against messing with the gun. Yes, it's a free country and one can do whatever one wants with his or her gun, as long as it's legal. I get into this topic more in the "Custom Glocks and Aftermarket Parts" in Chapter 20.

Just keep in mind that by buffing parts, changing parts for non-OEM and customizing parts in general, you're going to change tolerances, which can affect performance, safety and reliability. Even something as simple as having your Glock Cerakoted can change tolerances. Can a Glock be modified by a competent gunsmith in order to perform better? You bet. Can it still be safe and reliable? Sure. However, the vast majority of Glocks with mechanical problems seen by armorers have gotten that way after being monkeyed with.

Another helpful tool we added to the toolbox of knowledge was how to conduct field inspections (see Chapter 16). Field inspections are when you test the serviceability of parts and the function of systems through specific actions without taking the pistol completely apart. There are certain field inspections you do with the pistol completely assembled and there are inspections you do to the slide and lower receiver by themselves. Field inspec-

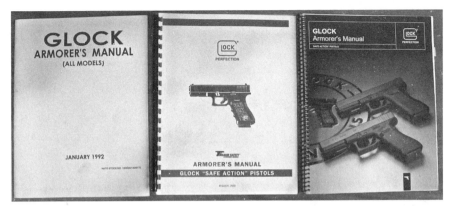

Armorer's manuals through the ages. Left to right: 1992, 2002 and 2014.

tions are very important for department armorers, but they're also important if you're looking over a used Glock you're thinking about buying.

If you've been through the armorer's course before and want or need to requalify, you'll be happy to hear the slideshow has been updated. I've heard horror stories of the more than 400 slides that had to be suffered through in years past. Now the slideshow has been cut to less than 150 slides, and all of them are high-quality graphics you can clearly see and will enjoy. Some are even moving graphics to demonstrate a process, such as how the various safeties work.

Also new is the armorer's manual. We got the new, updated 136-page armorer's manual, marked 07-2018, which covers everything up to and including the Gen5.

This 2018 armorer's manual includes Gen5, G19X and Slimline handguns, including G43X and G48.

The previous manual was written in 2014 and had 140 pages, and the one before that was printed in 2002 and had 72 pages. The 1992 manual had 41 pages (these manuals included a lot of empty space and unnecessary full-page graphics so the manual could be expanded to a size where it could actually be called a manual and not a pamphlet). The 2014 manual was a big improvement, thanks to high-quality pictures and graphics, as well as the addition of two separate sections; one for the Gen4, the other for the G42. The new 2018 manual starts with the "Gen4" section, which is the largest section, followed by a "Previous" [Generation] section and then the "Gen5 I G19X I Slimline" section.

If you are a Glock user, whether that be for carry, competition, duty, service, collector, lowly gun writer or whatever the case might be, I highly recommend the armorer's course. It's indispensable – both the knowledge you gain and the manual you receive. Another big plus, if you work on your Glock, as certified Glock armorer, you'll be able to order Glock OEM parts, which you can't do unless you're an armorer. Glock OEM parts are not only better than most aftermarket parts, they're also usually less expensive.

CHAPTER 19:
SUPPRESSORS

The Bureau of Alcohol, Tobacco, Firearms and Explosives (BATFE or ATF) officially calls them silencers, but don't use that term in front of a suppressor aficionado. Just call them "cans." This is one of the fastest growing sectors of the firearms industry. Since the first edition of this book, there have been major changes in laws governing how to get a suppressor. The ATF Rule 41F in 2016 had some big changes, mostly good, but some bad. The good news, under the new rule it is no longer required to get permission from the local Chief Law Enforcement Officer (CLEO), the CLEO just needs to be notified. This is great news, because under the old laws, people who lived in areas with anti-gun CLEOs were out of luck, just because of where they lived. Rule 41F removes this restriction. The bad news applies to those applying for a suppressor using a trust or corporation (details about this further in the reading) – now everyone listed in the trust or as a RESPONSIBLE PERSON of the corporation must submit two fingerprint cards and a passport photo. Previously this wasn't required. Additionally, a Form 5320.23 is required for every RESPONSIBLE PERSON. Suppressors that were approved prior to ATF Rule 41F, and Form 4s that were submitted/postmarked prior to July 13, 2016 are grandfathered in under previous rules.

With constant attacks on our gun rights, suppressors have fared no better and have been under renewed criticism as that "evil thing that assassins use," despite rarely ever being used in crimes.

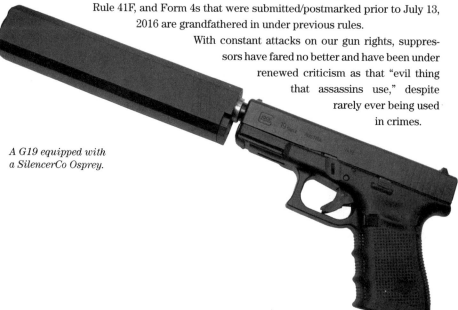

A G19 equipped with a SilencerCo Osprey.

At the time of this writing in mid-2019, 42 states allow for private ownership of suppressors. The eight states that still don't allow it are pretty much the usual suspects when it comes to draconian gun laws: California, Delaware, Hawaii, Illinois, Massachusetts, New Jersey, New York and Rhode Island. In February 2018, the BATFE listed nearly 1.49 million suppressors registered in the United States, up from 792,282 in 2015 (atf.gov; via Guns.com). Out of those 42 states, 40 now have a law making it legal to hunt with a suppressor. While hunting plays a very minor part in the Glock story, there are two Glock pistols listed on the

A G19 with an extended threaded barrel.

G17 with a Lone Wolf extended threaded barrel.

website as suitable for hunting; the G40 and G41. While I have yet to hear of anyone using .45 ACP for hunting, I have read that a 10mm can be an effective hunting caliber in a pistol.

The benefits to using a suppressor with your Glock are numerous, but in a nutshell, it just makes your entire shooting experience better. Obviously, it's going to be a whole lot quieter. Not only does this save your hearing, it makes it more pleasant for young and new shooters. While certainly not as quiet as depicted in movies and television, subsonic handgun loads will generally be at or under the acceptable level without hearing protection (though you should always wear hearing protection when shooting). The not-so-obvious reason to use a suppressor is that it mitigates some of the recoil, some say by as much as 30 percent.

PURCHASING A SUPPRESSOR

It requires a lot of waiting and patience. No one ever said government is fast. To purchase one, you'll need to live in a state where suppressors are legal. Next, you'll need to find a Class 3 dealer in your state, and you'll also need to fill out a BATFE Form 4 (Form 5320.4). The good news is that because they want your business and want to make the transaction go as seamlessly as possible, most Class 3 dealers will fill out and send in the appropriate forms for you. I've purchased suppressors from my Class 3 dealer and directly from manufacturers online. Here's how both transactions went down:

CLASS 3 DEALER

This one is the fastest way to do it. Go to your Class 3 dealer, pick out the suppressor you want, then pay for it. Give them your applicable paperwork (more on that to follow) and a check for $200 made out to BATFE. They'll fill out the Form 4 (or assist you in filling it out), you'll sign it, then they'll send everything in to BATFE. This is if the suppressor you buy is in stock. If not, your dealer will have to transfer it in. This used to take an additional one to three months, but electronic Form 3s have cut the wait time to two to three days for transfers between manufacturers, distributers and dealers.

Then the waiting game begins, which varies. It used to be about four to six months, but as more people learned you can legally own a suppressor, they became more popular. Unfortunately, no more people were allocated to deal with the resulting paperwork, so wait times grew to nine months, and sometimes even up to a year. The wait started to go down, but then the government shutdown in 2019 made it go back up again.

BATFE toyed with E-filing, which took one to three months, but that went away. Now wait times are all over the place, depending on which agent gets your paperwork. I purchased one suppressor, then four months later a second. It took 10 months to get the stamp for suppressor number one, and two weeks after that I got the stamp for suppressor number two. The paperwork was submitted four months later, yet came in only two weeks after the first suppressor's did. One suppressor took only 3.5 months. If you are lucky enough that your Class 3 dealer has a range on premises, you can shoot it during your long wait, you just can't leave the premises with it. It is, after all, yours. You just can't take possession of it.

After your stamp comes in, go pick up your suppressor and take it home, it's yours. Be sure to make many copies of the stamp paperwork, because the BATFE won't send you another if you lose it.

ONLINE SALES

This one takes a little longer. The first thing to know is that you'll still need a Class 3 dealer in your state. The next thing you do is purchase the suppressor from the manufacturer or retailer, either on its website or by phone. Once you do that, your Class 3 dealer will need to send them all their paperwork, and the source you purchased your suppressor from will need to submit to the BATFE the paperwork required to transfer the suppressor to the

U.S. Department of Justice Bureau of Alcohol, Tobacco, Firearms and Explosives	OMB No. 1140-0014 (01/31/2014) **Application for Tax Paid Transfer and Registration of Firearm**

ATF Control Number

2a. Transferee's Name and Address *(Including tradename, if any) (See instruction 2)*	**Submit in Duplicate to:** **National Firearms Act Branch** **Bureau of Alcohol, Tobacco, Firearms and Explosives, P.O. Box 530298** **Atlanta, GA 30353-0298**

1. Type of Transfer *(Check one)*

☐ $5   ☐ $200

Submit with your application a check or money order for the appropriate amount made payable to the Bureau of Alcohol, Tobacco, Firearms and Explosives. Upon approval of this application, this office will acquire, affix and cancel the required "National Firearms Act" stamp for you. *(See instructions 2h, 2i and 3.)*

2b. County

3a. Transferor's Name and Address *(Including trade name, if any) (Executors: see instruction 2k)*

3b. Transferor's Telephone Number and Area Code

3d. Number, Street, City, State and Zip Code of Residence *(or Firearms Business Premises)* if Different from Item 3a.

3c. If Applicable: Decedent's Name, Address, and Date of Death

The above-named and undersigned transferor hereby makes application as required by Section 5812 of the National Firearms Act to transfer and register the firearm described below to the transferee.

4. Description of Firearm *(Complete items a through h)*

a. Name and Address of Manufacturer and/or Importer of Firearm

b. Type of Firearm *(See instruction 1c)*

c. Caliber, Gauge or Size *(Specify)*

d. Model

Length *(Inches)*   e. Of Barrel: f. Overall:

g. Serial Number

h. Additional Description or Data Appearing on Firearm *(Attach additional sheet if necessary)*

5. Transferee's Federal Firearms License *(If any)*	6. Transferee's Special (Occupational) Tax Status *(If any)*	
(Give complete 15-digit number) (See instruction 2b)	a. Employer Identification Number	b. Class

First 6 digits	2 digits	2 digits	5 digits

7. Transferor's Federal Firearms License *(If any)*	8. Transferor's Special (Occupational) Tax Status *(If any)*	
(Give complete 15-digit number) (See instruction 2b)	a. Employer Identification Number	b. Class

First 6 digits	2 digits	2 digits	5 digits

Under Penalties of Perjury, I Declare that I have examined this application, and to the best of my knowledge and belief it is true, correct and complete, and that the transfer of the described firearm to the transferee and receipt and possession of it by the transferee are not prohibited by the provisions of Chapter 44, Title 18, United States Code; Chapter 53, Title 26, United States Code; or Title VII of the Omnibus Crime Control and Safe Streets Act, as amended; or any provisions of State or local law.

9. Consent to Disclosure of Information to Transferee *(See instruction 8)*. I **Do** or **Do Not** *(Circle one)* Authorize ATF to Provide Information Relating to this Application to the Above-Named Transferee.

10. Signature of Transferor *(or authorized official)*	11. Name and Title of Authorized Official *(Print or type)*	12. Date

The Space Below is for the use of the Bureau of Alcohol, Tobacco, Firearms and Explosives

By authority of the Director, This Application has been Examined, and the Transfer and Registration of the Firearm Described herein and the Interstate Movement of that Firearm, when Applicable, to the Transferee are:

Stamp Denomination

☐ Approved *(with the following conditions, if any)*

☐ Disapproved *(For the following reasons)*

Signature of Authorized ATF Official

Date

ATF Form 4 (5320.4)

To buy a suppressor, you will have to fill out a NFA Form 4 (Form 5320.4).

dealer. Again, where this previously took one to three months, it now takes only a couple days. Once they get the OK from BATFE, they will transfer the suppressor to your dealer, and you will need to go to the dealer and conduct business as if you are buying from the dealer directly, except you already paid for your suppressor. There usually will be a transfer fee, usually starting at $100, though it can on rare occasion be lower, it's all up to the dealer. Once you give the dealer your paperwork, you sign the Form 4, they'll submit it, and you'll start your wait.

Either way you go, it's a pretty simple process, it just requires a lot of waiting. In our "immediate gratification" society, this can sometimes be a little much for some people, and they choose to not purchase. Trust me, it is worth the wait.

Silencers Shop (Silencershop.com) has been proactive in making it as easy as possible to purchase a suppressor. What's great about this is they've been sitting down with the BATFE and American Suppressor Association (ASA) to simplifying the suppressor-buying process using the new rules set up by the ATF. This has allowed them to set up kiosks at Class III dealers that allow you to purchase a suppressor and submit all forms, photos and fingerprints from the kiosk in about 10 to 15 minutes. Some of the necessary submissions can even be done via Silencer Shop's smartphone app.

In addition to offering traditional Gun Trusts ($139) – which I cover below – they also offer a Single-Shot Gun Trust ($25) for each suppressor you buy, and a Lifetime Unlimited Single-Shot Gun Trust ($130). The premise behind the Single-Shot Gun Trust is that each suppressor has its own Trust – you don't have to collect fingerprints and forms from every trustee every time you want to buy a suppressor.

THREE WAYS TO FILE

The paperwork you need to submit to the BATFE depends on how you choose to purchase the suppressor. There are three ways to do it: as an individual, through a gun trust, or as a corporation. One thing to take into consideration, the BATFE changes rules/procedures frequently, it seems, especially in ironing out the details. Info found in this chapter is current when it was written, but please check current rules/regulations at the time of purchase.

If filing as an individual, you'll need an FBI fingerprint card, Form FD-258.

INDIVIDUAL

This method is the least favorable way, but it's the easiest. There really aren't any upsides, other than it takes the least amount of time to prepare for your purchase. You'll need to fill out the Form 4, then get a copy. You'll also need to be fingerprinted by your local law enforcement agency, using FBI fin-

U.S. Department of Justice
Bureau of Alcohol, Tobacco, Firearms and Explosives

Certification of Compliance with 18 U.S.C. 922(g)(5)(B)

Note: The Person Certifying to Citizenship Must Complete this Form. *(All entries Must be in ink, printed in CAPITAL LETTERS, and legible.)*

You Must complete this certification or ATF will not be able to act upon your application and the application will be returned to you.

18 U.S.C. 922(g)(5)(B) generally makes it unlawful for any nonimmigrant alien to ship or transport in interstate or foreign commerce, or possess in or affecting commerce, any firearm or ammunition; or to receive any firearm or ammunition which has shipped or transported in interstate or foreign commerce.

A nonimmigrant alien is an alien in the United States in a nonimmigrant classification. The definition includes, in part, persons traveling temporarily in the United States for business or pleasure, persons studying in the United States who maintain a residence abroad, and certain foreign workers.
The definition does NOT include permanent resident aliens.

1. Name under which the application was filed:
Last   First   Middle Initial   or Name of Corporation, Partnership, or Association, *(If applicable.)*

2. Name of person CERTIFYING to citizenship:
Last   First   Middle Initial

*If applying for a Federal Firearms License (*FFL*), All listed responsible persons MUST complete a CERTIFICATION.

3. What is your COUNTRY of citizenship?   Country Name *(list additional country(ies) below if applicable).*

If you are a citizen of the UNITED STATES, skip to question 7.

4. Immigration and Naturalization Service (INS) issued alien number or admission number:

5. Are you a NONIMMIGRANT alien? Answer "Yes" ☐ or "No" ☐

If you answered "No", skip to question 7.

6. If you answered "Yes" to question 5, you must answer the following questions:
   a. Are you in possession of a valid hunting license or permit lawfully issued in the United States Answer "Yes" ☐ or "No" ☐

*If you answer "Yes", complete the following:
   Hunting License/Permit Number, if any   Expiration Date, if any   State of Issuance

   b. Are you an official representative of a foreign government who is accredited to the United States Government or your Government's mission to an international organization having its headquarters in the United States? Answer "Yes" ☐ or "No" ☐

   c. Are you an official of a foreign government or a distinguished foreign visitor who has been so designated by the United States Department of State?
   Answer "Yes" ☐ or "No" ☐

   d. Have you received a waiver from the nonimmigrant alien prohibition from the Attorney General of the United States? Answer "Yes" ☐ or "No" ☐

*If you answered "Yes" to question 6a. or 6d., You must submit appropriate documentation in support of your "Yes" Answer.

7. Under penalties imposed by 18 U.S.C.924, I certify that the statements contained in this certification of compliance with 18 U.S.C. 922 (g)(5)(B) form, and any attached statements in support thereof, are true and correct to the best of my knowledge and belief.

Signature of Individual Who is Identified in Question 2: _____   Date: _____

ATF Form 5330.20
Revised April 2006

Two copies of form 5330.20 will need to be filled out and sent in if filing as an individual.

gerprint cards, Form FD-258. Additionally, you will need to fill out two Form 5330.20 forms, certifying your citizenship. All forms and fingerprints will need to be taken into your Class 3 dealer at the time of purchase, to be sent in to the BATFE. You will need to do this entire procedure for every suppressor and National Firearms Act (NFA) item you purchase.

GUN TRUST

When ATF Rule 41F was first published, everyone thought it would negate the benefits of using gun trusts and corporations to purchase suppressors. It is a lot more legwork, but the benefits are still very much so.

First, anyone listed in the trust can be in possession of the suppressor, without you being present. It will still need to be stored at the address listed on the Form 4, but if someone is named in the trust, they can take it to the range for the day. Second, along that same lines, it also shows a clear path for inheritance of the suppressors when the owner of the gun trust passes away. Purchasing a suppressor using a gun trust will, of course, require you to set up a gun trust in advance. It's best to use a local lawyer familiar with your state laws, but there are online resources as well. Generally, the cost will be around $200 to $500 to set it up. I used SilencerCo's online gun-trust generator and it worked perfectly ($130). You will need to take your gun-trust paperwork to your Class 3 dealer at the time of purchase, so it can be sent to the BATFE. Once you set up a gun trust, it's a "make it and forget it" proposition, with no further work to maintain the trust. ATF Rule 41F has taken away some of the benefits of the gun trust. As I wrote earlier, now everyone listed under the trust must get two sets of fingerprints, a Form 5320.23 and a passport photo for each suppressor you're submitting paperwork for. The process has been simplified somewhat in that most police departments have upgraded to a digital system for collecting fingerprints, so if you're doing multiple suppressor, you can go back at a later date and the police department will just print you two more copies.

CORPORATION

This is the method I used when I first started purchasing NFA items. I filed it under a limited liability corporation (LLC). It has all the perks of the gun trust, and anyone listed as a RESPONSIBLE PERSON in your corporation can be in possession of the suppressor (once again, ATF Rule 41F has affected this method, and all these RESPONSIBLE PERSONS will also need two sets of fingerprints, a Form 5320.23, and a passport photo). The only downside compared to a gun trust is you must maintain your corporation in good standing. That's the primary difference. So, every year, you will need to file your paperwork for your corporation. Purchasing under a corporation is the best method if you already own a corporation, but no one really forms a corporation just to purchase a suppressor or NFA item. It's much less work over the long haul just to make a gun trust. When you purchase your suppressor, you'll need to present to your Class 3 dealer the articles of organization paperwork for your company, as well as a certificate of good standing.

After I purchased my first four NFA items, I realized I didn't want to have to deal with the additional task of needing to file paperwork for the LLC because of NFA items (more importantly, if something happened to me, I didn't want my wife to have to worry about it), so I got the gun trust and transferred everything to that. It cost me extra in tax stamps, but it simplified things for me.

SilencerCo uses a piston like this one for two of its more popular models. The piston serves two functions: as an adaptor to thread the suppressor to various pistols, and as part of a Nielsen Device.

Here the SilencerCo piston is assembled into what serves as a Nielsen Device. It is then inserted into the suppressor and screwed into position.

SUPPRESSOR OPERATION/MAINTENANCE

Using a suppressor on a rifle or rimfire is simple: You just attach it and go, whether it's direct thread or quick attach. Centerfire pistol suppressors are a little trickier. Rifle barrels don't move, and it's the same with rimfire – even rimfire pistols have a fixed barrel. A centerfire semi-auto pistol has a moving barrel – in fact to cycle the action it's required that the barrel move. The barrel moves back a short distance before it unlocks from the slide. At that point it starts to tilt up. With the slide locked to the rear, the barrel is tilted up by a few degrees. If you attach an object to the end of that barrel, such as a suppressor, it makes the barrel work harder to tilt up. This in turn makes it harder for the slide to disengage from the barrel, which makes it difficult for the slide to function. The Nielsen Device serves like a buffer, and it allows the barrel to tilt up, and the slide to cycle as it needs to.

For this chapter, I used a SilencerCo Osprey. For the Osprey, SilencerCo uses a piston, which serves two functions. First, it serves as part of a Nielsen Device. Second, it is an adaptor – there are different pistons for different pistol brands and models, and for different calibers. The piston is assembled into a Nielsen Device with two other parts, then inserted into the suppressor, which is then threaded onto the barrel via the piston.

I currently have two other pistol suppressors "in jail" – at my FFL dealer, awaiting the stamp from the BATFE. The Alpha Dog Alpha-9, and SIG SAUER SD9, though neither of those were used in testing for this book.

When I attended the Glock Armorer's Course in 2019 for re-certification, we were told by the instructor that Glock makes suppressors, but they are not for sale in the United States. I do not have additional information on this at this time.

OPERATION

An understanding of what makes noise when you shoot a gun is an important part of understanding suppressors. Sometimes, people new to suppressors have an unreasonable

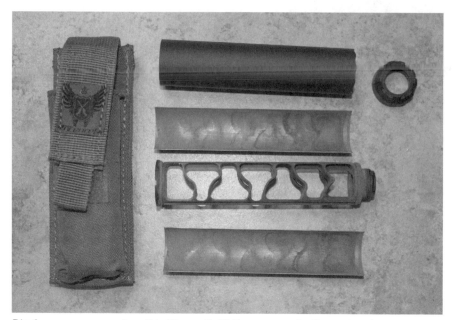

Rimfire suppressors such as this SilencerCo 22 Sparrow require the most maintenance. Unfortunately, not all are as easy to disassemble as the Sparrow.

expectation of what a suppressor is going to do for them, particularly with centerfire rifle suppressors. Most of this comes from not understanding where that noise comes from.

There are three things that make noise when you shoot a cartridge: the cartridge explosion, the action of the firearm, and the bullet as it breaks the sound barrier. All of these have to be taken into consideration.

The explosion when the cartridge is fired is the only part of the process the suppressor is actually suppressing. The suppressor traps the gases as the bullet is leaving the barrel, thus reducing the noise. This is why revolvers cannot be suppressed, because with a suppressor at the end of the barrel the gas will follow the path of least resistance and most of it will go out the front of the cylinder. There is one exception to this, as far as I know, in the 1895 Nagant revolver. This revolver uses the cartridge casing to seal the gas so that it all exits out the front of the barrel.

Second is the action. The suppressor has no control over this, and the only thing you can do to mitigate this is to shoot out of a non-semi-automatic firearm. In a rifle such as a bolt action, the action does not work as the bullet fires, and can be quietly cycled by the shooter after the bullet is down range. Of course, this does little good for handguns, as there are no practical pistols that do not come in semi-automatic.

Third is the bullet as it breaks the sound barrier. The suppressor also has no bearing on this. When people shoot suppressed firearms, this is the thing that makes the most noise, and leaves people with the most disappointment. There is a simple answer for this: purchase ammunition specifically made with subsonic loads. Unfortunately, not all cartridges can be fired with subsonic loads.

The 9mm bullet travels at a supersonic speed, so you'll need to purchase subsonic loads like this one from HPR.

Rimfire cartridges are very effectively suppressed. Even supersonic loads are relatively quiet compared to other cartridges. I've fired standard .17 HMR and .22 Winchester Magnum cartridges out of my SilencerCo .22 Sparrow (check with your manufacturer, not all rimfire suppressors can shoot these cartridges), and they suppress well. But with .22 Long Rifle subsonic loads, there's almost no noise, especially with a bolt-action rifle. A staple gun or BB gun makes more noise. I've used CCI subsonic .22 ammo, and it is some excellent stuff – quiet, reliable and pretty clean.

Handguns can also be effectively suppressed. Subsonic loads are pretty easy to find, and more manufacturers are making more subsonic loads. Some cartridges, such as .45 ACP, are all subsonic, unless you're running +P. Probably the most common cartridge to find subsonic ammo in is 9mm. The most notable thing you'll hear is the action of the handgun.

Centerfire rifles are the most difficult to suppress and leave new suppressor owners with the greatest disappointment if their expectations were based off Hollywood movies. The suppressor still does its job, just not as well as in the other two. Let's look again at the third cause of rifle noise. We already know that the only part of the process the suppressor has any bearing on is the gas that leaves the end of the barrel after the explosion that takes place when the cartridge is fired. And we know the sound from the action can only be affected if you're shooting a bolt-action rifle instead of a semi-automatic. That third factor is the toughest one to overcome, because the rifle cartridges used in military style rifles, mostly the 5.56, 6.8SPC, .308, etc., travel at more than 2,600 feet per second, and most 5.56 ammo is over 3,000 feet per second. Rifle bullets need to be this fast so they are effective when they impact on the target, and so they can stabilize in flight. Rifles fire relatively small bullets compared to pistols, and they rely on that high velocity to be effective on target.

Rifle suppressors, such as this YHM .30-cal can, require almost no maintenance. Most also can't be disassembled like rimfire suppressors.

An AR15 chambered in 5.56 shooting a subsonic load will be no more effective than shooting a .22 Long Rifle. The other side to this is bullet stabilization. The .308 Winchester is notoriously difficult to stabilize in subsonic ammunition, and most suppressor manufacturers have a warning about shooting subsonic .308 out of their suppressors. The danger comes when the bullet fails to stabilize out of the barrel, which can lead to baffle strikes on the suppressor. A baffle strike is when the bullet hits a baffle in your suppressor.

Just think about something traveling at 3,000-plus feet per second hitting a metal object that's attached to the end of a rifle. Nothing good comes of that. At the very least, you're out an item that you've invested good money in. The worst-case scenario is property damage and/or serious injury to people.

While I reported rifles are typically not as easy to suppress as handguns, and aren't as quiet, one of the biggest exceptions are rifles chambered in .300 Blackout. Subsonic .300 BO rounds are very quiet.

MAINTENANCE

Maintenance on suppressors is simple enough, but it can vary drastically between manufacturers, so make sure to check the instructions for your specific model. Across the board, the biggest threat to a suppressor is internal moisture. It's best to remove the suppressor after firing to allow air to circulate through it to speed up evaporation. If your suppressor is hot after firing, this will greatly increase the speed of evaporation. It's recommended not to store your suppressor on your firearm, but if you do, store it muzzle down with the action open to allow airflow.

Pistol suppressors are very simple to maintain, they're a lot like Glock pistols in that they require very little. Most manufacturers recommend taking the piston assembly apart and cleaning that. Manufacturers vary significantly on what to use for cleaning this, so once again consult with your manufacturer. The main chambers of most pistol suppressors are not made for disassembly, and most manufacturers advise against regular maintenance. Some even tell you never to clean it. Solutions left inside can, at worst, cause damage to internal components, or at the least leave behind sludge that compromises effectiveness. Many manufacturers point out that flat-out neglect of a suppressor is preferable to improper maintenance. The best thing to do is just blow it out with pressurized air to get rid of any loose fouling.

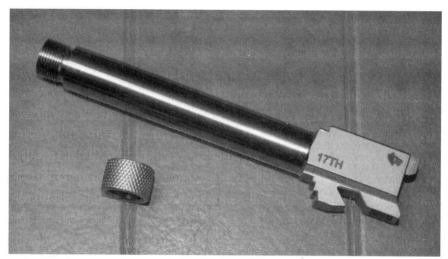

The Lone Wolf threaded barrel makes a very good aftermarket choice if you can't get your hands on a Glock threaded barrel.

Rifle suppressors are the easiest to maintain, as there is no piston assembly to disassemble. For most, maintenance should be kept to a minimum, or avoided altogether (I like the sound of this, much like what yard chores should be), depending on manufacturer. Some will tell you to use a hydrocarbon-based solution, like WD-40 or Kroil, to clean it every 2,000 to 3,000 rounds. Some will tell you not to clean it at all.

Rimfire suppressors get the dirtiest, so most are made to be disassembled. Many manufacturers recommend every 200 to 300 rounds; my .22 Sparrow needs to be cleaned every 1,000 rounds or so. Follow your manufacturer's disassembly instructions, and recommendations for cleaning.

THREADED BARREL OPTIONS

At the time the first edition of this book was written, Glock did not make OEM threaded barrels for sale, at least in the U.S. The Glock website now lists nine different models of threaded barrels available: G17 Gen4 (1/2x28), G17 Gen5 (1/2x28), G17 (M 13.5x1 LH, Gen1 – 4 only), G19 Gen4 (1/2x28), G19 Gen5 (1/2x28), G34 Gen5 (1/2x28), G21 Gen4 (.578x28), G21 (M16x1 LH), and G23 (M14.5x1 LH). (M stands for Metric, and LH stands for Left Hand, and references a European threading, not common in the U.S., however the major suppressor manufacturers do make adapters for it. For Glock pistols, LH barrels are for Gen1 through Gen4 only).

When suppressors started to become popular with civilian shooters, there were three primary manufactures of aftermarket threaded barrels for Glock pistols: Storm Lake, Lone Wolf and Bar-Sto. All make good barrels, though the Storm Lake and Bar-Sto are a little pricey for a barrel. The Lone Wolf falls more in line with the price of a Glock OEM barrel. With my deadline fast approaching, the testing I did was limited, but I did get my hands on

SilencerCo's line of threaded barrels is a great choice to fill the void left by Glock. It's an outstanding barrel.

a Lone Wolf barrel. Accuracy is good, and it worked reliably. Mine was the forged stainless model for the G17, and runs about $125. The nice thing about it is that it uses standard land-and-groove rifling, so you can use lead cast bullets with it. I dropped it in all four generations of G17, and it fit all of them with no gunsmithing. I expected as much. As far as workmanship, I didn't see any machining marks and it looks good.

Shortly before the first edition was finished, SilencerCo started making its own line of barrels. If you can't buy a barrel from the manufacturer of your gun, then buy one from the manufacturer of your suppressor. The very first suppressor I ever fired was a SilencerCo suppressor, and I've been a big fan of the company ever since – I now own three of its models. They work well, are well-designed and of high quality. I found the same thing holds true for its barrels. In regard to quality and performance, I would put the SilencerCo barrels up against any other aftermarket threaded barrel. They are outstanding. The workmanship on them is also excellent, with no machining marks and all precision machining. The barrel for the G17 that I have has an MSRP of $220. Available in models for the G17, G17L, G19, G21, G22, G23, G26, G34, G43.

As the Glock aftermarket parts cottage industry has boomed, there's probably dozens of companies making threaded barrels for Glock now. Glock is the most popular maker of handguns, so any new company that wants to enter the market naturally looks to the Glock. So, if a company exists to make aftermarket parts for handguns, chances are pretty good they make them for Glock. And if they make parts, then they probably make barrels, and if they make barrels, they most likely make a threaded one. There's a lot of options when it comes to threaded barrels.

WHICH SUPPRESSOR TO BUY?

An important thing to consider when making your choice of which suppressor to buy is what caliber should you get? There is more to it than just buying a suppressor for the specific caliber you want. For example, if you want to buy a suppressor for your G17 9mm, you don't have to buy a 9mm suppressor. In fact, most companies make suppressors that are multi-caliber (but you should confirm the model is multi-caliber before you buy).

If you buy a suppressor made for a .45 ACP, the suppressor will work with all the calibers smaller than it. So, the .45 ACP suppressor would work with .40 S&W and 9mm pistols (and some with .300 Blackout). The same holds true with rifles: If you buy a .30 caliber rifle can, it will work with 5.56, 6.8 SPC, etc.

There are tradeoffs, however, and then there are other factors that can cancel out that tradeoff, but cause yet another tradeoff. For example, if you buy a .45 suppressor to use with your 9mm, it gives you flexibility, because you can use it for more of your handguns. It's a better value for your money, because it's typically the same price, or just slightly more. But there is a trade off in slightly decreased decibel reduction, because more gas is allowed to escape. It's not a lot, with a .45 hole and a .356 bullet going out of it, you're talking .10 of an inch. With a rifle it's even less, a .30 hole with a .223 bullet coming out of it is .07 inches. So, it's not a lot of gas escaping, and unless you're very experienced with suppressors, you probably won't notice a discernible increase in sound.

And here's the other factor I mentioned: When you use a larger caliber suppressor for multiple calibers, the can itself is physically larger, so there's more room to trap gas. A .45 can is larger than one for a 9mm, so if you use the .45 can with a 9mm, it has more room to trap that gas, even though it allows a little bit more of it to escape. So, the physically larger suppressor mitigates the inefficiency caused by using a .45 can with a 9mm. In the end, the trade off to using a multi-caliber suppressor is you have a larger suppressor than you would if you used one specific to the smaller caliber.

If you're looking to purchase your first suppressor, unless you know you're only going to be using it with a specific caliber, get the larger, multi-caliber suppressor. Buy a .30 caliber can for your rifle and a .45 caliber can for your pistols. This way you have all of your firearms covered. Then, down the road, if you have the inclination and the money, purchase caliber-specific suppressors. But this is just a recommendation.

Another thing to keep in mind: suppressors are rated by cartridge, not the caliber of the bullet. For example, if you own a .30 caliber rifle can, and it's only rated up to .308, you can't use it with a .30-06 or anything more powerful (again, check with your maker on which calibers you can and can't use). The same holds true with the pistol suppressors; if you own one made for a .45, you probably won't be able to use it with a .44 Magnum Desert Eagle. Make sure to read which specific calibers your can is rated for, and if you have any questions, contact the manufacturer of your suppressor.

Suppressors also have different ratings, such as full auto and short barrel. Handgun suppressors are designed for short barrels, since handguns have short barrels, but not all rifle suppressor are rated for that. Even ones that are, might only be rated to a certain length. For example, you might have an AR with an 8.5-inch barrel, but a can that's only rated for a 10.5-inch barrel. Make sure to check the rating of your suppressor before shooting – you can cause damage to your suppressor. The full-auto rating is self-explanatory, if you're shooting a full auto, and your suppressor is not rated for full auto, don't attach it to your gun, it will get damaged from the heat.

CHAPTER 20:
CUSTOM GLOCKS AND AFTERMARKET PARTS

Glock has gotten so big, Glock isn't "just Glock," an entire cottage industry has spawned off of Glock. There are dozens of companies that make aftermarket custom parts and accessories, with new ones sprouting up all the time. At least a dozen companies make custom Glocks for you to purchase, or you can send in your Glock and armorers will work their custom "magic." And then there's the relatively new, but fast-growing segment of PCCs – that's Pistol Caliber Carbine – many of which are based off Glock magazines. Some even incorporate your Glock pistol into the carbine.

One fairly recent trend that's becoming more common is non-Glock Glocks. Several companies that have been making Glock slides, barrels and other parts used with the Glock frame, have now started making their own frames. The frames use Glock parts internally (both OEM and aftermarket parts), but the frame looks very different. So, it's a non-Glock handgun that is based off the Glock design. Most of these guns are named in a manner that still uses Glock model numbers, such as "17" and "19." For example, the

Keanu Reeves training for the movie John Wick 2 *with his Taran Tactical Innovations Combat Master Glock G34. (Photo by Taran Butler)*

The TTI Combat Master G34 model
used in the John Wick *movies.*
(Photo by Taran Butler)

handgun from Faxon firearms is named FX-19. It's hard for me to mentally classify these firearms, because here you have a company that is building a handgun from the ground-up as its own, however the design itself is not its own, because it's still Glock's design. I don't get into these guns a whole lot, because I think it's a little out of the scope of this book.

AFTERMARKET PARTS/ACCESSORIES

In this day and age of the "Insta-gun," it seems everyone with a camera or smartphone loves posting photos on Instagram of their customized guns with all OEM parts replaced with parts purchased for looks, first, and reliability/functionality, second. "Tacti-cool" as they call it. This is fine for competition Glocks, or casual shooting Glocks; but for me, all of my "go-to" and carry guns are pretty much stock. Those fighting guns are the guns I stake my life on, and I'm not concerned how those guns look, I'm only concerned how they perform. I'll upgrade sights to aftermarket, but that's about it. Glock makes each part with a very specific tolerance, and with very specific metals and polymers. Metals are hardened to a specific hardness, and are given a specific treatment/coating. Even something as simple as giving it a Cerakote can change the tolerances, even if just by a bit.

Here's an example, something as simple as the slide cover plate. Glock's OEM is polymer. A lot of the aftermarket parts are aluminum. Why is this a problem? It violates one of the rules in Glock assembly: Polymer to polymer, metal to metal. Each model of Glock is fine-tuned to the caliber it shoots, and one of the few differences between calibers is the spring-loaded bearing, made of polymer. There's a black one for .380/9mm, a white one for .40/.357/.45 GAP, and an Olive one for 10mm/.45. These typically don't wear out, because the polymer bearing surface only makes contact with the polymer slide plate cover. However, if it did wear, it would change the tolerances, having an effect on the extractor, which leads to failure-to-extract malfunctions. If this happens to your carry gun when you need it most, then suddenly that cool-looking slide cover plate with the Punisher logo just cost you your life.

Then there is the argument about legal issues with custom parts. Does a light-pull trigger get used against you in the instance where you need to defend yourself? I've read some smart people who have argued from both sides; and I've also read some "Internet lawyers" argue both sides, as well. Who's right?

It's just not worth it, and that's why I go plain-Jane stock on my fighting Glocks.

But for my non-carry guns, that's a different story. I like cool-looking guns as much as the next guy, and I'm not saying there's not a time and place for cool-looking guns. While I keep all of my fighting guns mostly stock, I do have my fun guns that I modify with flashy, custom parts. Those guns are first and foremost shooters, but I enjoy having them look good, too. Those are not guns I depend on for my personal defense, so if one of those has a problem at the range due to a custom part, no big deal, I can fix it.

I also want to clarify, I'm in no way reporting or implying that most of these aftermarket parts aren't high quality. I'm sure 99.9 percent of the time they function perfectly. However, as any Glock armorer can attest, if a Glock does break or have problems, a high percentage of the time it's non-Glock aftermarket parts, or someone has altered a Glock OEM part (like buffing down parts to make them smoother, for a better trigger pull. Again, that changes tolerances). I'm the same way with all of my self/home-defense guns. My home defense AR15s, for example, those all have triggers and parts designed for ruggedness. I don't put competition triggers on them, it's always a "combat" trigger or I keep the government trigger on it. Government triggers never break. But I have had fancy, cool-looking triggers break.

Is there likely to be a parts breakage or problem for the average shooter? No. Aftermarket parts made by reputable companies have been thoroughly tested, and tested again. The average shooter doesn't put enough rounds down range through his or her Glock for it to ever be an issue.

Now that you understand where I come from with the difference between my fighting guns and my fun guns, I've compiled a list of some aftermarket companies making some great parts/accessories. It's a huge cottage industry, and growing, so there's no way I can list them all, but these are ones I've personally used, had dealings with, or come across in my travels.

MAGAZINES

Aftermarket Glock magazines have been around for a while but haven't started catching on until the last four or five years. Glock makes such great magazines that are practically indestructible, it was hard for a lot of companies to compete. Add to that, the fact that Glock mags are relatively cheap, compared to pistol magazines from other brands. I personally like the design of Glock mags: polymer with a metal liner. That metal makes it more rigid, and especially having metal feed lips, that can be important. Especially in climates where it gets frigid. I've shot in temperatures down to -12 and even -18, with windchill far into the -20s, and I've had feed lips on polymer AR15 mags split when I was loading them. That's not as likely to happen with pistol mags, since they are loaded differently (push in and slide back) from AR mags, but it's still something to take into consideration.

However, there are some great aftermarket Glock magazines, and most are polymer. This list isn't conclusive, but these are ones I've personally tested/used.

On all of these magazines I did drop tests onto concrete with magazines filled to capacity with inert rounds (I loaded empty, un-primed 9mm cases with 124 grain FMJ bullets). I held the Glock at face height and hit the mag release to eject the mags onto the ground. I did this 10 times, unless otherwise noted. The results below do not include the fact that on occasion a round would come out, or a round would sometimes tilt inside the magazine. This is physics and has nothing to do with the magazine, it can happen to any of them. As long as the magazine doesn't break or disassemble, and keeps most of the rounds in it (usually only one round will pop out, sometimes two), then it's a win for that magazine. I know a lot of people do drop tests with empty magazines, because people typically drop mags after they've been emptied and they're reloading. However, I've been around enough 2nd Lieutenants and PFCs to know that when stress levels go up, wrong buttons can get pressed. Someone can do a reload and go to press the slide release with gloved hands and the next thing you know the mag drops out and the slide is still open. When you're on a two-way shooting range – when bullets are flying at you, not just from you – the last thing you want is for the mag that was accidently ejected to land on the ground and do an instantaneous disassembly.

PROMAG

This company has been at it for a while and makes excellent magazines. If you prefer Glock OEM mags made of polymer with a steel insert, these are the mags for you. Held side by side, it's hard to tell the difference between a ProMag and a GLOCK OEM mag, and that's a good thing. Standard capacity magazines generally run around

Since the G43 is made for concealed carry, this ProMag 50-round drum probably isn't that practical, but it sure is fun!

If you're looking for more magazine options than what Glock offers, but prefer Glock's metal-lined mags, take a look at ProMag. There are a lot of options, and they are extremely well built. Here we have extended-capacity magazines for (left to right) Glock .40-caliber models, G42, G43 and an FDE-colored 9mm mag.

The ProMag 9mm 50-round drums for (left) G17, G19, G26, G34; and (right) G43 Slimline. The G17 drum is perfect for PCCs that accept Glock mags.

Magpul also makes a beveled mag well that attaches via the grip hole.

Magpul Glock magazines come in several sizes for your shooting enjoyment. Shown here are the (left to right) 27-round, 21-round and 17-round 9mm Glock mags.

$22, (and by standard capacity I mean the capacity intended for that gun: G17 is 17 rounds, G19 is 15 rounds, G26 is 10 rounds, etc.), and extended-round magazines cost around $28-$33, including 27- to 32-round mags. ProMag also makes 50 round drum magazines for Glock that are $100 to $122, depending on make/model. The G17 model works great in the G17, G19, G26, G34 and is also a great fit for PCCs that use Glock mags. It also has a model for the G43, which is more for fun than anything else – the G43 is for carry, this drum mag is not – with an even crazier G42 model coming out in .380. I've personally used the G43 drum, G17 drum (I did not perform drop tests on the drums), and just about every magazine for Glock models ProMag makes, and all have performed perfectly, with no problems to report. They're well-made and very durable, just like Glock OEM mags. (promagindustries.com)

MAGPUL

Famous for polymer AR15 mags and AR accessories, Magpul started making Glock mags a few years back, and they're excellent. I admit, I was a little leery at first. Glock mags are pretty tough, as I mentioned. I could envision dropping a loaded mag on concrete and have cartridges flying everywhere. That never happened, and since I've been using Magpul mags, I've had no issues with them, and no breakages. It survived my 10-drop test onto concrete without any issues: no cracks, breaks, disassembly, etc. I feel comfortable buying any Magpul product and know it won't fail me.

I believe Magpul was the first company to use an orange follower in Glock mags, which I like. The Gen5 Glock mag followers look awfully similar. It only makes Glock PMAGs, called the GL9, for the 9mm Glocks. They come in standard capacities for the G17, G19, G26, as well as 10-round (restricted states) capacities, plus PMAGs in extended capacities of 21- and 27- round capacities, and an extended 12-rounder for the G26. Magpul also makes the GL L-Plate, which is a magazine floor plate that replaces the floor plate on the GL9, and is designed to fit in extended magazine wells used in competitive shooting.

Speaking of magazine wells, Magpul also makes the GL Enhanced mag well for Glock, that attaches via the grip hole. It allows for faster reloads, yet isn't so big that it prints when carried concealed under the shirt. It comes in four models: two for compact models (G19,

The Magpul Speedplate attaches to Glock OEM magazines and makes for speedier access to spare magazines, as well as a good shock absorber for dropped mags.

G23, G32, G38 and G35) in Gen3 and Gen4 (www.magpul.com), and two for standard models (G17, G17L, G22, G24, G31, G34, G35 and G37) in Gen3 and Gen4.

Another Magpul accessory made specifically for Glock OEM magazines is the Speedplate, for use on any 9mm and .40 S&W Glock OEM magazine. It's the pistol version of Magpul's Rangerplate, and provides a grip for pulling magazines out of your mag carrier, and to provide extra cushion from impact. It won't work with Magpul Glock mags, but it works with Glock OEM mags. Not only is it great for making it easy to grab mags out of the carrier, I also like that it adds extra cushion when mags drop out and hit the deck.

ELITE TACTICAL SYSTEMS (ETS)

ETS engineers made a name for themselves with their see-through magazines that were not only functional, but strikingly good-looking, too. A clear magazine in which you can see the rounds stacked on top of each other looks pretty awesome on a rifle such as an AR-15, but it doesn't have the same effect in a handgun, since the grip conceals the magazine inside of it. ETS has that covered, too, because it of-

ETS came to market with an orange transparent 31-round magazine (left) marketed for the G18. It sold so well, ETS introduced more colors, including red and blue. Here they're loaded with Black Hills 115-grain FMJ. (instagram.com/robb_manning #robb_manning.glock.book)

The 12-round ETS mag for the G42, here loaded with Black Hills Honey-Badger rounds, a very potent load.

fers extended-round magazines, with a 31-round 9mm magazine, so there's a whole lot of see-through magazine extending past the grip exposing the rounds stacked on each other. ETS mags come in a transparent smoke-gray color, but when the company introduced its Orange 31-round mag, it really caught my eye. It's marketed as being for the G19, but works in all the non-slimline 9mm models. It's very cool, and it does grab your attention. They've been so popular for ETS that it added blue and red models.

The 12-round G42 magazine is a welcome addition for anyone carrying the G42. Twelve rounds are always better than the factory six rounds, especially when talking about a .380 ACP. It's long for concealment, but works as a good backup mag.

ETS has a 40-round 9mm magazine on the way, but it wasn't available at the time of this writing.

In my past experience, clear, hard polymer is often more brittle than other polymers, and so I was a little leery about drop-testing the ETS mags. I started with the 31-round mag, and the first drop onto concrete revealed no issues at all. The second drop, though, the baseplate came off, inducing an instantaneous unload of the mag. Fortunately, most of the rounds stayed in the mag, and the two that didn't were sitting about 6 inches from the felled magazine, just next to the follower and mag insert. The baseplate and spring, however, I heard ricocheting around my garage and after about 15 minutes of searching I found the spring. The baseplate still hasn't been found to this date. None of the parts were damaged, and I was able to snap on another baseplate and it was just fine. So, the polymer didn't break or crack, it held up fine, it just had too much flex, allowing the baseplate to come off. If you're at the range, it won't be an issue dropping an empty mag on the ground, but be cautious of dropping mags with rounds still in them.

It turned out to reveal a bit of a silver lining that this happened, because if it wouldn't have happened, I wouldn't have learned the ETS mags will also accept Glock OEM baseplates (I used the ETS mag insert). More importantly, this means the ETS mag will also accept the Magpul Speedplate that I mentioned a few paragraphs ago. So, I took that same ETS mag and parts, and with the Magpul Speedplate installed I was able to do 10 drops onto concrete with no problems at all. This extra cushion is enough to keep the ETS mag from the instantaneous disassembly that it had without it.

As for reliability, the ETS mags functioned perfectly, I didn't have any malfunctions with any of them. That's important, because reliability is a big reason people are so fond of Glocks. If a magazine were to make a Glock unreliable, it wouldn't last long on the market.

The Jagemann Glock magazine was one of the first non-Glock Glock mags the author purchased, and he's never had any issues with reliability or durability.

I'm impressed with how thick ETS made the feed lips on its mags. They seem to be very rugged and have held up well so far. These are well-made mags, my only concern is the baseplate popping off. I'd definitely buy more of these, though, and replace the baseplate with the Magpul Speedplates. (www.etsgroup.us)

JAGEMANN SPORTING GROUP

The Jagemann mag feels like a little bit thinner polymer than the other mags, and I was a bit concerned about this when I first started using them a couple years ago. I've done prior drop tests with these mags on a couple of occasions, without any problems, and for this test onto concrete, still no issues. In fact, not even a single round came out, or even moved at all, which reinforced my confidence in these mags. Jagemann has its background in the automotive industry, starting in 1946. The company then moved into brass ammo casings, where it's become one of the largest independent brass case makers in the U.S. Jagemann decided to tap into its experience with automotive polymers and expanded into polymer handgun magazines.

Jagemann makes magazines for the G17, G19, G42 and G43, and in six different colors. These mags include an extended baseplate for extra grip when grabbing the mag, though it's not for increasing mag capacity, with the exception of the G17 mag, which is 18 rounds. The mags are high quality, with tight tolerances, and they cost only around $12 each. I will buy more of these without hesitation. (www.jagemannsportinggroup.com)

CUSTOM PARTS

I typically like everything to be organized in a particular fashion, and the sections of this book are no exception. I wanted a part about custom Glocks, and a part about custom parts for Glock. The challenge in trying to organize this, and keeping within the size constraints of the book, is where to draw the line between listing a company as making custom parts, or listing a company that makes custom Glocks. Many companies offer both. It's kind of a fine line between the two. The difference is a company selling custom parts will sell you parts, and you use those parts to customize your Glock. A company making a custom Glock will send you a Glock that's completely customized, you do nothing. This is done either of two ways, either you purchase a custom Glock as a completed product, or you send in your Glock, armorers work their magic, and they send you your customized Glock.

There are a few companies listed below – Zev, Lone Wolf Distributers and Grey Ghost Precision (GGP) – that sell parts, as well as custom Glocks. I include them in custom parts because that's what they're mostly known for. These three also sell a complete handgun, but I don't classify it as a "custom Glock," because zero percent of it is a Glock. The complete gun they sell is based off the Glock design, but they make everything, including the frame. (But you could take any part off of their complete gun, and swap it with an OEM part from a stock Glock.)

ZEV

Zev has been making aftermarket Glock parts for awhile, is one of the bigger names in the industry and well-respected. I've been an admirer of Zev products for awhile, but have limited hands-on experience shooting them, so I can't write in great detail about them. I

This G34 barrel from Zev is very accurate, and the dimpled, burnt-bronze finish looks great. (instagram.com/robb_manning #robb_manning.glock.book)

do have one of its G34 "dimpled, burnt-bronze" barrels, and it's outstanding, and very good looking. Judging from it, and from handling other products, Zev's stuff is very well-made. The barrels use pre-hardened chromium 416R stainless steel, like that used in match-grade rifle barrels. Each barrel is then cut rifled and inspected for rifling groove dimensions. The barrel is then double honed until a surface finish of 16 RA (roughness average) is reached. As a comparison, a 42 RA would be a bead blasted surface finish, and 4 RA would be a mirror finish. Just looking at the barrel though, you don't need fancy numbers and measurements to see the ultra-smooth finish. (www.zevtechnologies.com)

HYVE TECHNOLOGIES

Hyve specializes in aluminum CNC parts for your Glock, including mag releases, slide cover plates, magazine baseplates and triggers. Its parts are finely made, then anodized in vibrant colors that really stand out, making for great "Insta-guns." Or you can order the parts in black. Colors include: blue, OD green, copper, red, violet, tan, gray and black. Hyve also makes other parts for Glock that aren't as flashy, such as magazine springs and takedown pins. It recently started offering barrels and slides as well. I decked out my G43 in various Hyve parts for photos, but the black and white photos here in this book won't do it justice.

Hyve makes some great-looking Glock custom parts across the color spectrum. This G43 has a copper-colored mag release, slide cover plate (not visible in this photo), mag baseplate and extended mag baseplate. The trigger is copper with a blue trigger safety. (instagram.com/robb_manning #robb_manning.glock.book)

However, you can have a look at my Instagram feed (**instagram.com/robb_manning — #robb_manning.glock.book**). The parts are well-made, drop-in and I haven't had any problems at all with reliability. Though I don't have many rounds through the gun with these parts so I cannot vouch for durability and wear and tear. As I noted earlier in the book, I don't use my G43 much for carry anymore, but if I started to again, given my feelings about aftermarket parts for self-defense guns, I'd most likely switch back to OEM. But aside from that, Hyve parts are well-made in addition to looking good. Maybe after a couple thousand rounds through this gun with these parts, I'll start to change my mind about non-OEM parts on my fighting guns. (hyve-technologies.com)

This Lone Wolf G34 slide looks futuristic. It features quality construction and performs flawlessly.

This is not a laser gun; it's a G34 with a Lone Wolf Signature Series slide, Pattern No. 20. This one has been given a Winter Battleworn Cerakote finish.

LONE WOLF DISTRIBUTERS

One of the very first aftermarket parts I bought for one of my Glocks was a Lone Wolf threaded barrel, before Glock made threaded barrels. It's always performed well, with no problems, and has a good fit and finish.

Your eyes aren't playing tricks on you. Alpha Wolf (Lone Wolf Distributing) makes a barrel for your G42 that converts it to the Russian 9x18 Makarov cartridge. (instagram.com/robb_manning #robb_manning.glock.book)

Lone Wolf has been making Glock barrels and parts for a long time, and it is one of the largest. The company earned a loyal following making competitively priced products that performed well, and in recent years has added some higher-end products that are made in the USA, as part of the ALPHA WOLF line.

Lone Wolf now makes a custom part for every part for Glock, including the Timberwolf frame (which comes in large and standard size frames). It even offers complete pistols. One of my favorite things Lone Wolf offers is the Signature Series slides. I've seen pattern No. 20 through No. 23, and they are sharp-looking. A piece of art, really. Lone Wolf loaned me one of its Pattern No. 23 slides for the G34, and it looks like something out of a science-fiction movie. It put a cool looking Winter Battleworn Cerakote finish on it and included a G34 barrel with its "Frost Bitten" finish. It looks sexy, and it shoots great, too. I didn't get it until the last minute, so my range time with it is limited to just one session, but by the time you've read this I will have enjoyed more time at the range with it.

Something else Lone Wolf makes, if you're into com-bloc calibers like the 9x18 Makarov, but have always wanted a modern polymer gun chambered in 9x18 Mak, your wishes have been answered. Lone Wolf makes a 9x18 Mak conversion barrel for the G42. There's one that's threaded, and one that's not. I'm a collector of com-bloc weapons, so I think this is pretty cool. I was surprised at how nicely it shoots out of the G42. I thought it would be a little snappy, but it's not at all.

Aside from fun, there is a benefit: You've just upgraded the power of your G42. It's only a slight upgrade, the 9x18 Mak falls somewhere between a .380 ACP and 9mm Luger, and the bullet has a slightly larger diameter. Comparing off-the-shelf ammo from Hornady Critical Defense, the 90-grain FTX load, out of a 4-inch barrel the 9x18 Mak ammo has 11 more ft/lbs of energy at the muzzle, and 17 ft/lbs more energy at 50 yards. It's listed as having the same 1,000 fps muzzle velocity, though that's the only place I've found that they have the same velocity. Looking at reloading manuals, the 9mm Mak has anywhere from 70 to 200 fps increase for a comparable bullet weight/style. Of course, this is a barrel change that's not condoned by Glock, as the only thing it officially condones is swapping out .357 SIG barrels for .40 S&W, and vice versa. (www.lonewolfdist.com)

GREY GHOST PRECISION (GGP)

I first learned of Grey Ghost through the company's Grey Ghost Gear (GGG) soft line of gear, bags, pouches, slings, etc. (greyghostgear.com). When I eventually learned it also had a full

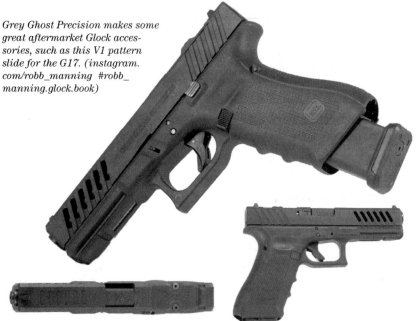

Grey Ghost Precision makes some great aftermarket Glock accessories, such as this V1 pattern slide for the G17. (instagram. com/robb_manning #robb_ manning.glock.book)

If you've ever used GGP products, you're familiar with the skull/ghost logo, seen here on the RMR cutout cover. (instagram.com/ robb_manning #robb_manning.glock.book)

The Grey Ghost Precision barrel, partially seen through this ejection port, uses a proprietary twist rate and is very accurate. (instagram.com/robb_manning #robb_ manning.glock.book)

line of Glock parts, I was a little baffled at first. To me it was like learning Under Armour also made gun accessories. It did not compute. Gear/Accessories vs. Gun Parts. There's generally not a lot of crossover, and when it happens, it's usually the case of a gun company that has become successful offering a line of gear to complement the guns, but it's usually an afterthought, and the products are not usually made by that company. Not the case here. Both divisions of the company – GGP and GGG – make outstanding products. I've used my GGG backpack for several years now, and the messenger bag for over a year. I'm newer to the GGP side of things, as I've only been testing its products since writing this book.

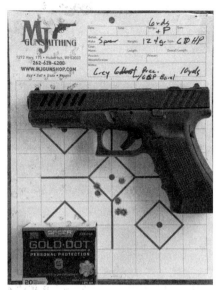

The GGP barrel and slide make for an accurate gun. Six shots at 10 yards, using Speer 124-grain 9mm +P GDHP.

I have the G17 Gen4 slide in pattern V1, and though I haven't logged a lot of rounds through it yet (I'm sitting at about 150) it's worked perfectly thus far. It shipped as a stripped slide and I've installed all OEM Glock parts in it, plus the GGP Glock match-grade barrel with a black nitride finish. I have the RMR cutout version, so I can mount a Trijicon RMR optic with no plate needed. Since I am planning on mounting an RMR, for sights, I decided to use some plastic Glock sights I had on hand. I didn't see a need for more expensive sights since it's going to have an RMR mounted on it. It's not going to be a carry gun anyway, since I don't typically carry a full size G17, it will be mostly a fun gun.

GGP uses a proprietary twist rate, and accuracy is outstanding. GGP also sells a slide completion kit of upgraded internal parts. This is a little bit out of the scope of this book, because it would make your Glock into a non-Glock, but GGP also makes a proprietary frame that uses OEM Glock internal parts, as well as a complete pistol called the GGP Combat Pistol. (greyghostprecision.com)

Faxon Firearms is known for making high-quality gun parts. Here's one of its barrels for a Glock G17: flame fluted, threaded and with a chameleon PVD finish. (instagram.com/robb_manning #robb_manning.glock.book)

FAXON FIREARMS

Faxon has been making high-quality AR-15s and Glock parts for years now, but a few years back become most famous for its new ARAK-21 rifle, which combines elements of both AR and AK designs into one rifle. Prior to firearms, Faxon has been machining precision metal parts for defense, automotive, medical and aerospace industries since 1978. Faxon knows what it's doing. Faxon makes some excellent barrels. I have the G17 "flame fluted, threaded, chameleon PVD finish, 416-R, Nitride, match series" barrel. It's made of 416-R Stainless steel and uses conventional rifling so you can shoot cast bullets with no worries. Finishing it off is an 11-degree target crown. It's a high-quality barrel, and very accurate, as well as being great looking. Faxon makes some great-looking slides, except unfortunately they don't make Glock slides, but slides for a competitor's handgun. However, Faxon makes a complete handgun called the FX-19, which is based off the Glock design and uses Glock parts, which leads me to believe it makes Glock-compatible slides for this handgun, so I'm not sure why the company doesn't sell one separately. Faxon makes great products; I'm hoping it continues to expand into the Glock aftermarket parts category. (faxonfirearms.com)

PATRIOT ORDNANCE FACTORY (POF)

POF is most famous for its gas-piston ARs, but the company now makes a Glock slide that's worth mentioning. It's called the G-Series Gentlemen's Slides, "for patriot gentlemen who appreciate a reliable tool with a touch of class and uniqueness." I have the P34 Gen4 model and it's well-made in addition to being good-looking. It's machined from 17-4 stainless steel and given a Nitride heat treatment for durability and corrosion resistance. It has an optics cut for a Trijicon RMR and comes with a cover plate. Also available in G17 and G19 models with optics cut, in Gen3 or Gen4. Models for G42 and G43 are also available, but without optics cut.

POF is known for its AR15s, but is now also making a Glock slide for the G34. It only comes in black. The author had it Cerakoted in WWII bazooka-green and military-ammo-can-yellow highlights (Cerakote by www.mjgunshop.com). (instagram.com/robb_manning #robb_manning.glock.book)

Another angle of the POF Glock slide. This angle shows the Zev G34 barrel (dimpled, burnt bronze). (instagram.com/robb_manning #robb_manning.glock.book)

The machining looks good, as to be expected from POF, with no rough machining marks visible. I love the patriotism that POF puts into its products, and this slide is no different, highlighted by the WWII era Army star and banner on the slide, which is also the POF logo. The rear slide serrations are chevron shaped, and the slide has front has ventilation cuts. It comes stripped, ready for OEM or aftermarket Glock parts. It's not completely

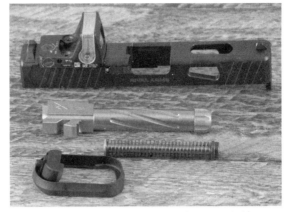

Rival Arms, an up-and-comer in the Glock accessory market, makes a solid lineup of Glock accessories.

stripped though, unlike the other slides I own, this one came with a pre-installed firing pin channel liner. It comes only in black, but would be perfect for a patriotic Cerakote job. So, I had the slide Cerakoted by MJ Gunsmithing (www.mjgunshop.com). It's a WWII bazooka green with military-ammo-can yellow highlights. It looks outstanding. Stay tuned to my Instagram feed for photos. (pof-usa.com)

RIVAL ARMS

A new kid in the gun industry, Rival makes everything you need to build a Glock G17, G19, G26, G34 or G43 (in Gen3 or Gen4) upper assembly (including barrel and guide rod), plus the mag extension, frame pin kit (in stainless steel or titanium), grip plug, mag extension and extended slide lock. Slides are CNC machined from 17-4PH stainless steel billet and Quench-Polish-Quench thermo-chemical case-hardened. All frames, except for the G43, come with optics cut for RMR or DOC optics. Barrels are CNC machined from 416R stainless steel billet, with a target crown muzzle, and given a BORSLICK Boron Nitride DCD (Dynamic Compound Deposition) inner bore treatment that's supposed to help resist heat and carbon buildup. As far as carbon buildup, it seems to be pretty easy to clean, but I don't know if it's noticeably different from a standard Glock barrel, which I don't find difficult to clean, to begin with. Barrels get a low-temp vacuum PVD coating in black PVD, Bronze PVD or Graphite PVD.

I have the G19 slide with RMR cut and the Bronze PVD threaded barrel. I used the Rival Arms slide completion kit, then added the two-piece flared mag well. The machining on everything is flawless, which makes for a perfect drop-in fit. Rival Arms engineers state they have tighter tolerances in their parts than factory, and I believe it. Of course, while that's all well and good, tighter tolerances are not always better, especially when it comes to reliability. So far, however, I haven't had any reliability issues at all, it ran perfect out the first time and every time. I don't have a huge round count through it, though, since I haven't had it that long. With this kind of quality and attention to detail, along with a good-looking product, I think Rival Arms is going to blow up and be a major player in the Glock-accessory game. Considering the company has only been around a couple years, Rival Arms got it right on the first try. (rival-arms.com)

TANGODOWN

I've been using TD products since the company first came out with the ARC magazines for AR15 rifles. TD makes a host of accessories for Glock, most of which by teaming up with Larry Vickers (Vickers Tactical: www.vickerstactical.com). TD makes one of my favorite mag baseplates, the Vickers Tactical Floor Plate, which is wider than a Glock OEM baseplate, so it's easy to grasp. They're highly regarded by those that use them, and for example, are included with Wilson Combat custom Glocks. I'm also a fan of the Vickers Carry Trigger. It has a flat, wide face that's com-

The slide, barrel and extended mag well are all from Rival Arms. The company is relatively new to the market, but it makes high-quality Glock accessories. (instagram.com/robb_manning #robb_manning. glock.book)

fortable to press. The flat face and low trigger safety allow the user to get a low finger press on the trigger, which changes the leverage dynamics, making it feel lighter. This includes only the trigger, not the whole trigger assembly with trigger bar, so it's not a drop-in install, though it's still pretty easy. It's a good upgrade over the OEM trigger, and at only $40, it's about the cheapest trigger you can find.

The TD Glock product I've had the longest is the Vickers Grip Plug, which doubles as a takedown tool for your Glock (see photo in the Wilson Combat section of this chapter). It's

The TangoDown Vickers Grip Plug includes a takedown tool for your Glock.

The TangoDown Vickers Tactical Carry Trigger is a solid upgrade over an OEM trigger. The wide, flat face and low trigger safety make for a light, smooth trigger press.

The TangoDown Vickers Floor Plate is one of the best aftermarket Glock baseplates on the market. The wide footprint makes it easy to grasp.

also a slight grip extension, so when the mag is installed, the back of the grip is level with the magazine, giving you a little more hand space at the bottom of the grip. Once installed, just give it a good twist and the takedown tool comes out for use. (tangodown.com)

FACTR

FACTR is so new to the game that it offers only one product: a trigger. Well, two actually, a trigger for Gen3/4 and a trigger for Gen5. It's a very good trigger, though, with a lot of detail that sets it apart from other offerings. It's kind of a "best of both worlds" approach to trigger design. At first glance, it looks like a straight trigger, but a closer look and you'll see it has a very slight curve. This offers all of the benefits of a straight trigger, but with a slight curve that cradles the finger. The trigger face is predominantly flat, but the edges have a bevel for comfort. As I said, the best of both worlds. Straight, but slightly curved. Flat face, with beveled edges.

The FACTR website says its trigger has decreased pre-travel, which it does, but let's break down what is meant by pre-travel to explain where the FACTR trigger is better. Pre-travel is the first initial portion of the trigger pull from the start, up until the firing pin is released (or "breaks"). That includes "take-up" (or "slack" as it's sometimes referred), which is from the resting point up until resistance is met; the "wall," which is the very first resistance; and "creep," which is from the wall up until the trigger breaks. Glock OEM triggers have about a quarter-inch of take-up and about a quarter-inch of creep. The FACTR trigger cuts out most of the creep portion of pre-travel. It has little to no overtravel, and I found the reset to be slightly shorter than a Glock OEM trigger, which is pretty good to start with.

The FACTR trigger pull weighed in at 5.5 pounds for around the first 25 pulls, and by about 50 pulls in, it was at 4.2 pounds, which is where it seems to have settled in.

It ships with a Glock OEM trigger bar and a reduced power striker safety spring (to reduce trigger pull weight – since the striker safety would push out of the way due to reduced spring tension, the trigger pull weight is reduced). It does still incorporate all three Glock safeties, and my initial testing doesn't indicate the reduced power striker safety spring would hinder that particular safety device, though it would take me a lot of shooting to draw a conclusion on this. Made of 6061 T-6 Aluminum. (factrusa.com)

AMERIGLO

I'm a huge fan of AmeriGlo CAP sights. A few years ago, I was at a shooting event and Dave Spaulding was the handgun trainer. We got to talking about the sights he designed for AmeriGlo, called the CAP (Combat Application Pistol) sights. He got input from an eye surgeon, who happened

The FACTR trigger, pre-install. It's made of 6061 T-6 aluminum and comes with a Glock OEM trigger bar and reduced power striker safety spring (not shown).

The FACTR trigger installed on a G19 Gen5. It takes the benefits of a straight trigger face, and the comfort of a curved trigger and blends them together.

to be a shooter, to develop sights for fast front sight acquisition in a crisis. Most sights have a square notch in the rear sight, and a round aiming point on the front sight, which the eye surgeon said can confuse the brain, even for a fraction of a second. CAP sights use a square front sight aiming point, which is easier to position within the square notch of the rear sight (in other words, "Square peg in a square hole," vs. "round peg in a square hole").

Dave sent me a set of his sights, and I can say, they are the fastest sights on target I have used. I installed them on my every day carry G19 Gen4, which was my go-to handgun until the Gen5 came out. The rear sight comes in a standard configuration that has a luminous index line below the square notch, that's lined up below the front sight aiming point; as well as a Spaulding model that has a flat black serrated rear sight with no luminous index line. The absence of anything on the rear sight is supposed to reduce clutter and make for faster acquisition, but between the two, I personally prefer to have the index line for low light. The sights are all metal with glow-in-the-dark tritium, and will set you back about $90 for the set. (ameriglo.com)

NIGHT FISION

I found Night Fision at SHOT Show, as I was checking out the booths, and was pretty im-

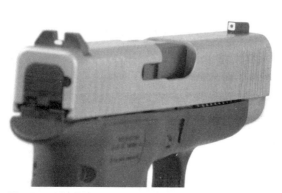

The AmeriGlo Dave Spaulding CAP sights are outstanding. The fastest-to-acquire sights the author has used. Shown here on a G48.

The author's G19 has had Spaulding CAP sights on it for several years now. They're very fast to target.

pressed. The company sent me an Accur8 set of sights, which are the official sights of Paul Markel's Student of the Gun. It calls their aiming points "Perfect Dot," and are made using the same material used in bulletproof glass, so yes, they're very tough. It's a large circle that's hard to miss in daylight. At the center of the front sight color ring is a tritium capsule and a second is found under the square notch on the rear sight. I found them to be very bright, a result of what Night Fision says is 30 percent more tritium than the leading competitors.

The Night Fision Accur8 sights, pre-install. These are for standard-size Glocks.

I don't know how much tritium other companies use, but I can say these are definitely brighter than most I've used.

In daytime use, the rear sight tritium dot is subdued, so all you really see is the bright front sight ring, which gets back to what I mentioned a couple paragraphs ago, about cutting out clutter to make it easier to find the front sight. But, the rear sight dot really pops in low light, which I like. During rapid fire drills, I was able to acquire the front sight and get it on target very fast. These well-made sights are CNC machined from steel and use Swiss tritium. The front "Perfect Dot" ring comes in 5 different colors. It will set you back $117 for a front and rear set. I'm still new to these sights, but I've become a big fan. (www.nightfision.com)

MISCELLANEOUS ACCESSORIES

FAB DEFENSE

FAB Defense is an Israeli company that's been making tactical and firearm accessories for a long time, many of which I use personally, and has a great lineup of Glock products. I like FAB's Scorpus Covert IWB Holster, it's the thinnest Kydex I've used, which really cuts down on bulk when trying to conceal. It's also designed well. You won't have to worry about it shifting or moving during draw. I've also used both the G42 and G43 mag plus-4 extensions. They look absolutely nothing like Glock, looking kind of awkward, but they work very well. It's not the typical mag extension that's just a hunk of aluminum or polymer, these are designed to be easy to grab the mag for reloads, and to provide a full hand grip for better handgun control while shooting.

One of my favorite Glock items from FAB Defense is the Cobra Quick Deployment Folding Stock. Simply slide the adapter into the famous Glock grip hole, just like you would any other grip hole plug, and it's ready to go. No modifications are necessary. It's a very tight fit and will require a lot of pushing, but it's designed that way so it's very snug with no play. It has a cheek rest, a rubber butt pad, it deploys quickly and locks securely open or closed. It's designed to work even with many OWB holsters. The only drawback: You'll need to register

If you want to mount an optic to your Glock, the FAB Defense GIS can make that happen.

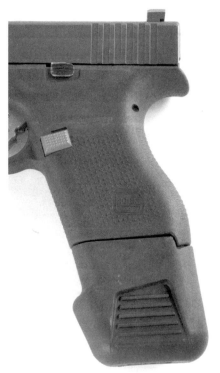

The FAB Defense Cobra Quick Deployment Folding Stock is reminiscent of pistol-stock attachments found on Lugers and other WWI-/WWII-era handguns. To use one, though, you'll need an NFA stamp from the BATFE.

The G42 and G43 (shown) mag plus-4 extension boosts your capacity to 10 rounds. It gives you a full hand grip and provides an easy grip for mag reloads.

your Glock as an SBR prior to using it. Is it worth it? I don't know, I haven't gotten my stamp back yet, so I haven't used one. But, I guess for me it was worth $200 to find out.

The GIS is a polymer picatinny scope mount for Glock. It uses two points of contact for stability. It slides onto the accessory rail, locking in place, then a pin replaces the OEM trigger pin, securing the rear of the GIS at that point. It sits high enough so the factory sights can still be used. The GIS has its own underside accessory rail molded into it, so you don't lose that space when its mounted to your Glock. You can still mount lasers and/or lights. Some might be scratching their head at the purpose of this one. It does look kind of silly mounted to a pistol; kind of overkill. But

The Scorpus Covert IWB Holster is designed well and is tough, yet cuts down on extra bulk, thanks to the thin polymer.

FAB Defense intends it more for PDW (Personal Defense Weapon) use, like with a stock and vertical front grip. I can see that, but for me to turn my Glock into a PDW in that type of configuration, I'll have to wait for my NFA stamp. (www.fab-defense.com, with US store: www.fab-defenseus.com)

WHEELER ENGINEERING

Glock had a good sight tool for installation/removal, but then it went to the current one, and it's not good. The first time I used it, it broke. There are some good sight tools on the market, and I suggest getting one of the aftermarket ones. The one I use is from Wheeler Engineering.

It's solid, heavy duty and all metal (except for the slide protection pads). A big plus is that you can use it with any handgun, not just Glocks. And it can be adjusted for flatside sights or angled, to get optimal push angle. It's a professional-grade sight tool, but priced at just over $200, it's a bargain. (www.wheelertools.com)

WISCO HOLSTERS

There's a lot of great options when it comes to holsters, but I happened upon this little gem of a company because it sells locally to me. When the G48 was first announced, I knew I'd need something to carry it in so I could test it for this book, but not many companies were making holsters for it, and

If you plan on changing out the sights on your Glock and other pistols, get a good sight tool like this one from Wheeler Engineering.

none could get me a holster right away. So, I was put in contact with Wisco Holsters – a one-man, local holster maker – and he sent me a Kydex holster within a week, including a matching double mag carrier. It's as professionally made as my other holsters from large holster makers. Fit and finish is excellent. The edges are smooth with no sharp corners. Wisco also offers great options for hardware. I chose belt fasteners that can be attached or removed without taking the belt off. Yet it stays firmly on so there's no worries of it coming off when you draw your gun. It's also fully adjustable for retention tightness. (wiscoholsters.com)

Wisco Holsters makes an excellent Kydex holster that's comfortable, works well and looks good. The belt clip on the holster allows for fast on/off without taking off the belt. (instagram.com/robb_manning #robb_manning.glock.book)

BRAVO CONCEALMENT

Bravo Concealment has been around for a long time, and the company makes great Kydex holsters. I can remember when it was a small company, working out of the garage, and now Bravo is an established holster companies in the industry. It's easy to see why. BC holsters are very well made, high quality and the prices don't break the bank. I own several, both IWB and OWB, for many models of Glock. The most current one I own is for the G43X. (www.bravoconcealment.com)

MAG PUMP

When you shoot a lot, loading magazines can get tedious. I've done hard testing on guns when I fired so many rounds that, after loading all the mags, at the end of the day I had blisters on my hands. Not a big deal, you just suck it up and go with it. But, you don't have to. I've used a lot of very good loaders, and many excellent ones. My favorite loader has always been the one I remembered to pack in my range bag. The Mag Pump is relatively

Here is a Bravo Concealment holster with the G43X. It is compatible with a gun with a threaded barrel, although the author doesn't have one on his G43X.

new to the market and it's become my instant favorite. It comes with adapters that make it compatible with most handgun mags on the market, and more are available from the website. After the adapter is inserted, stick in your magazine, round-count holes facing up and lock it in place. It's stays put until you pull the lever that releases the magazine. I like the Mag Pump because ammo doesn't have to be fed into it any certain way. Just dump your box of ammo into the hopper, pump the handle lever until your mag is loaded, then unlock the mag and go. Dump, pump and go! The handle lever is easy, even including the last round, and mag-view ports are visible so you can see how full it is. It's available only in 9mm, .223 (AR15) and 7.62x39 (AKM/AK-47) at this time. The MSRP is $150 for the standard model, and worth every penny. Pro ($250) and Elite ($400) models are also available. (magpump.com)

The Mag Pump uses adapters to make it compatible with most handgun magazines on the market. It's simple: Dump, pump and go. (instagram.com/robb_manning #robb_manning.glock.book)

SNAGMAG

This is one of those products that I wonder where it's been all my life. I believe in carrying an extra magazine, I really do. Because of the "excrement happens" life outlook. Stuff does happen, and it always happens at the worst time. And it would suck to have a gun but no ammo, because something happens to the mag that's loaded (or *supposed* to be loaded) into your carry gun. Mags can fail, jam, fall out, etc. Which is why I firmly believe in carrying at least one spare magazine.

But in reality, I usually forgo the extra mag for sake of expediency. For my daily routine, carrying an extra mag kind of sucks, for lack of a better term. I hate carrying one on my belt, if I'm being honest. For one, the carrier has to be threaded onto the belt early on in the belt-feeding process so it's on the weak-hand side of your waist, which means that once your handgun/holster is on and the belt is buckled, it's a pain to add or remove. Second, it's not comfortable, especially when sitting. Whereas the handgun/holster is a larger protrusion, the extra mag is smaller and is more uncomfortable. I don't like to just let the extra mag free-float around my pocket, because it's not fast to grab amongst the other stuff I carry in my pocket.

The SnagMag clips to the inside of your pocket like a carry knife – and to prying eyes that like to look at that area of a human torso, it looks like a pocketknife, too. It keeps the mag in perfect position for it to be grabbed so that it's oriented for a quick reload, and a tab on the SnagMag keeps it place when you draw the mag, so the holster doesn't follow the mag out of your pocket.

Halle Berry training for John Wick 3 *with her TTI Combat Master Glock G19. Yep, she's a shooter. One of us. (Photo by Taran Butler)*

For me, this has been a revolutionary development in my spare-mag carry, now I have no excuse. (www.snagmag.com)

CUSTOM GLOCKS

When I think of high-end custom handguns, I think of 1911s. Sure, there are other guns used – the Browning Hi-Power, the CZ 75, just to name a couple – but the 1911 is king of the custom gun. Maybe that's because so many companies are making 1911 pistols, so the choices are endless. But there's only one company making a Glock, and that's Glock. There are some clones out there, and as we discussed earlier, there are several companies making just about everything on a Glock except the receiver. There's even the Polymer80 (www.polymer80.com) for those who choose to "roll your own" Glock receiver. But that's not what I'm writing about here. I'm writing about companies taking a Glock handgun, making it "their own," and selling it as a custom Glock. For this book, I had to draw the line somewhere as to what's a Glock and what's not a Glock. So, I include in the custom Glock category guns that started off with a Glock-serialized frame and were customized from there. In other words, to be a custom Glock, at some point in the supply chain someone would have had to purchase an actual Glock handgun. Some companies use the Glock design, with Glock parts (usually non-OEM), but make their own frames, so these companies were not included.

I don't have experience with all the companies out there, but I do have experience with a couple of the best. Other notable companies that I'm familiar with, and want to mention, though I've never fired their guns so I lack the first-hand experience to write about them, include: Taran Tactical Innovations, which designed the custom Glocks used in the John Wick trilogy, (tarantacticalinnovations.com), Suarez International (suarezinternational.com), Robar (robarguns.com) and ATEi (ateiguns.com).

One of the most innovative products I've seen comes from Full Conceal (www.fullconceal.com). FC armorers take a Glock frame, cut it just above the grip, work their magic and come away with a Glock that folds in half. I've handled one at SHOT show, and they seem well made; but I've never shot one.

WILSON COMBAT

I've been a fan of Wilson Combat for years now. I've even been fortunate enough to get to know Bill Wilson through various articles/projects I've been involved with. My first introduction was a WC Recon Tactical model AR15, chambered in 6.8 SPC, and after that an AR

Like everything made by Wilson Combat, the WC Vickers Elite custom Glock is superb in quality and performance.

chambered in .308. I got that one when it was still the ".308 Project," as Bill named it. It was pricey, and some might scoff at paying that much for an AR15, but when you pull an AR15 out of the box, mount a mediocre scope on it, and are consistently shooting one-half MOA with it, that's a keeper right there. Then a couple years ago I assigned one of my writers an article about the new (at the time) WC EDC X9. After he did the testing and wrote the article, he told me in an email, off the record, "This is THE best handgun I've ever shot." After Bill was kind enough to send me one too, I have to concur.

By now you're probably wondering what this all has to do with Glock. I'm getting there.

The top of the Wilson Combat Vickers Elite custom slide reduces glare and is nicely done.

I'm establishing how highly I think of the guns that roll out of the Wilson Combat shop. I'll just say this: If Wilson Combat makes it – or customizes it – if I have the money I want one. I at least have to shoot it.

So, when I found out Wilson Combat was putting out a custom WC Glock, I had to get one in my hands. The demand was high, and it was tough to get one at first. Initially, it was only offered as a customization to one of your Glocks. Send Wilson Combat one of your Glocks, the custom work order form, along with a check or credit card number, and in X-number of weeks you get back a WC custom Glock. You can pick and choose any of the upgrades WC offers, with as few or as many as you want. It's a great option if you already own a Glock and want something specific done to it.

Another option WC offers, are two packages that WC has teamed up to offer. One option is the Paul Howe package. If you're not in the gun or

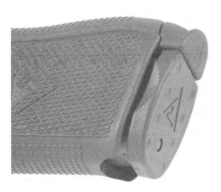

The WC Vickers Elite package ships with TangoDown mag baseplates and grip plug (with a Glock takedown tool, as described earlier in this chapter).

The WC Vickers Elite had front serrations before Glock did. And it looks better.

military community, you might not be familiar with the name Paul Howe. He's a retired U.S. Army Master Sergeant of 20 years, 10 of which were spent SFOD-D, better known as Delta Force. If you've seen the movie, or better yet, read the book "Blackhawk Down," Paul Howe was there. He's now the founder/owner and lead instructor for Combat Shooting and Tactics (CSAT) training program.

The WC Paul Howe package for Glock uses a Gen4 Glock in either G19 or G26, and includes a full fit Wilson Combat Barrel, 4.5 lbs. action tuned, stippled WC starburst pattern frame, stippled thumb pads with WC logo, Paul Howe cut on trigger guard, a black Armor-Tuff finish on the slide, WC square notch battle sight with AmeriGlo tritium, Paul Howe wide slide top serrations, and CSAT logo on the slide. The package starts at $1,500.

The second package is the Larry Vickers Elite package. Larry Vickers has a higher profile in the gun community, and comes from the same SFOD-Delta background as Paul Howe. The Vickers Elite package for Glock starts with a Gen5 in either G19, G17 or G45, and has a stippled frame with Vickers Tactical logo, stippled thumb pads with WC logo, Duty action tuned, black armor-tuff slide, battlesight with green fiber-optic front sight, wide slide top serrations, and front cocking serrations. Vickers has also teamed up with TangoDown for Glock accessories, which are used on the WC Glock package, including Tactical magazine release, grip plug, magazine baseplate (on all three magazines), trigger pad and slide stop. The front cocking serrations were designed into this gun prior to Glock releasing the FS variant for the Gen5. It's noticeable on the left side of the slide, because the serrations have been made around the Glock logo and the "19 Gen5" logo. The package starts at $1,430.

Wilson Combat sent me a Vickers Elite model, and it's everything you'd expect from a gun from WC. It's designed as a duty/fighting gun, which means it doesn't have a super-light match/competition trigger, it's a carry trigger. Mine averaged about a 4.9-pound pull. Mine shipped with the original Glock box, backstraps, cleaning accessories, three mags equipped with TangoDown/Vickers baseplates, plus the original Glock sights and mag baseplates in a Ziploc bag. (www.wilsoncombat.com)

The Wilson Combat Vickers Elite Custom G19 fired at 7 yards, using Federal 124-grain HST JHP.

ADM made a limited run of custom Glocks, and they're some of the best custom Glocks on the market, in terms of performance.(instagram.com/robb_manning #robb_manning.glock.book

AMERICAN DEFENSE MANUFACTURING

I won't write much about this one because it's a very limited run, not many were made and only ADM knows if it will ever make more. ADM is known for making high quality ARs, and it briefly touched into custom Glocks. I feel obliged to mention it, because it's one of the best I've shot and is the most accurate G19 I've shot. It's a G19 Gen3 frame with custom cuts and stippling. Danger Close Armament did the stippling for ADM, and I'm normally not a big fan of most stippling jobs done on polymer guns, but Danger Close did an outstanding job. The thumb pads above the trigger guard front have been cut, leaving a nice shelf to rest your thumb, and the cutout is nicely stippled. The mag release has a scallop cut and has been smoothed out. The Gen3 finger grooves have been removed, and the beavertail has been smoothed as well.

ADM used an Agency Arms mag well, and two different triggers in its builds, either a Zev or an Overwatch Precision. Mine came with a Glock OEM trigger. The slide is machined by ADM, and uses mostly

This is what you call center mass: The ADM G19 shot 15 rounds of SIG Elite 147-grain FMJ at 20 yards and made this outstanding group. (instagram.com/robb_manning #robb_manning.glock.book)

OEM Glock internal components. ADM used two different barrel manufacturers for its Glock builds, S3F and Agency Arms. Mine came with neither, and after talking with ADM, mine was a barrel blank that they finish machined the outside of. To finish the whole thing off, ADM gave the slide a TiN coating, which looks incredible. The firing pin and firing pin safety were both given a TiN coating, as well.

I'm new to TiN as a firearms coating, and didn't know a lot about it from a firearms aspect, so I did some research on it. It is the abbreviation for Titanium Nitride, which is a gold-colored ceramic hard coat applied via PVD (Physical Vapor Deposition). It's been used in medical equipment and tools for awhile now (if you have drill bits that are gold in color, they are most likely TiN coated). (www.americandefensemanufacturing.com)

PISTOL CALIBER CARBINES (PCC)

One growing segment of firearms is Pistol Caliber Carbines (PCC), and it's booming. The predominant platform PCCs come in is ARs, but that's not the only one. Glockophiles have been asking for Glock to make a PCC for years, but it hasn't taken the leap yet, though I hear, "soon." We'll have to see about that. Until then, a lot of companies are making PCCs that are compatible with the Glock magazines you already own. It goes back to the old West, and probably even before that, when given the poor logistics at the time (there was no Amazon Prime to ship you whatever you wanted overnight) it made sense to have your pistol shoot the same cartridge as your rifle.

The upsides to a PCC are many. For me, the best part is it gives you the stability of placing a stock in your shoulder. I'm a much better shot with a rifle than I am with a handgun. Depending on which PCC you're looking at, longer barrels are a big plus, too. Some of them come with full-length barrels, and I was surprised at the accuracy of a 9mm bullet coming out of a 16-inch barrel. You can go the other direction and get a super compact PCC with a 5-inch barrel. With these you're not really gaining anything in barrel length, but it still improves accuracy because you still have the support from the stock, or pistol brace, depending on how you have it configured.

This is as good of a place as any to cover the situation with SBR vs. Pistol. A stock on this PCC with a 5-inch barrel would make this an SBR (Short Barrel Rifle), which means it would need ATF approval in the form of a Form 1 approval and stamp. Or you could purchase a pistol brace that goes on a special buffer tube (in the case of the AR style PCCs), that gives the firearm the classification of pistol, so no Form 1 need be approved. These pistol braces, at the least, brace to your arm for added stability; and at best, depending on the ATF, can be shouldered like a conventional stock. The reason I have to give worse/best case scenario is the ATF has reversed positions on whether or not you can shoulder a pistol brace. The agency has gone back and forth so many times it's not funny, and reflects the silliness of the laws governing SBRs. A funny thought about this whole situation: An AR Pistol PCC isn't really a carbine, so we shouldn't call it a Pistol Caliber Carbine. According to ATF rules, it would be a Pistol Caliber Pistol, which is uhhhhh, a pistol.

PCCs also give you more options in using optics/lights/lasers, which pistols don't give you, and since most AR style PCCs use a lot of standard AR parts, you have access to a lot more upgrades, such as better rifle triggers. There's some good handgun triggers out there, but I don't think any can top the rifle triggers on the market.

Probably the biggest benefit to PCCs, they're loads of fun to shoot. And 9mm ammo is far cheaper than 5.56 ammo to shoot, so you can shoot more.

There are a lot of PCCs on the market. A good percentage of AR makers make at least one PCC model, but to keep it applicable to this book, I'm only including ones that are centered around the Glock magazine. Even then I could write a whole book about PCCs, so I'm just going to narrow it to the couple that I have spent a good amount of time with: the CMMG Banshee and Ruger PC Carbine. I've shot the Rock River Arms PCC, and that's a great gun, and I know Wilson Combat and American Defense Manufacturing also make a PCC, and I'm quite sure those are stellar.

CMMG BANSHEE 300 MKGS, 900

The Banshee AR line is CMMG's most compact configuration it offers, coming in AR SBR's and AR Pistols. This model takes Glock 9mm magazines, making it a perfect companion to those who carry a Glock pistol. When choosing which model I wanted, I chose this AR pistol because I wanted a 9mm AR that was as small and lightweight as I could get, just for ease of use in tight quarters (which, for me, is in and out of my Polaris Ranger Side-by-side UTV, conducting pest/vermin control at my remote cabin). I like the additional stability/accuracy the AR pistol offers (as compared to just carrying a Glock pistol). I'm a decent pistol shooter, but a far better rifleman. And, for me, the pistol brace is mostly just a "placeholder" until I get my SBR stamp back from the ATF.

It uses a Radial Delayed Blowback (RDB) operating system, not the traditional blowback system used by other Pistol Caliber ARs. With a traditional blowback system, the weight of the bolt and the recoil spring is what keeps the bolt in battery long enough to clear dangerous chamber pressure when the gun is fired. To adjust for the power of the cartridge, since there's a limit on the strength of the spring (to allow for the bolt to cycle reliably), the solution is to make the bolt heavier, which makes for a heavier firearm. CMMG's RDB system has a rotating bolt head, so when

The CMMG Banshee is extremely compact, making it very handy, especially in tight confines.

The Banshee 300 MkGs is well-made, looks good, and the 9mm is cheaper to shoot than a 5.56 AR. Equipped with a Shield Sights SIS mini red dot (with cover), it's very fast on target and surprisingly accurate, given its short barrel.

The Ruger 9mm PC Carbine uses Glock OEM 9mm magazines, as well as compatible after-market magazines. It has a more traditional rifle look to it than do AR-type PCCs.

the gun is fired, the bolt head must rotate and unlock before moving out of battery to cycle, ensuring enough time for the chamber pressure to hit a safe level. The result is a far lighter firearm. Mine weighs in at 4 pounds, 13.5 ounces, and that's with a Shield Sights SIS mini-red dot attached (no magazine inserted).

Like all of the CMMG rifles I've shot, the Banshee is high quality and very well made. Being compatible with Glock mags makes it extremely handy. For me, it has a utilitarian purpose, but aside from that, it's a lot of fun to shoot. (cmmginc.com)

RUGER PC CARBINE

This one isn't specific to the Glock mag, it's actually made with Ruger's SR-Series/Security-9 magazine in mind, but Ruger is smart enough to know there's a whole lot more Glock mags out there than Ruger mags. So, it comes with a handy adapter that allows it to accept Glock mags. Ruger's PC Carbine isn't AR based, it's a conventional rifle that looks more like a 10/22. It's a Takedown rifle based on the same system as the 10/22 Takedown, which makes it very convenient and very portable. It comes with an 18-inch barrel and is extremely accurate. The receiver has a rail on top for optics to improve accuracy and speed. It's quick and handy with a little red-dot optic, but a low-magnification scope works well, too. It comes in a standard model, and in an AR-style free-float aluminum handguard. In early 2019, Ruger also released a model chambered in .40 S&W, which seems like a pretty nice option.

I was at the Ruger media event where it launched the PC Carbine, out at Gunsite. Fifteen writers/editors were there, and we put more than 3,000 rounds of 9mm through it without a single hiccup. We put it through some pretty rigorous training, and I was very impressed. Accuracy was most impressive, far better than I had anticipated.

As much as I love the AR15, I like having a 9mm carbine that's not another AR, and looks more like a traditional hunting rifle. It now comes in a couple different configurations and colors, including one with an AR-style aluminum free-float handguard, and also a U.S. Flag Cerakoted version. Available in 9mm and .40 S&W. (www.ruger.com)